New Feminist Research Ethics

New Feminist Research Ethics re-examines the place of the ethical in feminist research and identifies new priorities for feminist researchers. As urgent social, political, and environmental challenges demand new ethical sensibilities, contributors revisit the relationship between feminism and research to ask what it means to be an ethical feminist researcher now. They explore how hierarchies of privilege have shaped our understandings of research ethics and question how evolving understandings of feminist research ethics sit alongside formal institutional ethics processes. Contributors also situate feminist research ethics in the context of a broader ethics of care and repair. Importantly, *New Feminist Research Ethics* acknowledges the need for feminist ethical research frameworks that encompass multiple perspectives and draw from diverse traditions of knowing. This volume brings together established and emerging scholars and perspectives from sociology, history, gender studies, archival studies, cultural studies, and architecture. It was originally published as a special issue of the journal *Australian Feminist Studies*.

Maryanne Dever is Co-editor of *Australian Feminist Studies*. Her research focuses on feminist literary and archival studies. Her previous Routledge edited collections include *Archives and New Modes of Feminist Research* (2018), which won a Mander Jones Prize from the Australian Society of Archivists, and *Fashion: New Feminist Essays* (2020), co-edited with Ilya Parkins. She is currently Pro-Vice-Chancellor (Education and Digital) at the Australian National University, Canberra, Australia.

New Feminist Research Ethics

Edited by
Maryanne Dever

LONDON AND NEW YORK

First published 2023
by Routledge
4 Park Square, Milton Park, Abingdon, Oxon, OX14 4RN

and by Routledge
605 Third Avenue, New York, NY 10158

Routledge is an imprint of the Taylor & Francis Group, an informa business

Chapters 1–5, 7 and 9 © 2023 Taylor & Francis
Chapter 6 © 2021 Niamh Moore, Nikki Dunne, Martina Karels and Mary Hanlon. Originally published as Open Access.
Chapter 8 © 2021 Xin Liu. Originally published as Open Access.

With the exception of Chapters 6 and 8, no part of this book may be reprinted or reproduced or utilised in any form or by any electronic, mechanical, or other means, now known or hereafter invented, including photocopying and recording, or in any information storage or retrieval system, without permission in writing from the publishers. For details on the rights for Chapters 6 and 8, please see the chapters' Open Access footnotes.

Trademark notice: Product or corporate names may be trademarks or registered trademarks, and are used only for identification and explanation without intent to infringe.

British Library Cataloguing-in-Publication Data
A catalogue record for this book is available from the British Library

ISBN13: 978-1-032-45207-4 (hbk)
ISBN13: 978-1-032-45208-1 (pbk)
ISBN13: 978-1-003-37591-3 (ebk)

DOI: 10.4324/9781003375913

Typeset in Myriad Pro
by codeMantra

Publisher's Note
The publisher accepts responsibility for any inconsistencies that may have arisen during the conversion of this book from journal articles to book chapters, namely the inclusion of journal terminology.

Disclaimer
Every effort has been made to contact copyright holders for their permission to reprint material in this book. The publishers would be grateful to hear from any copyright holder who is not here acknowledged and will undertake to rectify any errors or omissions in future editions of this book.

Contents

	Citation Information	vi
	Notes on Contributors	viii
1	Research from the Heart: Friendship and Compassion as Personal Research Values Jennifer Douglas	1
2	Feminist Research Ethics and First Nations Women's Life Narratives: A Conversation Kath Apma Penangke Travis and Victoria Haskins	18
3	Beyond Formal Ethics Reviews: Reframing the Potential Harms of Sexual Violence Research Shaez Mortimer, Bianca Fileborn and Nicola Henry	34
4	Archives as Spaces of Radical Hospitality Jamie A. Lee	48
5	A Screen of One's Own: The Domestic Caregiver as Researcher During Covid-19, and Beyond Cathy Smith	57
6	Towards an Inventive Ethics of Carefull Risk: Unsettling Research Through DIY Academic Archiving Niamh Moore, Nikki Dunne, Martina Karels and Mary Hanlon	72
7	Learning to Stand with Gyack: A Practice of Thinking with Non-Innocent Care Lisa Slater	92
8	The Use/Less Citations in Feminist Research Xin Liu	104
9	Embracing Amateurs: Four Practices to Subvert Academic Gatekeeping Michelle Moravec	114
	Index	129

Citation Information

The chapters in this book were originally published in the journal *Australian Feminist Studies*, volume 36, issue 108 (2021). When citing this material, please use the original page numbering for each article, as follows:

Chapter 1
Research from the Heart: Friendship and Compassion as Personal Research Values
Jennifer Douglas
Australian Feminist Studies, volume 36, issue 108 (2021) pp. 109–125

Chapter 2
Feminist Research Ethics and First Nations Women's Life Narratives: A Conversation
Kath Apma Penangke Travis and Victoria Haskins
Australian Feminist Studies, volume 36, issue 108 (2021) pp. 126–141

Chapter 3
Beyond Formal Ethics Reviews: Reframing the Potential Harms of Sexual Violence Research
Shaez Mortimer, Bianca Fileborn and Nicola Henry
Australian Feminist Studies, volume 36, issue 108 (2021) pp. 142–155

Chapter 4
Archives as Spaces of Radical Hospitality
Jamie A. Lee
Australian Feminist Studies, volume 36, issue 108 (2021) pp. 156–164

Chapter 5
A Screen of One's Own: The Domestic Caregiver as Researcher During Covid-19, and Beyond
Cathy Smith
Australian Feminist Studies, volume 36, issue 108 (2021) pp. 165–179

Chapter 6
Towards an Inventive Ethics of Carefull Risk: Unsettling Research Through DIY Academic Archiving
Niamh Moore, Nikki Dunne, Martina Karels and Mary Hanlon
Australian Feminist Studies, volume 36, issue 108 (2021) pp. 180–199

Chapter 7
Learning to Stand with Gyack: A Practice of Thinking with Non-Innocent Care
Lisa Slater
Australian Feminist Studies, volume 36, issue 108 (2021) pp. 200–211

Chapter 8
The Use/Less Citations in Feminist Research
Xin Liu
Australian Feminist Studies, volume 36, issue 108 (2021) pp. 212–221

Chapter 9
Embracing Amateurs: Four Practices to Subvert Academic Gatekeeping
Michelle Moravec
Australian Feminist Studies, volume 36, issue 108 (2021) pp. 222–235

For any permission-related enquiries please visit:
http://www.tandfonline.com/page/help/permissions

Notes on Contributors

Maryanne Dever is Co-editor of *Australian Feminist Studies*. Her research focuses on feminist literary and archival studies. Her previous Routledge edited collections include *Archives and New Modes of Feminist Research* (2018), which won a Mander Jones Prize from the Australian Society of Archivists, and *Fashion: New Feminist Essays* (2020), co-edited with Ilya Parkins. She is currently Pro-Vice-Chancellor (Education and Digital) at the Australian National University, Canberra, Australia.

Jennifer Douglas lives and works on the traditional, ancestral, and unceded territories of the xwməθkwəy̓əm (Musqueam) people. She is Associate Professor in the School of Information at the University of British Columbia, Vancouver, Canada, where she teaches courses on personal archives, archival arrangement and description, and archival research and scholarship. Her research interests include personal and intimate archives, the emotional dimensions of archival work, person-centred approaches to archival theory and practice, and archival representation and its histories.

Nikki Dunne is Research Officer with *Family Carers Ireland*. She is a sociologist working on the intersection of gender, family, and care labour migration issues, centred on labour and migration in the framework of global capitalist economy. This has extended into an interest in distance relationships, exploring the ways in which feminised migration impacts on familial caregiving.

Bianca Fileborn is currently Senior Lecturer in Criminology in the School of Social & Political Sciences at the University of Melbourne, Australia. Their research examines innovative and victim-centred justice responses to street harassment, sexual violence and LGBTQ+ communities, and sexual violence in the night-time economy and live music spaces.

Mary Hanlon is College Professor at Okanagan College, Kelowna, Canada. She has a PhD in Sociology from the University of Edinburgh, UK, with research themes including transnational social movements and related activism (online and offline), work and labour rights, environmental justice, global fashion and apparel production and consumption, digital sociology, and knowledge dissemination.

Victoria Haskins is Professor of History and Co-director of the Purai Global Indigenous History Centre at the University of Newcastle, Australia. Since basing her first book on the story of the life of her great-grandmother, a white activist for Aboriginal citizenship rights in the 1930s, she has published extensively on gender, domestic labour, and cross-cultural relationships in settler colonial and imperial histories.

NOTES ON CONTRIBUTORS

Nicola Henry is Professor and Australian Research Council Future Fellow in the Social and Global Studies Centre at RMIT University, Melbourne, Australia. Her research investigates the nature and impacts of sexual violence, including legal and non-legal responses to these harms. Her current research focuses on technology-facilitated abuse and image-based sexual abuse.

Martina Karels is Assistant Professor of Communication Arts at St. Francis College, Brooklyn, USA. She received her PhD in Sociology from the University of Edinburgh, UK. Her research combines theories of social memory and performance to explore memory-making and remembrance in everyday life, particularly in public spaces, art, digital archives, and activism.

Jamie A. Lee is Associate Professor in the School of Information at the University of Arizona, USA, where their research and teaching attend to critical archival theories and methodologies, multimodal media-making contexts, storytelling, and bodies. Lee's book, *Producing the Archival Body* (Routledge, 2021), interrogates how power circulates and is deployed in archival contexts in order to build critical understandings of how deeply archives influence and shape the production of knowledges and human subjectivities. Lee has published in *Archivaria*; *Archival Science*; *Journal of Critical Library and Information Studies*; *Peitho: Journal of the Coalition of Feminist Scholars in the History of Rhetoric and Composition*; and *Media, Communications, & Cultural Studies*. They have also published book chapters related to archival studies, media studies, art and culture, and the history of American sexuality. For more on their research: www.thestorytellinglab.io

Xin Liu is Senior Lecturer at the Center for Gender Studies at Karlstad University, Sweden. She has published articles in journals such as *Parallax*; *Catalyst: Feminism, Theory, Technoscience*; *Australian Feminist Studies*; *MAI: Feminism & Visual Culture*; and *Feminist Review*. Her research projects are located in the intersection of environmental humanities, critical race studies, science and technology studies, social theory, digital media research, and feminist theory.

Niamh Moore is Senior Lecturer in Sociology at the University of Edinburgh, UK. She has a background in interdisciplinary research, encompassing ecofeminism, and work on archiving, both community archiving and archiving research data. She has published *The Changing Nature of Eco/feminism: Telling Stories from Clayoquot Sound*; co-authored *The Archive Project*; and co-edited *Participatory Research in more-than-Human Worlds*.

Michelle Moravec is Associate Professor of History at Rosemont College, Philadelphia, USA. She sits on the American Historical Association's Digital History Working Group and serves on the *Journal of Women's History* editorial board. Her most recent publications include 'Feminist Bestsellers: A Digital History of 1970s Feminism' in the *Journal of Cultural Analytics* and 'Digital Historical Practices' in the *Journal of Women's History*.

Shaez Mortimer is PhD Candidate and Research Assistant in the Social and Global Studies Centre at RMIT University, Melbourne, Australia. Her research explores LGBTQA+ people's experiences of sexual violence and seeking support, as well as queer and feminist research methodologies. She has a background in community work, advocacy, and violence prevention.

Lisa Slater is Settler Colonial Scholar and Associate Professor at the University of Wollongong, Australia. Her work examines Indigenous-settler relations, in all of its messy, complex materiality. Firstly, she seeks to reveal what culturally and emotionally drives policymakers, such as government and non-government agencies, and 'progressive' settlers' engagement with Aboriginal Australians, and how it plays out in concrete local forms. Secondly, she examines how Aboriginal people utilise cultural initiatives to contest settler colonialism and affirm sovereignty. Her projects have a strong focus on remote and rural Australia. Her monograph, *Anxieties of Belonging in Settler Colonialism*, was published in 2019 (Routledge).

Cathy Smith is Australian Architect, Interior Designer, and Senior Lecturer in Interior Architecture at UNSW, Sydney, Australia, where she was also the inaugural Turnbull Foundation Women in Built Environment Scholar (2018–2022). Her interdisciplinary scholarly research focuses on issues of social equity, property tenure, placemaking, and urban renewal, focusing particularly on meanwhile interiors and architecture and DIY procurement.

Kath Apma Penangke Travis is Postgraduate and Research Student and Lisa Bellear Indigenous Research Scholar at Victoria University, Melbourne, Australia. Kath has spent many years examining her ancestral family history, and her research seeks to explore ways in which archival stories can be re-claimed, re-authored, and re-patriated by First Peoples to address individual, family and community identity, and intergenerational healing.

Research from the Heart: Friendship and Compassion as Personal Research Values

Jennifer Douglas

ABSTRACT
This article reflects on the author's efforts to center friendship and compassion as in research that is highly personal and intimate, as well as on the ways that friendship and compassion, as research values, can sit in tension with university research ethics board (REB) approval processes. The article includes three research case studies to explore how procedural ethics review by REBs overlooks certain types of research harms and obscures the important role of relationships in determining research outcomes. The article concludes with a call for research from the heart.

Introduction: Thinking about Friendship in/and Research

It's a Saturday morning in August, and my research assistant Alex and I are seated at a local artist's kitchen table, sharing bread we brought and a fruit salad she prepared for us. We're talking about her daughter, Lara Gilbert, a young writer and aspiring doctor who died by suicide in 1995 when she was just twenty-two and whose archives Alex and I have been working with. We're also talking about her artwork, about her late partner, a jazz musician, and around and through it all, about grief, loss and memory. We're having this meeting because Alex and I are about to publish an article that references her daughter's archives as well as an art installation she assembled that incorporated archival materials in different ways. In email discussions about permissions to use a photograph of the installation in the publication, we decided to meet in person and now I think we're all a little nervous and uncertain. Alex and I discussed on the drive to her apartment how strange it might be to meet this woman for the first time, when we already know so much about her family life from our work in the archives. We've felt a bit voyeuristic: peeking into her daughter's diaries at the archives and being shown and permitted to handle some of the intimate objects she assembled in the art installation on a visit we made to the gallery that now owns it. And now here we are, at her kitchen table that is also part of her studio, taking tentative steps to get to know each other.

We learn a great deal in conversation about the artist's intentions for and feelings about the installation, about the context of her daughter's archival collection, about her daughter and what she was like as a young girl, and about the artist's childhood, too. The conversation, a bit awkward at first, flows more easily as we sip our tea and share some stories. She asks me questions about why I'm interested in her daughter's archives and I tell her about the death of my own daughter and my subsequent focus on grief in recordkeeping. As parents who have both experienced the loss of a child (under vastly different circumstances) perhaps we are more easily able to establish a kind of trust between us; I feel we might be developing some rapport.

This is not research. We have no formal ethics agreement in place; nothing we say in this space together, none of our conversations – conversations that have got right to the heart of my research questions on the connections between grief and archives – can or will be 'used' in my work. This is a friendship developing, I think; a friendship developing *around* and *because of* my work, yes, but one I must keep separate from my work, unless or until it is sanctioned by my institution.

In this article, I want to think more about the role of friendship in research, as well as about ideas of intimacy, vulnerability and compassion. In particular, I want to think about these ideas in the context of research ethics and specifically in the ways these ideas are in tension with research ethics as framed by institutional review ethics boards (REBs). In the meeting I describe above, I felt that tension deeply. I found researching in the Lara Gilbert archives extraordinarily moving and difficult. Lara Gilbert and I were born two years apart and shared many of the same childhood interests; reading her diaries was a deeply *familiar* experience, and though our lives also differed in many respects, I felt I could understand or relate to Gilbert in some ways. I was also extremely upset by and angry about abuse Gilbert described experiencing in her diaries. I felt, as Catherine Hobbs has put it, that I needed to 'do right by' her (Hobbs 2012), and meeting with her mother was part of that *doing right by*. We were publishing an article on her archives, her mother hoped to have a chat with us, and we were more than happy to meet her; but then if that chat turned into a moving discussion about records, grief and love, and if her mother began to talk about her own archival materials, what then? Is this still a chat? Is it research? What do I want it to be? What is it allowed to be? How do we move from friendship – especially new, fledgling friendship – to research? Should we? And if we do, how will that shift affect the nature of our chat? At what stage do I seek formal ethics approval for this friendship and this chat? How would I insert a consent form into our relationship? Would I want to? Would such formality cool this new relationship? What kind of role is there for friendship in research, for research in friendship?

I don't pretend in this article to have answered all the many questions my work so far has raised for me. I present this research storey instead as one of several examples where I am encountering and approaching questions related to friendship, to relationships, and to 'doing right by,' in my recent research projects. This article is primarily reflective in tone; through the examples I discuss, my aim is to surface ethical issues that I believe many researchers face but that are not always shared in formal spaces like research journals. Friendship enters into the article this way too; as I intend this as an invitation to share and work together, the article itself may be experienced, I hope, as a gesture of research friendship.

Relationality and Personal Research

In a paper co-written with Dolly Sen, Anna Sexton calls for the 'emergence of a larger body of knowledge on the complexities, benefits, challenges and rewards of friendship as an aspect of co-inquiry' (Sexton and Sen 2018, 884). Sexton and Sen, together, describe how their friendship developed throughout and informed the course of Sexton's research project. Sen, a participant in Sexton's study, describes research as 'a razor wrapped in power and privilege,' and argues that 'something has to change;' for her, 'friendship as methodology' was 'the best process for me to tell my storey unhindered and more truthful than it has ever been told before whilst being a research participant' (Sexton and Sen 2018, 886). Sexton draws on Lisa H. Tillmann-Healy's work on 'friendship as method,' in which Tillmann-Healy describes how she engages 'friendship as a method of inquiry,' where though she might employ 'traditional forms of data gathering' including participant observation and interviewing, the 'primary [research] procedures are those [used] to build and sustain friendship: conversation, everyday involvement, compassion, giving, and vulnerability' (Tillmann-Healy 2003, 731, 734).

This work has given me language to describe a kind of relationality that has been integral to my own research process. My research focus for several years has been on understanding recordkeeping[1] as a kind of grief work; as a scholar of archival studies, I have been asking how closer attention to the emotional dimensions of recordkeeping can inform – and possibly transform – the ways that archivists carry out their work with record creators, donors and researchers. In 2018, I received funding for a project that aimed to explore the connections between recordkeeping and grief work through three research activities: (1) interviews with bereaved parents about how they make, keep and use records as part of their personal grief work; (2) interviews with archivists about how grief (and other emotions) is part of archival work; and (3) research in bereavement collections, a term I have used to describe archives that are wholly or in part created through a grieving process. This research activity on grief and records was preceded by a more-or-less failed study on online grief communities, where drawing on Appadurai's (2003) work, I was interested in studying how online grief communities (i.e. the types of communities that develop in particular online platforms centered on experiences of grief) function as aspirational archives. My research focused on online communities created and nurtured by bereaved parents and considered the types of memory work carried out by parents as both a means of remembering and a means of continuing a relationship with their child (see Mitchell et al. 2012; Bailey, Bell, and Kennedy 2015).

My research interest in grief and recordkeeping is deeply personal. My work over the last near decade has been profoundly influenced by my experience of the stillbirth of my second daughter, Anja. In the early stage of my grief, which coincided with the final stage of my doctoral work, I found myself unable to work on my dissertation project, which suddenly seemed absolutely trivial; however, as a junior scholar about to go on the job market, I also felt unable to stop working. Increasingly, as a means of trying to keep working at something that felt meaningful, I shifted my attention to what I was beginning to recognize as a particular type of memory work in the online grief communities that provided almost the only emotional outlet for my own grief and longing for my daughter. Eventually, I began to widen my study of the connections between grief and archives to think first about the creation of records as a means of working through grief, and then about the work of archivists and how grief might play a role in their relationships with others (creators, donors, researchers) and with the records in their care.

Of course, all research is personal to some extent (England 1994; Jaggar 1989; Loughran and Mannay 2018), but some research is *more* personal, and some projects are inherently more intimate than others. My work on grief and recordkeeping is one of those projects where intimacy – in this case, intimate relationships, intimate acts, and intimate records – is pronounced. Each phase of the research project outlined above has involved some kind of intimate relationship, involving the disclosure of intensely personal information that often made both teller and listener vulnerable and required some negotiation of trust. In the interviews I conducted with bereaved parents, for example, the stories shared with me were of deeply personal loss and trauma, while even in archival research, working through folders and files, the intimate details of other people's lives are revealed, sometimes, but not always, intentionally.[2]

How do we, as researchers, deal with such intimacy, with the inherent relationality of intimate research? If we work at research institutions, we will be guided in practice by REBs, which dictate procedures around participant recruitment, procurement of informed consent, risk assessment and mitigation of harms, and the confidentiality of participant data. However, many researchers have called attention to the rather constrained views REBs take regarding what aspects of research require ethics overview (e.g. REBs focus on recruitment and consent but rarely on data analysis and representation), as well as who requires 'protection' (e.g. REBs focus on mitigating harms to research subjects while ignoring or obscuring the impacts of research on other parties, including the researcher, research assistants, and other stakeholders).

One such critique comes from Denise Turner and Rebecca Webb, who discuss the 'binary of "ethics" and "Ethics"' (Turner and Webb 2014, 383). Citing Simon Blackburn, they define Ethics as 'the institutional discourse of ethical research' and ethics as 'the relational ethics of actual research practice' (Blackburn 2001; Turner and Webb 2014, 383–384), and explore how 'Ethics' operates sometimes at the expense of 'ethics.' Both Turner and Webb work with research populations considered vulnerable: in Turner's case, bereaved parents and in Webb's, children. Their article describes how REB protocols, designed to protect vulnerable participants, were used to uncritically and paternalistically assess vulnerability, a process that resulted in removing agency from participants as well as misjudging how the risk of harm manifested in their research. In Turner's research, for example, bereaved parents were judged to be vulnerable, but Turner shows how participating in the research project empowered them by providing an outlet to share their stories and their child's memory, while other research participants – assistants involved in data analysis – *were* negatively affected but had been overlooked as being at risk because they were not research subjects, but rather part of the research team.[3] In this way, Turner and Webb's work calls attention to the myopic assessment of vulnerability and understanding of relationality by university REBs; they are not alone in doing so.

Feminist Research Practices and the Problems with REBs

Many feminist researchers have questioned the ability of institutional ethical review to adequately address the full range of ethics-related questions and concerns that can arise during the research process. Ethics review is essentially intended to protect the research subject from harm: to protect those who *are researched* from the *researchers*. Institutional ethics review in Canada is guided by the Tri-Council Policy Statement: Ethical Conduct for Research Involving Humans (2018), which is primarily concerned with risk to participants, informed consent, and confidentiality of participant data. The policy directs researchers to identify risks of participation in research, as well as steps to mitigate those risks; to explain how informed and ongoing consent will be obtained; and to explain the steps that will be taken to ensure participant anonymity or confidentiality. This approach to ethics review mirrors the processes described by Edwards and Mauthner (2014, np) at universities in the United Kingdom, which 'usually require researchers to obtain written ethical approval from any collaborating organizations involved in the research and to ask research participants to sign a consent form basically stating that they have had the nature and purpose of the research explained to them and that they fully and freely consent to participate.'

Edwards and Mauthner critique this approach for being overly simplistic: 'Such an approach,' they explain, 'implies an either/or position: either consent is informed, participants are protected, and so on, or they are not.' The typical approach of REBs, they add, is also overly deterministic, implying also 'that all the ethical issues involved in a research project can be determined at the start of the project being carried out, that any potential harm may be offset by research participants' stated willingness, and that an ethics committee sanctioned project is by definition an ethical one.' Edwards and Mauthner echo other feminist researchers in suggesting that 'the aim appears to be to avoid ethical dilemmas through asserting formalistic principles, rather than providing guidance on how to deal with them' (Edwards and Mauthner 2014, np).

This claim highlights several limitations of REBs as arbiters of what is ethical in research. Feminist researchers critique the REB emphasis on principles rather than process (England 1994), arguing that this approach creates rigidity, emphasizes the distance – deemed necessary – between the researcher and her subject, and assumes that if the principles of harm reduction and informed consent guide the development of the research design, the research that is carried out will be unproblematic. DeVault and Gross (2014, np) have suggested that as 'research ethics review' became 'increasingly institutionalized, many qualitative researchers have shared with feminists the sense that routinizing ethical review work can work against the inductive, improvisational character of qualitative research.'

The ethics review process seems to imply that all research steps and their attendant risks can be identified before the research takes place, and that the researcher is able to control them. In 1994, Kim England called attention to the neopositivist empiricism that underpins such assumptions and 'specifies a strict dichotomy between object and subject as a prerequisite for objectivity.' 'Such an epistemology,' England goes on to argue, 'is supported by methods that position the researcher as an omnipotent expert in control of both passive research subjects and the research process.' While both 'feminism and the so-called postmodern turn in the social sciences' presented 'a serious challenge to the methodological hegemony of neopositivist empiricism' (1994, 81), feminist scholars – and other qualitative researchers – have continued to point to similar kinds of epistemological scaffolding in contemporary ethics review procedures. England suggested that research should be seen as a process rather than a product, as 'an ongoing, intersubjective (or more broadly, a dialogic) activity' (1994, 82), but institutional ethics boards remain focused on procedures, on controlling research before it begins, and underestimate the process and complications of *doing* research.

Another serious – and connected – critique aimed at ethical review boards relates to how the focus on harm and risk is not necessarily matched by a commitment to *care*.

Although the relationship between the researched and the researcher has been central to determining what is ethical and what is not, Judith Preissle and Yuri Han argue that 'it has been abstract principle rather than caring that frames most conventional thought about this relationship' (2014, np). This focus on principle at the expense of care is evident in the research examples provided by Turner and Webb; REB review focused on consent procedures and risk assessment, i.e. on 'Ethics,' to protect participants, but failed to consider how a caring research design could empower and extend compassion to participants or to acknowledge the multiple individuals who participate in research projects and require care.

Friendship in/and Research: Three Case Studies

In this section, I turn to three examples of how ideas about vulnerability, intimacy, friendship and care have affected my understanding of the ethical dimensions of my research work and call attention to the inadequacies of institutional ethics review to address these dimensions.

Researching Online Grief Communities

After nine years, I rarely turn to the blog I used to post to every day as an outlet for my grief and a means of connecting with other parents. Our 'cohort' has mostly moved offline, the most intense days of grief and need behind us. Every once in a while though, I come back, write a few paragraphs, hit post and feel better. One Friday in February, overwhelmed by months of teaching and parenting through a global pandemic and having passed Anja's birthday by with barely a pause, I write a post about the ongoingness of grief and the fears I have that my daughter is mostly forgotten. This post calls them back, that old cohort of 'loss mamas.' 'I think of Anja every time I dig my hands deep into the rich, red earth of my garden,' one writes. She is recalling another blog post I wrote in the first year after Anja's death on a visit to New Brunswick, where the mud that lines the bed of the marshes near my inlaws' home is thick and red and oozing and where I reflected on the strangeness of grieving so far from the only place I had ever held her. It still amazes me, this connection we forged, through distance and time, how we remember with and for each other, how we continue to hold each other up even now, nearly a decade later.

When I set out to study online grief communities, I knew I had to work carefully. As a participant in these communities, I could reflect on my own use of and connection to them. I had been a reluctant but desperate joiner; reluctant both because I hated the situation I was in and because I was not an 'online' person at that point, and desperate because there were so few places where I felt safe talking about my daughter and my grief. I knew many other participants in these spaces felt the same way and wondered how I could protect these spaces and ensure they remained safe as I turned a research eye toward them.

In 2012, when I first began this project, I found writing on the ethics of research in online communities scarce, although I think it was mostly that I did not know where to look. I consulted the guidance provided by my university research ethics board, and found that according to them, since the communities I was thinking about operated 'in the open' on the web, they were considered to have no expectation of privacy and therefore I was not required to seek their consent to study them. This did not sit right with me, though when I talked to some colleagues they assured me that it would be acceptable to write about what people posted to websites and blogs that were not moderated or password protected.

Several times I tried to write an article about aspirational archives and online grief communities but each time I found myself incapable of finishing: it simply *felt wrong*. I replayed online conversations about feeling misunderstood by those who had not lived through the death of a baby and remembered the feeling of intense relief – and *release* – I had felt when I first found these spaces and experienced the kind of support and understanding they provided. Could I really put them on display and open them up for scrutiny? Sure, they were not closed spaces, but did that make them truly public? The thought of turning a research lens on these community spaces made me profoundly uncomfortable.

Eventually, I discovered scholars writing about the ethics of online research (for example Morrison 2011; Luka and Millette 2018; Cowan and Rault 2018; Moravec 2017); Malin Svenginsson's assertion that 'even if a certain internet medium admittedly is public' (2009, 77) it might not be experienced as public by its users resonated deeply with me, but I also knew that I understood how true it was because of the relationships I had developed and continued online. When I stopped writing the article, each time it was because I was thinking: I cannot do this to my friends, to these people with whom I have relationships. And then, I knew, too, that that feeling must be extended outward, to other communities that operated online in 'intimate publics' (Morrison 2011; Berlant 2008) of their own making.

In their recent work, The Feminist Data ManifestNo, Cifor et al. (2019) 'refuse to understand data as disembodied and thereby dehumanized and departicularized' and 'commit to understanding data as always and variously attached to bodies.' Here, the connection between a body and her data, or the traces she leaves through her actions or presence online, is emphasized, so that as researchers, we have to think about the person behind the post. This is a kind of consideration that goes beyond determining how we can attain informed consent from community posters, contributors and lurkers, or how we can ensure confidentiality in publication of findings, to considering whether even beginning to make those efforts is a violation of friendship or a repudiation of care. I believe there is a great deal to be gained from better understanding how online grief communities function, but I have never been able to determine how to study these communities without feeling I am exploiting and extracting from them – without feeling like I am trespassing on a relationship. I put the many false starts of that article away, though I have written about the difficulty of *trying* to do this research; that in itself, I fear, might be too much.

The guidance on my university REB website still asserts that 'if you are using *publicly available* information from a social networking site (i.e. information that you do not need a social networking account or password to access) and no other non-public source to obtain your data, this research is exempt from review under Article 2.2 of the Tri Council Policy Statement.' (emphasis in original, https://ethics.research.ubc.ca/sites/ore.ubc.ca/files/documents/social_networking_sites-GN-June_2012.pdf). They warn that 'intellectual property rights protections or dissemination restrictions imposed by the owners of the site' and state that 'it is up to individual researchers to familiarize themselves with these requirements.' This is a perfect illustration of adherence to principle with no advocacy for care: any other researcher with less understanding of the complex dynamics and relationships that make up the online communities I tend to in my own research process is free to come and turn their lens upon them.

Archival Research and Human Subjects

When Alex and I arrived at the University of Victoria Archives, we were prepared to encounter difficult material, having understood from the description of the Lara Gilbert fonds that it would contain records related to Gilbert's experience of depression and her death from suicide. The fonds includes Gilbert's childhood diaries, where she wrote about her love of Michael Jackson, about school, friends and crushes. I noticed that she and I used the same kind of diaries. I remembered buying them at a little shop in Fan Tan Alley, not that far, really, from where we sat in the basement of the university library. Gilbert's diaries turned darker in her teen years, as she started to recover memories of childhood sexual abuse by a family member. She wrote about depression, about being hospitalized, about being sexually assaulted by an orderly while she was hospitalized. When it was time for a lunch break, Alex and I emerged from the archives in a stereotypical state of shellshock: blinking in the sunlight, feeling 'out of time,' more than two decades past the time where Gilbert lived and on a different university campus, but also feeling deeply affected by – and deeply protective of – Gilbert's experiences.

There is no ethical review process for archival research. The Canadian TCPS2 policy explains that archival materials are considered publicly available and therefore not subject to REB review. As Heidi McKee and James Porter point out 'boxes of papers' are not human subjects. They are not 'living persons with whom you can negotiate consent and collaborate' (2012, 60). McKee and Porter go on, however, to suggest that there are reasons why researchers might *treat* archives as human subjects, arguing that in some ways, 'as an extension of the person, representing her thoughts, feelings, ideas, words, and even body,' archival 'papers are also people' (2012, 78, 60) As with the data traces we leave behind on the web, archival materials are 'always and variously attached to bodies'; they cannot be 'dehumanized and departicularized' (Cifor et al. 2019; see also Lee 2017, 2021). Indeed, the work of archivists, from appraisal and selection to arrangement and description, stresses the connection of archival material to the person who created it, keeping all of the materials of a single creator together, naming a collection after its creator, and centering finding aids around a biographical sketch (Douglas 2018; Caswell 2014; Iacovino 2010).

McKee and Porter argue that there needs to be 'a shift from seeing the archives as *documents* to seeing the archives as *persons* – perhaps not persons in the IRB [institutional review board] sense of subjects, but persons as research participants' (2012, 77). While we may not be able to consult with the creator of an archives we can consider our responsibilities to them as persons and participants by asking ourselves questions about our motivations for doing and publishing research; about what kind of consent might have been provided by the archives creator, i.e. what the creator might have understood would happen to her records and how they would be used; and by thinking more deeply about what is public and what is private in archives and whether there are 'times and circumstances' when the archival material available to us as researchers should nevertheless 'not be used, should not be accessed, should not be made public' (McKee and Porter 2012, 70).

Our ethical responsibilities to archival subjects as research participants extend too to how we represent them in our writing, how we 'help the dead, who do not know they are dead, finish their stories' (Birmingham 2008, 144; Kirsch 2008). This is a responsibility Alex and I have certainly felt. We have been concerned to 'do right by' (Hobbs 2012) Gilbert as we think about how we can or should continue her story. On the first page of one of her childhood diaries, Gilbert left a clear message to potential readers: 'Do Not Look in Here!!! This is my Diary!! This is Lara Gilbert's LIFE!!' (Lara Gilbert fonds). It was easy to feel like trespassers in these papers full of family secrets, and detailed descriptions of Gilbert's depression, treatment and suicidal ideation. When I think about my own childhood diaries being read by researchers, I want to protect Gilbert's childish dreams and fears from scrutiny. But Gilbert left a note to her mother to keep her diaries private for a period of time, and then to try to publish them. Kirsch (2008, 24–25) extends the researcher's ethical responsibility to archival subjects to their descendants as well, and though Gilbert has no descendants, her mother has played a prominent role in securing the archives' future; she also figures prominently in the archives' texts. Alex and I have thought about our responsibility to her, too, and to our representation of the mother-daughter relationship. There are things we know now about the archives because we have sat around a table with Gilbert's mother, and our research might benefit from formalizing that relationship with an ethics agreement that allows us to incorporate these conversations into our analysis of the Lara Gilbert fonds. In fact, we have come to a potentially uncomfortable moment where we might need to decide whether we bring the friendship into the research or take the research out of the friendship. It is also an instructive moment, illustrating the intimate connections that archival materials have to lived lives, to bodies in the world outside the reference room and academic journals.

Intimate Interviews and Research Relationships

I am always a little bit nervous before I start an interview, but this time I am more anxious than usual. I have known Claire virtually for eight years, but we have never met in person. She was one of the first bereaved mothers I 'met' online. In the early days of my grief, I found her blog, written about the stillbirth of her son (who died only three months before Anja) and the grief that then engulfed her. I commented on one of her posts, and then she commented on one of mine. After several weeks of comments on each other's blogs, we exchanged email addresses and have kept up a correspondence ever since. We write on our children's birthdays, other significant dates, when we are especially sad or angry, and often just to check in. But we have never seen each other's faces, or heard each other's voices. Will it be weird? I wonder. Will we be awkward? I sit in the tiny, sterile room at the university where I have decided I have the most privacy to conduct these interviews and sign in to Skype. She signs on. She smiles at me. The tears come right way. 'Hello,' we both say at the same time. We recognize each other immediately.

Between December 2018 and March 2020, I carried out a series of interviews with bereaved mothers, whom I recruited through the online grief communities I belong to. After deciding not to study these communities as aspirational archives, I was nevertheless interested in the type of memory work bereaved parents engage in, especially when recordkeeping is part of their grief work. I thought if I interviewed individual parents about their personal record making and keeping practices I could keep the online communities out of the study and, by building member checks into my research design, ensure parents had agency over their stories and how they were represented.

Alex and I took great care completing our REB application, ensuring that our research design included many opportunities for participants to exert agency over their stories; we used a semi-structured interview protocol that allowed me, as interviewer, to follow participants' lead and we returned transcripts to participants to edit before they approved them. We also attempted in our application to communicate how participants who might at first glance appear to be extremely vulnerable as grieving parents could also experience the research process as empowering, explaining why anonymity might not be the preferred condition for a mother who worries her child will be forgotten.

The attention we paid to agency and vulnerability in our research design helped us to practice an ethics of care, but overall the REB process also made it difficult to always give priority to care over principle. For example, letters of initial contact and consent forms had to be prepared in advance and include some formulaic elements; even written in the 'lay language' the REB advocated, these formal research instruments and rules about when and how to communicate made 'friendship as method' difficult to enact at key points in the process. Because several of the women I interviewed were known to me before the interviews, the scripted communications felt particularly distancing and cold.

The interviews themselves were extremely intimate. I submitted to the REB a semi-structured interview protocol, with scripted questions and an acknowledgment that the interview would likely stray from the script to follow participants' interests and emphases. These interviews did not only stray, they completely broke down the interview structure, becoming what Marianne Paget (1983; quoted in DeVault and Gross 2014) terms 'search procedure,' or the state an interview achieves when 'the conversation can unfold as a collaborative moment of making knowledge' (DeVault and Gross 2014, np).[4] I not only asked questions and listened to answers, but also shared my own experiences of bereavement with the women I interviewed, and sometimes they asked for advice or wanted to know how I had navigated some aspect of grief. For example, several times a conversation evolved about sibling grief and parenting while grieving. Two of the parents knew I had living children older than theirs and wanted to know how I had talked to them about Anja's death, how they behaved and reacted, and whether I could share what had helped and what had not. In a more standard interview protocol, I might have tried to shift the conversation back to their own experiences, but it felt disingenuous and even a bit cruel to deflect or ignore their questions. The effort required to maintain the distance between researcher and researched that, as England (1994) points out, underpins assumptions about the researcher's ability to protect the researched from harm, was impossible to sustain in the context of our relationship to each other as bereaved parents with shared experiences of trauma; even if it had been possible to maintain, in this case, it would have felt entirely *un*ethical to remain stoic and detached in response to participants' disclosures. To not have shared parts of my own experience would have rendered the research exercise entirely extractive; sharing some of my own experience did not erase the power imbalance that is inherent in research but it introduced some reciprocity to the relationship, a little give in the midst of the usual taking.[5]

One ethically ambiguous part of this project was virtually overlooked by the REB process: the representation of research findings in published writing and conference presentations. While REBs are concerned with participants' anonymity and/or confidentiality in research dissemination, when it was time to write articles about ideas of records and recordkeeping in bereavement, I was struck by how much leeway I had to shape the representation of their stories, confidential or not. Even as I tried to center participant voices and experiences through the use of long quotations, I was aware of the questions England (1994, 86) asks of this practice: is it a 'sufficient means of including "others," especially when those quotes are actually responses to unsolicited questions that came about through the researcher's disruption of someone else's life?'

Birch and Miller (2014, np) extoll a 'notion of participation [that] embodies specific ideals of how the researcher and researched should cooperate with each other in order to form a "good", honest and reciprocal relationship,' but then also note how at some point in a project 'research ideals of participation' will 'come into conflict with our personal goals of completing our projects and fitting into the requirements of the academic world.' As a research activity, writing (and other types of knowledge mobilization) is a space where participant and research motivations can diverge: the parents I interviewed wanted to tell stories about their babies; I needed to write a paper about recordkeeping. Writing a paper about how the recordkeeping practices of a group of individuals who, prior to the interview, had not conceived of records in the disciplinary contexts I operate in required significant interpretive work, and I know it is possible that some of the connections I have made in my writing, while unlikely to be harmful to participants, could be baffling, and potentially also distancing. One of the parent participants, Brooke, talked about how vulnerable she felt showing photographic records of her baby to people who she thought would not be able to look at them with love: after reading our disciplinary interpretation of their experiences, would the parents we interviewed feel we had looked with love (Douglas and Alisauskas 2021)?

Ellis (2007, 10) recounts uncomfortable encounters she had with past ethnographic research participants who felt she had misrepresented – and even maligned – them in published findings and muses:

'I suspect that even in those cases, many of us confused our roles. We became friends with those we studied because we couldn't help ourselves, and because it made our work easier while we were there. However, friendship was secondary to our research purposes, and when we left, our relational loyalties shifted to readers and professional associations. The problem comes not from being friends with participants but from acting as a friend yet not living up to the obligations of friendship.'

What does it mean to live up to the obligations of friendship in research once our participant-friends are no longer as intimately involved in the processes of research? How can we practice what Wilson (2008, 77) terms 'relational accountability,' or the imperative to 'be respectful of and help to build the relationships that have been established through the process of finding out information'[6] through all phases of the research including its dissemination and enactment? In our own writing (Douglas and Alisauskas 2021, 10), and as a direct response to Brooke's plea for others to look with love, Alex and I asked ourselves what it would mean to listen and write with love. We tried in our article to 'suspend disciplinary judgment and to listen to what record-making and record-keeping means to the parents we spoke with,' to center parents' own words and stories, and to center, too, 'their loss and their love and the ways these have shaped their understanding of what a record is and what it can do in the world.' The result, I think, is a new perspective on the value of records in individual lives, but like England, I am still left wondering, is it sufficient?

Conclusion: Enacting Compassionate Research Practices

Writing about research with 'intimate others,' (and echoing Turner and Webb's distinction between Ethics and ethics), Ellis (2007, 4) identifies two 'dimensions of ethics;' drawing on the work of Guillemin and Gillam (2004), Ellis differentiates between procedural ethics, 'the kind mandated by Institutional Review Board (IRB) committees to ensure procedures adequately deal with informed consent, confidentiality, rights to privacy, deception, and protecting human subjects from harm,' and 'ethics in practice, or situational ethics,' which 'deal with the unpredictable, often subtle, yet ethically important moments that come up in the field.' I have tried in the examples above, and especially in the short research vignettes scattered throughout this paper, to draw attention to some of these 'unpredictable moments' where the difference between procedural and situational ethics is palpable.

To these two 'ethical dimensions,' Ellis adds a third, which she calls 'relational ethics' and connects to Gilligan's (1982; 1988) and Noddings (1984; 1995) work on ethics of care. Relational ethics, Ellis explains, 'recognizes and values mutual respect, dignity, and connectedness between researcher and researched, and between researchers and the communities in which they live and work.' Ellis further argues that relational ethics 'requires researchers to act from our hearts and minds, to acknowledge our interpersonal bonds to others, and initiate and maintain conversations' (Ellis 2007, 4). In other work, Ellis still more explicitly specifies care as a value that must underpin at least some types of research; Ellis calls for 'compassionate research,' or research that 'emphasizes what we can do for participants, instead of what we can get out of them; that connects us with the other, instead of pulling us apart; that contributes to social justice, rather than only to the accumulation of 'data' or, worse, to the unread books and articles collecting dust on library shelves.' (2017, 54)

A focus on compassionate and relational research practices, which incorporates also elements of Tillmann-Healy's 'friendship as method,' might fill some of the gaps REB review leaves behind itself. Ellis lays out several 'premises' of compassionate research that guide her in work. These include reminders that 'stories are told differently in developing relationships:' when a 'relationship grows and trust is built' participants might 'share more intimately, seeking information, feedback, and mutual sharing from the researcher.' This type of sharing, Ellis argues, provides participants with more 'opportunity to work through, amend, delete, and add to the story in ways not possible with a stranger asking questions in a single interview.' The developing relationship between researcher and participant will also help the researcher learn how to 'read the participant in more nuanced ways,' to know 'what is appropriate to ask, how to follow up on ideas, and when to back off' (Ellis 2017, 56–57). In the different research scenarios I describe above, a compassionate research practice would sanction the kind of reciprocal disclosure and abandonment of researcher distance that characterized my interviews with bereaved parents, while also providing a touchstone for determining whether decisions Alex and I made more or less on our own about whether our representation of those conversations constituted '*doing right by.*'

A compassionate approach to research would encourage me to pay attention to the qualms I have had about exposing individuals like Lara Gilbert and the parent participants in online grief communities, who have ostensibly provided their material to scrutiny, but who, for many reasons, might not have imagined what such scrutiny could look or feel like. Ellis states that one of the goals of her work has been 'to interact with survivors in ways that honor, care for, and support them as they reflect on the tragedies they have endured' (Ellis 2017, 57). Although I might not have been entirely in the wrong to continue my work on online communities, I would not have been capable of ensuring that that work would 'honor, care for, and support' the community without the capacity to consult and converse with all of its members. Similarly, I can reflect on ideas about honoring, caring for and supporting participants to determine when material in an archival collection is – despite being publicly available – perhaps unnecessary to publicize in my own work.

Overall, Ellis's approach to compassionate research 'emphasizes the role of connection and feeling' (2017, 58) in decision making related to research design and ethics. Sometimes it has felt to me that connection and feeling are exactly what is missing from 'procedural ethics.' In my current project, I am trying to center connection and feeling, compassion and friendship, in the design of flexible, responsive and engaged project protocols and instruments. I am also trying to center connection and feeling, compassion and friendship, in the continuing evolution of my research relationships. As several feminist scholars practicing relational ethics have noted, it is not easy in these models to know when a project ends: how do we end a research relationship that is also a friendship (Duncombe and Jessop 2014)? This question is at the front of my mind as I consider the questions about friendship and research with which I opened this article. Will our conversations around the table with our artist friend evolve into a formal research relationship? If so, what will change in our friendship and in our research, and how will we navigate one kind of relationship within the other? I have not yet been able to answer these questions, but I know that when I do, the answer will come not from my university ethics board, but from my heart.

I gratefully acknowledge the financial support of the Social Sciences and Humanities Research Council of Canada through the Insight Development and Insight grant programs. I am especially grateful to the parents who participated in my research on bereavement and recordkeeping, to Lara Wilson, Director of Special Collections and University Archivist at University of Victoria Archives, for her guidance with the Lara Gilbert fonds, to Carole Gilbert for kitchen table conversations and emails, and to Alex Alisauskas for her innumerable contributions to the research projects described here.

Notes

1. As an archival studies scholar, I use *recordkeeping* as a term that encompasses acts of record creation, use, organization and preservation by records creators and by archivists and other records professionals.
2. While archival donors can set restrictions on public access to collections or parts of collections, usually for a set period of time (e.g. until ten years past the death of the donor or

twenty-five years from the time of donation), thereby controlling access to particularly private or intimate records, there are other ways sensitive material may be inadvertently made available; record collections are often large and cover wide swaths of time so that even their creators may be unaware of what is documented and preserved in them. Even the most controlled archives can contain areas of wilderness.
3. Regarding attention to research team needs in 'emotionally demanding research' see for example: Kumar and Cavallaro (2018), Rager (2005), Tilley (2003).
4. See also Hollway and Jefferson's (2013) discussion of 'psychosocial subjects' and the ways in which 'unconscious intersubjective dynamics' affect the co-creation of meaning in qualitative interviewing.
5. This type of sharing is not appropriate in every research relationship, and many research questions can be answered without it. Researcher sharing in interviews can also be problematic. For nuanced discussions of researcher disclosure in qualitative interviewing see for example Miller (2017); Harris (2015); Ellis and Burger (2002).
6. The principle of relationality in Indigenous research methods has significantly impacted my thinking about friendship in research, but more broadly underscores the urgent need for reciprocal, respectful and accountable research in and with over-researched populations and in particular with and in Indigenous communities. On relationality in Indigenous research methodology see also Kovach 2017; Kovach 2021; Archibald 2008.

Disclosure Statement

No potential conflict of interest was reported by the author(s).

Funding

This work was supported by Social Sciences and Humanities Research Council of Canada: [Grant Number 430-2018-00182].

References

Appadurai, Arjun. 2003. "Archive and Aspiration." In *Information is Alive: Art and Theory on Archiving and Retrieving Data*, edited by Joke Brouwer, and Arien Mulder, 14–25. Rotterdam: NAI Publishers.

Archibald, Jo-Ann. 2008. *Indigenous Storywork: Educating the Heart, Mind, Body, and Spirit*. Vancouver: UBC Press.

Bailey, Louis, Jo Bell, and David Kennedy. 2015. "Continuing Social Presence of the Dead: Exploring Suicide Bereavement through Online Memorialisation." *New Review of Hypermedia and Multimedia* 21 (1–2): 72–86. doi:10.1080/13614568.2014.983554.

Berlant, Lauren. 2008. *The Female Complaint: The Unfinished Business of Sentimentality in American Culture*. Durham, North Carolina: Duke University Press.

Birch, Maxine, and Tina Miller. 2014. "Encouraging Participation: Ethics and Responsibilities." In *Ethics in Qualitative Research*, edited by Tina Miller, Maxine Birch, Melanie Mauthner, and Julie Jessop. np online. London: SAGE Publications. doi:10.4135/9781473913912.

Birmingham, Elizabeth (Betsy). 2008. "'I See Dead People': Archive, Crypt, and an Argument for the Researcher's Sixth Sense." In *Beyond the Archives*, edited by Gesa E. Kirsch, and Liz Rohan, 139–146. Carbondale: Southern Illinois University Press.

Blackburn, Simon. 2001. *Ethics – A Very Short Introduction*. Oxford: Oxford University Press.

Caswell, Michelle. 2014. "Toward a Survivor-Centred Approach to Documenting Human Rights Abuse: Lessons from Community Archives." *Archival Science* 14 (3–4): 307–322.

Cifor, Marika, Patricia Garcia, T. L. Cowan, Jasmine Rault, Tonia Sutherland, Anita Chan, Anna Lauren Hoffman, Niloufar Salehi, and Lisa Nakamura. 2019. *Feminist Data Manifest-No*. Retrieved from: https://www.manifestno.com/.

Cowan, T. L., and Jasmine Rault. 2018. "Onlining Queer Acts: Digital Research Ethics and Caring for Risky Archives." *Women & Performance: A Journal of Feminist Theory* 28 (2): 5–16. doi:10.1080/0740770X.2018.1473985.

DeVault, Marjorie L., and Glenda Gross. 2014. "Feminist Qualitative Interviewing: Experience, Talk, and Knowledge." In *Handbook of Feminist Research: Theory and Praxis*, edited by Sharlene Nagy Hesse-Biber. np online. Thousand Oaks: SAGE Publications. doi:10.4135/9781483384740.

Douglas, Jennifer. 2018. "A Call to Rethink Archival Creation: Exploring Types of Creation in Personal Archives." *Archival Science* 18 (1): 29–49.

Douglas, Jennifer, and Alexandra Alisauskas. 2021. "'It Feels Like a Life's Work': Recordkeeping as an Act of Love." *Archivaria* 91: 6–37.

Duncombe, Jean, and Julie Jessop. 2014. "'Doing Rapport' and the Ethics of 'Faking Friendship.'." In *Ethics and Qualitative Research*, edited by Tina Miller, Maxine Birch, Melanie Mauthner, and Julie Jessop. np online. London: SAGE Publications. doi:10.4135/9781473913912.

Edwards, Rosalind, and Melanie Mauthner. 2014. "Ethics and Feminist Research: Theory and Practice." In *Ethics in Qualitative Research*, edited by Tina Miller, Maxine Birch, Melanie Mauthner, and Julie Jessop. np online. London: SAGE Publications. doi:10.4135/9781473913912.

Ellis, Carolyn. 2007. "Telling Secrets, Revealing Lives: Relational Ethics in Research with Intimate Others." *Qualitative Inquiry* 13 (1): 3–29. doi:10.1177/1077800406294947.

Ellis, Carolyn. 2017. "Manifesting Compassionate Autoethnographic Research: Focusing on Others." *International Review of Qualitative Research* 10 (1): 54–61. doi:10.1525/irqr.2017.10.1.54.

Ellis, Carolyn, and Leigh Berger. 2002. "Their Story/My Story/Our Story: Including the Researcher's Experience in Interview Research." In *Handbook of Interview Research*, edited by Jaber F. Gubrium, and James A. Holstein. np online. Thousand Oaks: Sage.

Elm, Malin Sveningsson. 2009. "Question Three: How do Various Notions of Privacy Influence Decisions in Qualitative Internet Research?" In *Internet Inquiry: Conversations about Method*, edited by Annette N. Markham, and Nancy K. Baym. SAGE Publications. Chapter doi:10.4135/9781483329086.n7.

England, Kim V.L. 1994. "Getting Personal: Reflexivity, Positionality, and Feminist Research." *The Professional Geographer* 46 (1): 80–89. doi:10.1111/j.0033-0124.1994.00080.x.

Gilligan, Carol. 1982. *In a Different Voice: Psychological Theory and Women's Development*. Cambridge, MA: Harvard University Press.

Gilligan, Carol. 1988. "Remapping the Moral Domain: New Images of Self in Relationship." In *Mapping the Moral Domain: A Contribution of Women's Thinking to Psychological Theory and Education*, edited by Carol Gilligan, Janie Victoria Ward, Jill McLean Taylor, and Betty Bardige, 3–21. Cambridge, MA: Harvard University Press.

Government of Canada. Panel on Research Ethics. 2018. *Tri-Council Policy Statement: Ethical Conduct for Research Involving Humans – TCPS 2* https://ethics.gc.ca/eng/policy-politique_tcps2-eptc2_2018.html.

Guillemin, Marilys, and Lynn Gillam. 2004. "Ethics, Reflexivity, and 'Ethically Important Moments' in Research." *Qualitative Inquiry* 10 (2): 261–280. doi:10.1177/1077800403262360.

Harris, Magdalena. 2015. "'Three in the Room': Embodiment, Disclosure, and Vulnerability in Qualitative Research." *Qualitative Health Research* 25 (12): 1689–1699. doi:10.1177/10497232314566324.

Hobbs, Catherine. 2012. "Personal Ethics: Being an Archivist of Writers." In *Basements and Attics, Closets and Cyberspace: Explorations in Canadian Women's Archives*, edited by Linda M. Morra, and Jessica Schagerl, 181–192. Waterloo, ON: Wilfrid Laurier University Press.

Hollway, Wendy, and Tony Jefferson. 2013. *Doing Qualitative Research Differently: A Psychosocial Approach, 2nd ed.* London: Sage.

Iacovino, Livia. 2010. "Rethinking Archival, Ethical, and Legal Frameworks for Records of Indigenous Australian Communities: A Participant Relationship Model of Rights and Responsibilities." *Archival Science* 10 (4): 353–372.

Jaggar, Alison M. 1989. "Love and Knowledge: Emotion in Feminist Epistemology." *Inquiry* 32 (2): 151–176.

Kirsch, Gesa E. 2008. "Being on Location: Serendipity, Place, and Archival Research." In *Beyond the Archives*, edited by Gesa E. Kirsch, and Liz Rohan, 20–27. Carbondale: Southern Illinois University Press.

Kovach, Margaret. 2017. "Doing Indigenous Methodologies: A Letter to a Research Class." In *The SAGE Handbook of Qualitative Research, 5th ed.*, edited by Norman K. Denzin, and Yvonne S. Lincoln, 214–234. London: Sage.

Kovach, Margaret. 2021. *Indigenous Methodologies: Characteristics, Conversations, and Contexts, 2nd ed.* Toronto: University of Toronto Press.

Kumar, Smita, and Liz Cavallaro. 2018. "Researcher Self-Care in Emotionally Demanding Research: A Proposed Conceptual Framework." *Qualitative Health Research* 28 (4): 648–658.

Lara Gilbert fonds. *University of Victoria Archives*. Victoria, BC.

Lee, Jamie A. 2017. "A Queer/ed Archival Methodology: Archival Bodies as Nomadic Subjects." *Journal of Critical Library and Information Studies* 2 (1). https://journals.litwinbooks.com/index.php/jclis/article/view/26

Lee, Jamie A. 2021. *Producing the Archival Body*. London: Routledge.

Loughran, Tracey, and Dawn Mannay. 2018. "Introduction: Why Emotion Matters." In *Emotion and the Researcher: Sites, Subjectivities, and Relationships*, edited by Tracey Loughran, and Dawn Mannay, 1–15. Bingley: Emerald Publishing.

Luka, Mary Elizabeth, and Mélanie Millette. 2018. "(Re)Framing Big Data: Activating Situated Knowledges and a Feminist Ethic of Care in Social Media Research." *Social Media & Society* 4 (2): 1–10. doi:10.1177/2056305118768297.

McKee, Heidi A., and James E. Porter. 2012. "The Ethics of Archival Research." *College Composition and Communication* 64 (1): 59–81.

Miller, Tina. 2017. "Telling the Difficult Things: Creating Spaces for Disclosure, Rapport and 'Collusion' in Qualitative Interviews." *Women's Studies International Forum* 61: 81–86.

Mitchell, Lisa M., Peter H. Stephenson, Susan Cadell, and Mary Ellen Macdonald. 2012. "Death and Grief On-Line: Virtual Memorialisation and Changing Concepts of Childhood Death and Parental Bereavement on the Internet." *Health Sociology Review* 21 (4): 413–431. doi:10.5172/hesr.2012.21.4.413.

Moravec, Michelle. 2017. "Feminist Research Practices and Digital Archives." *Australian Feminist Studies* 32: 91–92. doi:10.1080/08164649.2017.1357006.

Morrison, Aimée. 2011. "'Suffused by Feeling and Affect': The Intimate Public of Personal Mommy Blogging." *Biography* 34 (1): 37–55.

Noddings, Nan. 1984. *Caring, a Feminine Approach to Ethics and Moral Education*. Berkeley: University of California Press.

Noddings, Nan. 1995. "Caring." In *Justice and Care: Essential Readings in Feminist Ethics*, edited by Virginia Held, 7–30. Boulder, CO: Westview Press.

Paget, Marianne A. 1983. "Experience and Knowledge." *Human Studies* 6: 67–90. doi:10.1007/BF02127755.

Preissle, Judith, and Yuri Han. 2014. "Feminist Research Ethics." In *Handbook of Feminist Research: Theory and Praxis*, edited by Sharlene Nagy Hesse-Biber. np online. Thousand Oaks: SAGE Publications. doi:10.4135/9781483384740.

Rager, Kathleen B. 2005. "Compassion Stress and the Qualitative Researcher." *Qualitative Health Research* 15 (3): 423–430.

Sexton, Anna, and Dolly Sen. 2018. "More Voice, Less Ventriloquism – Exploring the Relational Dynamics in a Participatory Archive of Mental Health Recovery." *International Journal of Heritage Studies* 24 (8): 874–888. doi:10.1080/13527258.2017.1229109.

Tilley, Susan A. 2003. "'Challenging' Research Practices: Turning a Critical Lens on the Work of Transcription." *Qualitative Inquiry* 9 (5): 750–773.

Tillmann-Healy, Lisa M. 2003. "Friendship as Method." *Qualitative Inquiry* 9 (5): 729–749. doi:10.1177/1077800403254894.

Turner, Denise, and Rebecca Webb. 2014. "Ethics and/or Ethics in Qualitative Social Research: Negotiating a Path Around and between the Two." *Ethics and Social Welfare* 8 (4): 383–396. doi:10.1080/17496535.2012.745583.

Wilson, Shawn. 2008. *Research is Ceremony: Indigenous Research Methods*. Halifax & Winnipeg: Fernwood Publishing.

Feminist Research Ethics and First Nations Women's Life Narratives: A Conversation

Kath Apma Penangke Travis and Victoria Haskins

ABSTRACT
This essay offers a reflection on conducting historical research relating to First Nations women's lives and cross-cultural relationships in ways that are ethical and informed by feminist sensibilities. In dialogic mode, the authors work through issues and insights that have arisen in the process of researching the life story of Arrernte woman Minnie Undelya Apma, who was abducted as a child from her parents in Central Australia in 1920 by anthropologist Herbert Basedow and his wife Olive (Nell). The process of collaborative research between Kath and Victoria ignited a relationship of mutual understanding and empathy that yielded further enquiries. Fundamentally the process created a space for us to talk and think about the many ways we approach and understand the remarkable history of Minnie Apma's life, that includes how that story is told and by whom. We argue that there are meaningful ways for First Nations and Second Peoples researchers of First Nations' women's life narratives to work together, that will not only improve historical scholarship, but also help to build respectful relationships that counteract inequality and ongoing disempowerment of First Nations people in our society.

Introduction

We make this shared contribution as two historians, one, Kath Apma Penangke Travis, a First Nations Arrernte woman, and the other a white Australian Second Nations woman, Victoria Haskins.[1] We offer a feminist approach to the Indigenist approach proposed by Lester Irabinna Rigney (1999) who insisted that research supports self-determination struggles. Without offering a prescriptive model, our discussion suggests new avenues through which researchers of First Nations women's life narratives can contribute to archival research by theorizing and putting into practice oral (living) history. It reflects some of the questions and discussions we have had in the process of working together, as researchers and writers, on the life story of Kath's grandmother Minnie Undelya Apma. We were introduced to each other quite literally through the archives, when archivist Andrew Wilson, Senior Aboriginal Project Officer at the South Australian State Records, connected us at the end of 2015. Kath was then embarking on the journey to trace her family history, and Andrew knew that Victoria had uncovered a number of critical archival records relating to Minnie Apma's story, as part of her project on the history of Aboriginal domestic service. We have continued our conversations about Minnie's story, and about researching and writing First Nations women's histories more generally, ever since. In 2018 we presented together, on 'Whose Story is it? Aboriginal voices in history and research,' at the Australian Historical Association (AHA) conference, with another First Nations historian Aileen Marwung Walsh moderating. This written piece grows out of that conversation, and many others we have had over the years.

We present our thoughts and insights in a conversational or dialogic mode, believing this to be most appropriate to the intent and aims of both a feminist and a First Nations-centered decolonizing approach. It is not intended as a didactic or prescriptive text in any way; rather in using this form, we hope to stimulate and encourage other conversations and interactions (we draw inspiration here, too, from Whetung and Wakefield [2018]). Collaborations between First Nations and Second Nations researchers driven by the imperative to decolonize praxis raise fundamental questions about the ethics of historical research and production, as Kat Ellinghaus and Barry Judd discuss –

> we strive to find a scholarship of ethical engagement that repositions the processes of writing Australian histories about Indigenous peoples to include elements that exist beyond the colonial archive and are grounded in real life, active and dynamic engagement with contemporary Indigenous peoples and society. (2002, 59)

Conversations, 'yarning,' is established as a distinctive First Nations practice in historical research that requires researchers to step out of the 'ivory towers' of academia (Barker 2008; Bessarab and Ng'Andu 2010) and one that we draw upon here in some ways, to reflect on the possibilities and potentials of conversational collaborations. It is striking, given the particular silences in the archival records of women's voices, that such approaches are often utilized in the reconstruction of women's life histories via archival restoration and return (for example, Hughes and Trevorrow 2018). These in turn can be traced to the collaborative conversations of First Nations and Second Nations women scholars exploring the interconnections and entanglements of women's life stories (Huggins, Saunders, and Tarrago 2000), and correspond with the interest in feminist history and ethnography generally on the 'processes, products and possibilities' of collaborative – and resistant – research (Benson and Nagar 2006, 586). In our essay we begin by outlining the story of Minnie Undelya Apma – in Kath's words primarily – and then reflect individually on our own connection to her story, as the precursor to our conversation about the ethical issues that are raised for us both in the way we encounter and negotiate the archive.

Her-story: Minnie Undelya Apma

Minnie Undelya Apma was 11 years old when she was violently and abruptly stolen from her parents in 1920 from Central Australia by anthropologist, medical practitioner and geologist Dr Herbert Basedow and his wife Olive ('Nell'). Basedow was on his third expedition, funded by pastoral and mining company interests, ostensibly to examine Aboriginal people's health in the lower southern part of the Northern Territory. Loaded into the back of Basedow's camel-drawn buggy to Adelaide, Minnie was to be enslaved in the Basedow household, apparently invisible to government authorities for eight years, despite the protests of at least three deputations between 1922 and 1932 led by her father, a senior law man, and other Arrernte elders, demanding that Minnie be returned to her father and her country. Upon the sudden death of Basedow in 1933, Minnie was taken like a family heirloom by Basedow's unmarried sisters for further enslavement. Bound in servitude, unable to go home and unlikely to marry, it was never expected that Minnie would have children. Despite the odds, Minnie did – a son Charlie, born in 1942, and then a daughter, Margaret (Margie), born in 1943. Both were taken from Minnie's care in very different ways. Charlie was kept in the care of the Basedow sisters until 1963. He passed in 1996, unmarried and without children. Minnie's daughter – Kath's mother, Margaret – was taken and placed in a children's institution run by the United Aborigines Mission. Margie was then under their control for a further twenty-six years, during which time she had three children of her own – including Kath – all of whom were taken from her. Minnie finally returned to Alice Springs in 1958. Her parents had both passed without either ever seeing their daughter again. But Kath reunited with her grandmother in 1986, and with her mother and sisters, and has been on a quest over many years to find the family story. The importance of uncovering the truth to family reconnection saw Kath attend university for the first time in 2017, giving her the opportunity to retell her family story, in a her-storical biography, *Minnie, Mum and Me: The Black Headed Snake* (Travis 2019).

Our Stories: Finding Minnie Apma

Kath

As a First Nations woman, I understand the importance for future generations to know our family story. Disconnection, separation, isolation and transgenerational trauma has been an unfortunate fundamental experience for my family. Locating the family story was difficult – woven throughout the colonial archive lie the tangled stories of memory and trauma of my family, five women across three generations who had been forcibly removed from each other and family spanning from 1920 until 1969.

I knew that many women, including within my own family, might find the process difficult as we embarked on the journey. In fact I also knew that they may not espouse shared beliefs about the value of the written archival story, but I knew emphatically that they do share the standpoint of women, First Nations women. This standpoint reflects a common situation of exclusion and subordination in a social world ordered and divided by gender. Our individual experiences differed due to intersecting oppressions produced through institutionalization, separation and adoption (Jaggar 2004; Moreton-Robinson 2000, 88–89).

At age 50, I embarked on the process to find my story. Some might say it was a mid-life crisis, but when I did not know my family story, where I struggled to belong, where the intergenerational trauma was and continues to be prevalent through my family, it was important not just for me, but for my children and grandchildren, that I sought to locate and understand our family story. I wanted to create some form of cultural artefact that told our story, a legacy for generations. Narungga activist and poet Natalie Harkin (2014) describes the importance of First Nations people demonstrating creativity that shows the passionate, rich storytelling that emerges when First Nations release the stories captured in the archives and restore them as living cultural heritage. That was the purpose of the book I wrote.

The experience of accessing the archives is both chilling and intimate. It was a family snapshot into my own and my families lives lived under extraordinary surveillance, and yet I was compelled to the process, seeking the diamond, the gem that would reveal all.

Victoria had been identified to me as someone 'who knew about my nanna'. Victoria made contact with me immediately and I could not have prepared myself for the information she was sharing with me. In that moment she forwarded me references, names of archival locations where information about my family was held, names and places I had never heard of before. I could not believe people outside of our family would even know about Minnie, when we didn't even know.

Identity for me is more than just a name, beliefs, personality, looks and/or expressions: it consists of knowing the origins from where I came from, the stories that make up my family and about kinship. I was searching for a place of belonging and identity and so the accidental archival journey of re-authoring a new family narrative began. Using the references and names provided to me by Victoria I began wading deep through the maze of race-based Government policies, that included how First Nations people, women in particular were enslaved, put into institutions or adopted. It increased my appetite for truth telling and I wanted to find a way to honor and give voice to Minnie, my mother and myself, where our voices had not been heard before.

Victoria

I first came across Undelya (as I thought of Minnie then) in South Australia's Mortlock Library in 2005, as I was researching the history of the young women sent down from Central Australia to work in Adelaide in the 1920s. The policeman Sergeant Stott, official Protector of Aborigines, was the architect of this scheme, and it was Stott who authorized Basedow to take Minnie and another First Nations girl from Central Australia with him to Adelaide. An incredible document I found, a copy of a 1928 telegram from Minnie's father Charlie Apma to Basedow demanding that his daughter be returned to him, set me on Minnie's archival trail. As more and more records relating to her surfaced, and from them I started to piece together what happened, I could see how powerful and unique the story was, and I knew that if Minnie had had any living descendants, that these records would be hugely important to them. I asked Andrew Wilson at the State Archives if he could let any family members of either girl who might come to the archives know I might be able to assist them. When Andrew rang and told me that one of Minnie's granddaughters wanted to talk with me, it seemed like it was just meant to be.

In the first instance, I was pleased that I was able to help Kath, as a historian, to shortcut navigating these pretty traumatizing archives. It was gratifying, if uncomfortable, to position myself as an expert who could give back something of meaning to a descendant of a woman whose life-story I had been constructing. But as our friendship grew, the real privilege for me has been in Kath's generosity in sharing her continuing research journey with me – a journey that has expanded considerably beyond the cold-hearted archives of the state and taken her back to country and culture – and her invitation to me to absorb and appreciate the deepening and complicated meanings woven through the story of Minnie and her daughter and granddaughters. It is Kath's work and her sharing of that work every step of the way that has brought Minnie's voice out of the archives and back to where it belongs – with her own family.

Victoria

What is the significance for First Nations women today, of stories like Minnie's story? What do you see as your responsibility as a historical researcher as well as Minnie's direct descendant? What about your relationship with Margie and with other women of Minnie's family who you have met in the process?

Kath

The legacy of discriminatory treatment continues for many First Peoples in archives where their stories are still locked in police files, exemption files, child welfare reports and in some instances privately-owned records, meaning they are not always able to locate their story or own their identity. People whose family members were impacted on by government policies need to undertake extensive archival research in order to know their family history. In order to properly address the question of archive-as-source to archive-as-subject (Stoler 2002), the colonial archive has to be interrogated more thoroughly, particularly by First Nations people who refuse to be removed from the written record, or to face a future without an identity. My work is informed by Natalie Harkin's methodology that disrupts the colonial narrative and questions the construction of identity, arguing that the surviving archives of institutional remembering and forgetting can be reinvested with meaning through a cultural lens (Harkin 2014). By situating myself as a First Nations historian I am in the first instance positioning my standpoint in the same way, applying the method employed by Harkin to contest the historical record through a critique of the colonial archive as a site of persuasion through what she terms her sovereign expression. This emerging scholarship points to the importance of reauthoring our stories to provide a sense of identity. Family history is essential – it helps us to understand ourselves, it keeps memories alive, and most importantly it allows each generation to have an idea of who they are and where they come from. In First Nations families, culture and memories have been passed down through generations of storytelling. These stories help new generations connect to their history to know their story. As I researched and re-authored our family narrative, I was unraveling the settler fantasy that had attempted to silence our voices. I was able to do this, not because we were not in the archives but because we were, and it was addictive and satisfying. Women play an important role as storytellers, and as educators of their children and grandchildren about the family's legacy.

As a First Nations historian my communal responsibility is centered in sovereign (interconnected) First Nations women's ways of being, knowing and doing. Leading by example and empowering other First Nations women who are interested in understanding how to navigate the colonial archive, to share my experiences of how to re-author and repatriate our stories back to family and community. Knowing how to discover, share, and preserve our family history is an essential component to overcoming barriers and challenges for future generations.

We as First Nations people are agents capable and interested in research, and we have expert knowledge about ourselves so the power of authoring our family narratives, how we re-claim our stories – not ones written about us, but stories written by us as a method of re-writing history from a First Nations perspective – can play an integral role in understanding identity, for reconnecting to family and finding balance with a sense of belonging.

Kath

As you focused on your early research on the history of First Nations domestic service as it related to your own family, and then finding Minnie's story, what ethical considerations did you consider as to whether you would publish or not publish your findings?

Victoria

Wasn't this the first question you asked me after you found out who I was and that I had been researching Minnie's story – why haven't you published anything? Minnie's story, yes, was a dilemma to me. I don't know what it would have been like if I'd found her story in the archive and I *hadn't* had all that background with my own family history, but of course in an indirect way it was that background that brought me to Minnie's story in the first place.

Before I discovered my great-grandmother's story in the 1990s (a white woman who employed Aboriginal girls as servants and went on to become an Aboriginal rights' activist), I felt that I understood the arguments against Second Nations researching and writing First Nations histories at an abstract intellectual and political level. But recognizing my own family connection to this history helped me to grasp how confronting it can be to have others writing your own stories. My great-grandmother, Joan Kingsley-Strack (known in my own family as 'Ming'), had treasured many letters from and about the women who worked for her, giving me an awareness of the entangled nature of all archives, and of the power dynamics that gave, and continue to give, some people effective custody over the stories of others. In the process of researching and writing up the history of Ming's relationships with First Nations women, I sought out and found descendants of all the women I knew had worked for her then, and tried to make sure not only that they knew who I was and what I was doing and why, but also were agreeable to that. I also shared copies of all the material I had on their own ancestors with them, as well as what I was thinking and writing about their lives during the periods they were involved with my family: I wanted the history I told from these paper records to connect with their descendants as well as with me. I felt the process was true to what Ming would have wanted herself, and important for my own sense of integrity. The whole experience made me profoundly aware of the ethical responsibilities you have as a historical researcher and writer (for discussion see Haskins 2005, 10–11; Haskins 1998, 2000).[2]

When it came to Minnie's experiences, I absolutely had to have some level of consultation with her family, if only to make sure that they were aware of the material that was there, because of how significant it was. Before you reached out to me, Kath, I had given two conference papers about Basedow's taking of the two girls – one as a form of expose,

I suppose, of an injustice that had been relegated to a dismissive footnote in existing work on Basedow, and the other on the role played by his wife Nell – but Minnie's story felt too deep and too personal and too complex for me to publish anything without discussing it with family members. Also, importantly, there was an insurmountable silence at the heart of the story, because in none of the records I had found, did either of the two young women speak directly. I felt that there was a resistance in the records to my crafting of a workable narrative that could be in any way empowering to First Nations women (then or now) and I had no desire to replicate the way that Basedow – and Nell – had stolen them from their families to serve, literally, the project of colonization.[3]

Victoria

I know you've recently been working through the institutional processes of ethics at your university, so you can carry out your research on Minnie's life story. Do you think these kinds of processes are important and valuable? How have they helped or hindered your research and how could they be improved?

Kath

The transmission of knowledge within First Nations community through storytelling as a research method is increasing. Storytelling is regarded as essential for cultural continuity and survival for preserving and passing on cultural knowledge to future generations and is fundamental to First Nations identity, both personal and communal (Simpkins 2009; Geia, Hayes, and Usher 2013). My ongoing work as a First Nations historian relates to family history, recognizing that it is a valuable commodity to First Nations communities. I am guided in cultural practice by my Elders, community and family as way of strengthening community identity and agency through the use of auto-ethnographic methodology that is conversant with an epistemological and theoretical framework consistent with practice-based ways of knowing, being and doing (Martin and Mirraboopa 2003). This methodology is central to First Nations research and is my sovereign right to self-determination, one that gives voice to First Nations knowledge working towards a cultural framework that consists of the aspirations and needs of community (Dana-Sacco 2010; Grieves 2020). Thus research in this area is defined as being led by First Nations people, as a way of ensuring that our identities are not distorted or even discarded in order to consciously and imaginatively address the 'pain of being Aboriginal' as a particular form of social suffering (Adelson 2000). This practice draws on the analyses that have spanned two hundred years of white occupation and intervention where First Peoples, both individually and as a community, are left to mend the broken circles of family life. It offers a new response from First Nations peoples who are custodians of family historical information and who seek ways to share stories in order to restore and revive cultural practices (see Stone 2017; Adelson 2000; Haebich 2000).

I was introduced to ethics as a university requirement through coursework for my PhD. The coursework offered me a first glance at the National Statement on Ethical Conduct in Human Research 2007 (updated 2018) (National Health and Medical Research Council 2019). As I proceeded through the lengthy application process of obtaining ethics approval to do my research, it was difficult finding ways to answer questions that seemed intrusive and demanding. In order for me to be granted permission to proceed, the system insisted that I provide a different methodological approach that included Western terminologies, such as changing my language from 'gathering' to 'documenting', and 'yarning' to 'exploring', and required me to provide letters of authority from my family matriarchs to conduct yarning circles. These demands frustrated me, conflicting with my de-colonising methodological approach that speaks to the lived experiences of First Nations women.

The contemporary Human Research Ethics Committees (HREC) of Australian universities and the national ethical frameworks that direct their oversight of research involving First Nation participants mirror the historic work of the Aborigines Protection Boards; stifling the decision-making processes that First Nations peoples themselves are participants in and to whose authority and outcomes they adhere. The entire ethics application experience is indicative of how the ethics approval processes of Australian universities often function to achieve unethical outcomes by undercutting the ability of First Nations researchers and First Nations community participants to be 'self-determining' in establishing and agreeing to the terms on which research will be carried out in practice (Ellinghaus and Judd 2020). The existing Australian Institute of Aboriginal and Torres Strait Islander Studies (AIATSIS 2020; Davis 2010) research ethics framework, designed in consultation with First Nations researchers and communities, needs to be used to increase the contribution of First Nations knowledge to Australian research.

To move forward, the ethics processes must engage with First Nations voices, and focus on positionality and relationship to place and people, as well as foster long-term accountability to embedded knowledges (Moreton-Robinson 2003; Kwaymullina 2016), in order to allow more First Nations scholars to propose solid beneficial projects for First Nations Community to progress through the academy.

Kath

First Nations women have experienced and carry intimate her-stories of domestic service, and the government system of indenturing these women and their families before them, have gone mostly unacknowledged and still hidden from them. From a Second Nations Australian and historian what are your thoughts on how to increase collaboration between archives, Second Nations historians and First Nations communities, to not only have access to the stories, but how their stories are written and shared?

Victoria

These archives (as you know) are so painful and problematic, but they are also so important. Despite the lies and insults studded throughout them there is also truth within them – for a striking example of that, there's Charlie Apma's letter! Archives of state control can be dangerous, not to mention traumatic for those who have been subjected to them, and there are major challenges in efforts to decolonize them. The work of Natalie Harkin (2014, 2019, 2020) provides a striking example of contesting the archives' domination (I've given an overview of recent national and international scholarship on decolonizing archives in Haskins 2017, 51–55). The release of a 'Position Statement on the Right of Reply to Indigenous Knowledges and Information Held in Archives' in August 2021 (prepared by the

Indigenous Archives Collective, an association of people working in galleries, libraries, archives and museums) affirmed a series of principles asserting and protecting the rights of First Nations people in relation to historical records relating to them (Indigenous Archives Collective 2021). From my perspective, having First Nations archivists who are really committed to the work of collaboration and getting the histories out – truth-telling – to the wider community, *and* who understand absolutely the ethical issues in these often volatile archives, is critical. People like Andrew Wilson, hero of the South Australian archives. There are other archivists, both First and Second Nations, working around the world to build connections between Second Nations researchers and First Nations communities, but we need more of them.

It is also essential that Second Nations historians make the effort, and go out of their comfort zone, to spend time with First Nations people to get an understanding of the issues for First Nations people today and the significance of these histories. In doing so, they will need to reflect upon their motivations and purposes in working on such histories, to connect their intellectual work to their heart and soul (their values), and to be able to articulate that when they are speaking with First Nations people. That is a journey and a process, but of course ultimately a very positive one.

Victoria

How do First Nations researchers like yourself negotiate the kind of government records held on First Nations women like the records relating to Minnie? As a Second Nations researcher I find I am struggling to hear the voices of First Nations people – especially women – in the archives – how do you 'hear' them, do you hear them, what do you think Minnie and others would want from your research?

Kath

The records were as confusing to access and interpret as the institution (that is, the archive) itself. As a First Nations woman I have to negotiate what First Nations historian Lynette Russell (2005, 267) has referred to the 'incommensurable ontologies' of western and Indigenous knowledge systems. I navigated the colonial language through the lens of Arrernte cultural knowledge in order to rediscover identity, kin relationships, cultural practice and protocols, and bring Minnie out of obscurity and into the present, as a proud Arrernte woman in her own right. In this way the conventional positioning of individuals as the 'subjects' of the official archival record is disrupted: not doing so allows for the continued disempowering effect on First Nations whose lives have been so extensively documented for the purposes of surveillance, control and dispossession.

It is important to note that there has been and continues to be a 'silence' within the Australian collective history and memory. More importantly First Nations women have and continue to be marginalized, and subjected to various forms of violence, in a process both historical and ongoing in Australia, and our knowledge and practices are often omitted and rendered invisible, so not surprisingly Minnie's voice was and has not been heard. The absence of First Nations people's voices on (as well as in) colonial history feeds the historical fallacy that First Nations just 'disappeared', a colonial perspective that continues to impact all First Nations and contributes to entrenched health disparities compared with other Australians today.

Minnie was featured in photographs and newspaper articles but not about 'who' she was, rather about 'what' she was – un-civilised, black girl, sewing expert, untrained, wild, Aboriginal maid, lovable creature, to name just a few. The public was invited to see Minnie and the other young woman in the Basedows' custody in such a way as to highlight the process of civilization and applaud their domestication by the state. In these articles I could not hear her words, her truths. What was visible was the sadness in Nanna Minnie's downward-looking eyes in the many photographs, the same sadness mirrored in my own eyes.

But there is a duality to archival records in that, whilst they have in the past been instruments of oppression and the construction of a negative view of First Nations identity, they can in the present and future play an important reconciling role in recovering identity, memory and reuniting families. Since writing the book I have been able to reconnect to family 'on country'. I have had the opportunity to sit with my Aunties who have revealed many stories, but none more harrowing than how Nan's brothers thought she had died, they did not know where she had gone, and when she did return she didn't talk about her experiences and they did not ask. They loved her, and have shared with us so many amazing stories about 'who' she was.

The creation of my family artefact is compiled from a place of healing, and leaves a legacy for future generations to know the story in a First Nations narrative. It has afforded myself and children safe passage of return to country, to be connected and know their cultural kinship, relations and stories. Nanna Minnie would be proud that I have sought to re-claim, reauthor and re-patriate a new family narrative that 'talks blak' to the archives, so that her-storical truths can be heard.

Kath

Do you think historians have a role in disrupting traditional notions of archives in ways that support First Nations women in re-imagining records, where the oral may be privileged over the written?

Victoria

Oral histories have been and remain profoundly important for recovering and reconstructing First Nations history – the testimonies of the Aboriginal and Torres Strait Islander people who were removed as children from their families comes to mind immediately – but also for First Nations professional and academic scholars like yourself, who move fluidly between the roles of researcher and participant when conducting oral history research. Oral histories are well established in feminist and women's historical research method. Susan Geiger, historian of Tanzanian women's history, argues that historians who aspire to feminist practice should be testing the validity of the written record against the oral accounts of women, not the other way around. She further calls, as a matter of ethics, for thoughtful and explicit articulations of the relationship and distinction between the researcher carrying out oral historical research and what she terms 'the oral historian,' taking care not to represent this latter position as the interviewee or informant, but rather as a historian in their own right (1990, 174–6; see also Gluck and Patai 1991). There is a further complexity with First Nations historical method, I believe, where the practice of oral history is a longstanding fundamental mode of both recording and producing history. There are pre-colonial oral historical traditions that have their conventions and forms, and which are retained and continue to be passed down as sacred and incontestable truths, inseparably connected to place, law, and movement through space, with designated knowledge-holders who have the exclusive authority to speak (Tuhiwai Smith [1999] 2004, 144–5; Mahuika 2019; De Santolo 2019). I'm thinking here of the traditions you've referred to relating to Charlie Apma's country, for example, that complicate our understanding of Basedow's interest in taking his daughter, and Apma's determination in securing her return. In place of Geiger's 'oral historian', perhaps we might use the term 'knowledge holder'.

Historians learn to be sceptical of all records and archives – to read them against the grain – while also mindful of the need to read them along the grain as well, according to the mentality in which they were produced and therefore need to consider viewing the archives not as sites of knowledge retrieval, but of knowledge production (Stoler 2002). In 'hearing' (as with 'reading') histories that are orally transmitted, I want to suggest we consider the knowledge holder as being themselves an archive, a repository of records, and as such a locus of authority and power. That doesn't mean that oral histories and evidence can't be interrogated or challenged, but that they can be understood as a kind of living archive, on par with the repositories of officialdom, that produce knowledge. The ethical issues that arise here that need to be recognized and articulated concern the power relationship between the researcher (whether they are First or Second Nations) and the 'knowledge holder', which in crucial ways mirrors that between the researcher and the official archives. (I don't want to over-simplify here, but perhaps one could argue that just as a Second Nations historian often has privileged access to the official documentary archive, the First Nations historian can have privileged access to First Nations knowledge holders?) And of course there are times when a historian is both the researcher *and* the knowledge holder – especially when the subject is one's own family history, as is the case for both of us. If our agenda is the empowerment of First Nations women, we must recognize the disempowering effects of contesting First Nations knowledge holders; yet, we cannot ignore oral histories that we prefer not to critique. Instead I think it is crucial that we – regardless of our background as First or Second Nations historians – must engage thoughtfully, respectfully and genuinely with oral histories. Teasing out a more nuanced understanding of the role of the knowledge holder, is one of the ways in which historians can help to disrupt the hegemony of the official archival records.

Victoria

I'm finding that emerging Second Nations scholars, who are otherwise interested in and supportive of First Nations women, feminist issues and decolonization, are reluctant to carry out research – archival or otherwise – relating to First Nations histories now. They are concerned that their work – their voice – would not be valued or wanted by First Nations women or people generally. What would your advice be to scholars like this? How do you think we can build better collaborative relationships?

Kath

At first glance, this seemed a difficult question to answer so I have decided to answer based on my cultural knowledge as a First Nation woman, as a stolen generation survivor, then as an academic, historian and author.

First Nations know emphatically that they live inside the trauma and suspect that when we tell our truths it is not believed. I acknowledge there has been robust dialogue by numerous academic scholars on First Nation Nations' experiences particularly regarding the stolen generations, truth, testimony, trauma, memory and genocide. Anita Heiss notes that the 1990s saw increased discussion, both within and outside First Nations communities, on the issues of Second Nations writers writing about First Nations. For some Second Nations people working in this area, their case for doing so gains credibility as they are seen to be providing a voice (however indirectly) to First Nations. Some Second Nations historians focus on establishing what actually happened in the past through a methodical narrative, proclaiming their views on the policies and the broader question of why the government thought it was a good idea to remove children. Some even assert that the notion of truth is grounded in historical sources, without hearing our truths and draw mostly on archival materials (and sometimes oral history) to tell their stories (Heiss 2002).

It could be argued that the national amnesia has 'ended' since the late twentieth century, yet there is a contrasting and ambiguous variant of the silence taking shape. First, there was a complete silence about First Nations history from Second Nations historians, then they started to pay attention doing so in ways that employed silence in a different way – this time they silenced First Nations' voices by writing histories that were archivally-focussed and so privileged their own voices as experts in the archival research. This presumption of their expertise is symptomatic of the way in which our voices have been and continue to be systemically silenced by government policies and administrators. The unspoken advantage that Second Nations scholars as the dominant culture have over First Nations people, is that they can choose to look away from this history. It is the First Nations people who must directly confront the archives, and who have no choice but to go to the evidence within them, of colonial practices against First Nations people, to reconstruct our historical truths.

This history, our shared history, is neither simple nor pure. The collective refusal to speak the truth of this history allowed and continues to allow for the development of a fictitious national identity which ignores the brutal and ongoing impact on First Nations. The historical fallacy that First Nations people just 'disappeared' is a fundamental characteristic of the repressive colonial perspective that continues to impact me and my family today. My research highlights who would be included and excluded, calling into question the obscurity and theft of First Nations women's voices particularly.

Historians cannot rely on historical sources alone to tell their truth regarding the experiences of First Nations people. It may seem complex but it is not. Mutual recognition, relationship and understanding of our shared history is the foundation from which we can hope to move forward together.

Victoria

I get your point, and it's a very powerful one, that by being reluctant to raise their own voices on this history Second Nations historians imply that the historical truth, as such, is not at the very heart of the matter. But I think there's a genuine concern that by even doing this kind of research, Second Nations historians are replicating privilege and silencing First Nations people again. Second Nations historians, as outsiders, can certainly mis-hear and interpret oral histories they are told (Cruikshank 1990). But the compounding of the silencing in the archives of First Nations women, in particular, is especially problematic when they avoid engaging with custodians of oral histories (the knowledge holders), and I think Second Nations researchers need to be prepared to take the risk of being wrong, of being un-knowing. For me, what I've found in working with you (and with other First Nations historians), is the central importance of coming together and working collaboratively and sharing in everything we – that is, Second Nations historians – do, in all our research and writing.

Kath

For myself and my family the method of re-authoring our family story contests the dominant narrative and challenges the accepted HIS-storical version of this country's story. This power of re-authoring, how we re-claim our stories – not ones written about us, is integral in understanding our identity, kinship relationships and resets the agenda allowing us to focus on healing rather than trauma. Our sovereign right to tell First Nations family history in our voice is about untwisting the colonial voice, changing the story, empowering our women and families to have voice. We know as First Nations women that we are agents capable and interested in research, with expert knowledge about ourselves and for this reason we have to remain focused and assert our cultural authority, not just for ourselves but for our daughters, mothers, sisters, and community.

Notes

1. Kath Apma Travis Penangke is a proud *Imarnte* woman of the Arrernte people of Central Australia and sovereign to this continent. Throughout this paper we will be using the term First Nations People or First Peoples when referring to Aboriginal and Torres Strait Islander people across Australia. We will use Second Nations people as it relates to anyone who is not First Nations to Australia.
2. There have been several histories written concerning the Basedow family and Herbert Basedow himself, including one family history authored by a Basedow descendant. However none of these former histories were written in consultation with the descendants of either of the two First Nations girls he abducted.
3. There are some gendered comparisons that could be drawn between the Basedows and my great-grandmother in terms of their complicity in the removal of First Nations girls for domestic labor coupled with their rather contradictory advocacy at times for Aboriginal rights, but such a discussion is beyond the scope of this present paper.

Disclosure Statement

No potential conflict of interest was reported by the author(s).

ORCID

Victoria Haskins http://orcid.org/0000-0002-4226-2151

References

Adelson, Naomi. 2000. "Re-Imagining Aboriginality: An Indigenous People's Response to Social Suffering." *Transcultural Psychiatry* 37 (1): 11–34.

AIATSIS (Australian Institute for Aboriginal and Torres Strait Islander Research). 2020. *AIATSIS Code of Ethics for Aboriginal and Torres Strait Islander Research*. Canberra: AIATSIS.

Barker, Lorina. 2008. ""Hangin' Out" and "Yarnin": Reflecting on the Experience of Collecting Oral Histories." *History Australia* 5 (1): 09.1–09.1.

Benson, Koni, and Richa Nagar. 2006. "Collaboration as Resistance? Reconsidering the Processes, Products, and Possibilities of Feminist Oral History and Ethnography." *Gender, Place & Culture* 13 (5): 581–592.

Bessarab, Dawn, and Bridget Ng'Andu. 2010. "Yarning About Yarning as a Legitimate Method in Indigenous Research." *International Journal of Critical Indigenous Studies* 3 (1): 37–50.

Cruikshank, Julie. 1990. "Myth as a Framework for Life Stories: Athapaskan Women Making Sense of Social Change in Northern Canada." In *The Myths We Live By*, edited by Raphael Samuel, and Paul Thompson, 174–183. London: Routledge.

Dana-Sacco, Gail. 2010. "The Indigenous Researcher as Individual and Collective: Building a Research Practice Ethic Within the Context of Indigenous Languages." *American Indian Quarterly* 34 (1): 61–82.

Davis, Michael. 2010. "Bringing Ethics up to Date? A Review of the AIATSIS Ethical Guidelines." *Australian Aboriginal Studies* 2: 10–21.

De Santolo, Jason. 2019. "The Emergence of *Yarnbar Jarngkurr* from Indigenous Homelands: A Creative Indigenous Methodology." In *Decolonizing Research: Indigenous Storywork as Methodology*, edited by Jo-ann Archibald, Q'um Q'um Xiieen, Jenny Bol Jun Lee-Morgan, and Jason De Santolo, 239–259. London: Zed Books.

Ellinghaus, Katherine, and Barry Judd. 2020. "Writing as Kin: Producing Ethical Histories Through Collaboration in Unexpected Places. Researching F W Albrecht, Assimilation Policy and Lutheran Experiments in Aboriginal Education." In *Questioning Indigenous-Settler Relations. Indigenous-Settler Relations in Australia and the World*, Vol. 1, edited by Sarah Maddison, and Sana Nakata, 55–68. Singapore: Springer.

Geia, Lynore K., Barbara Hayes, and Kim Usher. 2013. "Yarning/Aboriginal Storytelling: Towards an Understanding of an Indigenous Perspective and its Implications for Research Practice." *Contemporary Nurse* 46 (1): 13–17. doi:10.5172/conu.2013.46.1.13.

Geiger, Susan. 1990. "What's So Feminist About Women's Oral History?" *Journal of Women's History* 2 (1): 169–182.

Gluck, Sherna Berger, and Daphne Patai, eds. 1991. *Women's Words: The Feminist Practice of Oral History*. New York: Routledge.

Grieves, Genevieve. 2020. "Just Tick the Box: A Koorie Woman's Experience of Negotiating the University's Ethics Process." In *The Meeting of Aesthetics and Ethics in the Academy: Challenges for Creative Practice Researchers in Higher Education*, edited by Kate MacNeill, and Barbara Bolt, 101–109. Oxon: Routledge.

Haebich, Anna. 2000. *Broken Circles*. Fremantle: Fremantle Arts Centre Press.

Harkin, Natalie. 2014. "The Poetics of (re) Mapping Archives: Memory in the Blood." *Journal of the Association for the Study of Australian Literature* 14 (3): 1–14. https://openjournals.library.sydney.edu.au/index.php/JASAL/article/view/9909/9798.

Harkin, Natalie. 2019. *Archival Poetics*. Sydney: Vagabond Press.

Harkin, Natalie. 2020. "Whitewash-Brainwash: An Archival-Poetic Labour Story." *Australian Feminist Law Journal* 45 (2), 1–15.

Haskins, Victoria. 1998. "Skeletons in Our Closet: Family History, Personal Narratives and Race Relations History in Australia." *The Olive Pink Society Bulletin* 10 (2): 15–22.

Haskins, Victoria. 2000. "Family Histories, Personal Narratives and Race Relations History in Australia." *Canberra Historical Society Journal* 45: 25–29.

Haskins, Victoria K. 2005. *One Bright Spot*. Houndsmills: Palgrave.

Haskins, Victoria. 2017. "Decolonizing the Archives: A Transnational Perspective." In *Sources and Methods in Histories of Colonialism*, edited by Kirsty Reid, and Fiona Paisley, 47–68. Oxon: Routledge.

Heiss, Anita. 2002. "Writing About Indigenous Australia–Some Issues to Consider and Protocols to Follow: A Discussion Paper." *Southerly* 62 (2): 197–207.

Huggins, Jackie, Kay Saunders, and Isabel Tarrago. 2000. "Reconciling Our Mothers' Lives." In *Race, Colour & Identity in Australia and New Zealand*, edited by John Docker, and Gerhard Fischer, 39–58. Sydney: UNSW Press.

Hughes, Karen, and Ellen Trevorrow. 2018. "'The Nation is Coming to Life': Law, Sovereignty, and Belonging in Ngarrindjeri Photography of the Mid-Twentieth Century." *History of Photography* 42 (3): 249–268.

Indigenous Archives Collective. 2021. "Position Statement on the Right of Reply to Indigenous Knowledges and Information held in Archives." https://indigenousarchives.net/indigenous-archives-collective-position-statement-on-the-right-of-reply-to-indigenous-knowledges-and-information-held-in-archives/.

Jaggar, Alison M. 2004. "Feminist Politics and Epistemology: The Standpoint of Women." In *The Feminist Standpoint Theory Reader: Intellectual and Political Controversies*, edited by Sandra G. Harding, 55–66. New York: Routledge.

Kwaymullina, Ambelin. 2016. "Research, Ethics and Indigenous Peoples: An Australian Indigenous Perspective on Three Threshold Considerations for Respectful Engagement." *AlterNative: An International Journal of Indigenous Peoples* 12 (4): 437–449. doi:10.20507/AlterNative.2016.12.4.8.

Mahuika, Nepia. 2019. *Rethinking Oral History and Oral Tradition: An Indigenous Perspective*. New York: Oxford University Press.

Martin, Karen, and Booran Mirraboopa. 2003. "Ways of Knowing, Being and Doing: A Theoretical Framework and Methods for Indigenous and Indigenist Re-Search." *Journal of Australian Studies* 27 (76): 203–214.

Moreton-Robinson, Aileen. 2000. *Talkin' Up to the White Woman: Aboriginal Women and Feminism*. St Lucia: UQP.

Moreton-Robinson, Aileen. 2003. "I Still Call Australia Home: Indigenous Belonging and Place in a Postcolonising Society." In *Uprootings/Regroundings: Questions of Home and Migration*, edited by Sara Ahmed, Anne-Marie Fortier, Mimi Sheller, and Claudia Castada, 23–40. Oxford: Berg Publications.

National Health and Medical Research Council, Australian Research Council and Universities Australia. 2018. *National Statement on Ethical Conduct in Human Research 2007 (Updated 2018)*. Canberra: National Health and Medical Research Council. www.nhmrc.gov.au/guidelines/publications/e72.

Rigney, Lester Irabinna. 1999. "Internationalization of an Indigenous Anticolonial Cultural Critique of Research Methodologies: A Guide to Indigenist Research Methodology and its Principles." *Wicazo sa Review* 14 (2): 109–121.

Russell, Lynette. 2005. "Indigenous Knowledge and Archives: Accessing Hidden History and Understandings." *Australian Academic & Research Libraries* 36 (2): 161–171.

Simpkins, Maureen. 2009. "Book Review: *Aboriginal Oral Traditions: Theory, Practice, Ethics* Edited by Renée Hulan and Renate Eigenbrod." *Great Plains Research: A Journal of Natural and Social Sciences* 19 (2): 242.

Stoler, Ann Laura. 2002. "Colonial Archives and the Arts of Governance: on the Content in the Form." In *Refiguring the Archive*, edited by Carolyn Hamilton, Verne Harris, Jane Taylor, Michele Pickover, Graeme Reid, and Razia Saleh, 83–102. Dordrecht: Springer.

Stone, Elizabeth. 2017. *Black Sheep and Kissing Cousins: How Our Family Stories Shape Us*. Oxon: Routledge.

Travis, Kath Apma Penangke. 2019. *Minnie, Mum and Me: The Black Headed Snake*. Melbourne: Self-published.

Tuhiwai Smith, Linda. (1999) 2004. *Decolonizing Methodologies: Research and Indigenous Peoples*. London: Zed Books.

Whetung, Madeline (Nishnaabeg), and Sarah Wakefield. 2018. "Colonial Conventions: Institutionalized Research Relationships and Decolonizing Research Ethics." In *Indigenous and Decolonizing Studies in Education: Mapping the Long View*, edited by L. T. Smith, E. Tuck, and K. W. Tang, 146–158. New York: Routledge.

Beyond Formal Ethics Reviews: Reframing the Potential Harms of Sexual Violence Research

Shaez Mortimer, Bianca Fileborn and Nicola Henry

ABSTRACT
Given the recent surge of research about sexual violence, it is timely to revisit the role of ethics in this field. This article examines two key frameworks which govern ethics in sexual violence research: institutional risk management and trauma discourse. While recognising the importance of these frameworks, we argue that they share a narrow conceptualisation of the potential harms of sexual violence research. Drawing on the legacy of decades of feminist research on sexual violence, we call for a deeper engagement with ethical and epistemological questions of knowledge, positionality and power. We argue that researchers need to consider the broader social and political contexts that shape survivors' lives and experiences of disclosure in undertaking ethical research. Sexual violence researchers must also consider the potential harms of their research on marginalised communities – from questioning who is included in research, to the implications of the responses to violence advocated for. Utilising insights from feminist, critical and intersectional traditions – and reflections on our own experiences as sexual violence researchers – we argue for ethical considerations to extend beyond risk management and medicalised trauma frameworks.

Introduction

Once marginalised as a 'niche' topic within women's studies, sexual violence research has moved closer to the mainstream of disciplines such as psychology, psychiatry, medicine, criminology, sociology, health sciences, law and other fields in recent years. Through qualitative and quantitative research, feminist scholars have brought greater attention to the lived experiences of victim-survivors, the failings of criminal justice systems, the lack of accountability for perpetrators, and the inadequacy of leaders in addressing this issue across institutional and interpersonal contexts. Greater public awareness of sexual violence has also been shaped by feminist activism and advocacy, and further fuelled by recent events such as the #MeToo Movement and high-profile cases of sexual violence across university, media and government settings (see e.g. Fileborn and Loney-Howes 2019).

With a wealth of new research emerging on sexual violence, it is timely to revisit the role of ethics in this field (Downes, Kelly, and Westmarland 2014). What principles and processes influence the ethical considerations of sexual violence researchers? How is the potential for harm in research conceptualised and addressed in practice? In this article, we argue that there are two main frameworks that govern ethical research on sexual violence. The first is a risk management approach to ethics, which is best exemplified by the institutional ethics approval processes that are required of researchers. The second is a trauma model, drawn from psychological literature and therapeutic practice. While we recognise that both approaches are necessary to undertaking ethical research on sexual violence, we argue that these models share a narrow conceptualisation of the potential harms of research, focused predominately on the risks of harm to individual participants, and which can overlook other important ethical considerations.

The first section of the article describes the risk management model of institutional ethics processes and its limitations. The second section examines the trauma model, explaining its origins and utility, then discussing feminist critiques of the model and applying these to a research context. It is important to note that although we address these models separately, they are not mutually exclusive; in fact, it is our observation that the trauma model is increasingly informing the ways that institutional ethics boards consider applications. The final section of the article explores a selection of ethical issues that we argue are missed or overlooked by risk management and trauma models. To conclude, we offer recommendations and points for reflection for scholars undertaking research in the field. We acknowledge that this is a complex area and one which requires ongoing discussion among feminist researchers. This article aims to overview some key concerns about the conceptualisation of ethics in sexual violence research, but we hope that further conversation and research will build from these observations.

The Risk Management Model

Human research ethics procedures are in place to safeguard and protect research participants from harm, while ensuring that research has the potential to benefit the broader community. In Australia, strict codes of conduct govern research, such as the *Australian Code for the Conduct of Research* (NHMRC 2007), and all university-based research involving human participants is subject to review by a human research ethics committee (NHMRC 2015). Ethical research is informed by the key principles of respect, merit, justice and beneficence (NHMRC 2007; Scott 2013). According to these principles, all research participants must be treated with respect and afforded their rights and autonomy as human beings (NHMRC 2007). Research must be methodologically sound and designed in a rigorous manner. The potential benefits of a project also need to be considered carefully against the potential risks and harms to participants, researchers and non-participants alike. As Scott (2013, np) notes, the principle of 'justice' means that 'the risk and benefit associated with research will be evenly distributed', while the related principle of 'beneficence' means that the research must have the potential to 'do good' or benefit the wider community – though how these concepts are understood in practice is far from certain (Whelan 2018).

Fundamentally, the institutional ethics process is concerned with risk: identifying and mitigating risk, ensuring that the risks associated with a project are outweighed by its potential benefits, and ensuring that participants have a sufficient understanding of the risks in order to give 'informed consent'. A risk management approach has been criticised for failing to take into account the complex, emergent and evolving nature of the ethical conundrums encountered during research. It assumes, for instance, that all (or most) risks *can* in fact be identified and mitigated ahead of time (Atkinson and Butler 2012; Downes, Kelly, and Westmarland 2014; Halse and Honey 2007; Whelan 2018).

Institutional ethics processes have been subject to feminist critique due to their basis in 'the hierarchical, objective traditions of the positivist paradigm' (Burgess-Proctor 2015, 125; see also Mulla and Hlavka 2011). For example, while informed consent is an integral component of ethical research, it has been criticised as relying on economic rationalist assumptions of the self-serving individual undertaking a cost/benefit analysis (see Mulla and Hlavka 2011). Julia Downes and colleagues (2014) note that institutional ethics processes originated in biomedical research and therefore do not necessarily address the unique ethical concerns of gendered violence research. As such, the requirements of institutional ethics can sit in tension to the values and ethics of feminist-informed research in this field. For example, the use of paper or electronic consent forms or participant information statements can directly compromise the safety of a participant if they live with their abuser (Downes, Kelly, and Westmarland 2014). Similarly, LGBTIQA+ participants may be at risk of 'outing' themselves to the people they live with if the participant information statement or consent form are discovered (Roffee and Waling 2017). For participants and researchers alike, there are significant safety concerns if interviews are conducted in the homes of victim-survivors of family violence, where perpetrators may be present (Fontes 2004).

These scenarios are not necessarily predictable from the outset of the project, and while human ethics committees should proactively address these safety and support issues during the ethics review stage, there is no guarantee that they will. Instead, the process often relies on the skills, experience and insights of the researcher and their support systems. As Downes, Kelly, and Westmarland (2014) argue, there is a need for better training and meaningful support for researchers who are often dealing with complex, sometimes rapidly changing or drawn out, ethical issues in the moment and as they arise.

This is not to downplay the importance of institutional ethics approval or risk management strategies as there are many examples of research that has caused harm to participants and communities (see Atkinson and Butler 2012; Halse and Honey 2007; Juritzen, Grimen, and Heggen 2011). Rather, our concern lies in the way that institutional ethics approval may work to reduce 'ethical research' to a technical and bureaucratic exercise where harm is neatly conceptualised as individual, predictable and manageable, when the reality is much more complex (Halse and Honey 2007; Whelan 2018). In a sharp critique of institutional ethics, Andrew Whelan (2018, 1) notes, 'the opportunity for a proper conversation about research ethics in the community of researchers is supplanted by an administrative exercise in 'box ticking''. The danger is that inexperienced researchers, or those without an understanding of feminist sexual violence research, may not consider the risks to themselves or participants beyond the requirements stipulated within the formal ethics review process. As we discuss below, the trauma approach to ethical sexual violence research attempts to bridge this gap. However, we argue it is similarly based on a narrow conception of harm and may likewise fail to capture broader ethical concerns for research in this field.

The Trauma Model

There are common assumptions about how survivors should react after sexual violence, how sexual violence will impact their lives, and how they might present during a research interview. Although not always specifically required by human ethics committees, the trauma model of sexual violence has had a strong influence on researchers and ethics review processes alike. We have observed that institutional ethics boards are increasingly using the principles and language of the trauma model as guidance. It is therefore worth investigating the foundations, impacts and critiques of the trauma model.

The trauma model is premised on the notion that rape or sexual assault is an event that is deeply distressing and life-altering for the victim-survivor. Although there are different definitions, Laplanche and Pontalis (1988, 465) define trauma as '[a]n event in the subject's life, defined by its intensity, by the subject's incapacity to respond adequately to it and by the upheaval and long-lasting effects that it brings about in the psychical organization'. In 1980, in response to the experiences of Vietnam War veterans, post-traumatic stress disorder (PTSD) was introduced as a new category by the American Psychiatric Association (APA) in their Diagnostic and Statistical Manual of Mental Disorders. PTSD is characterised by 'chronic trauma' – an experience outside the range of 'normal' human experiences, leading to a profound altered consciousness, recurrent and intrusive re-living of the experience, negative thoughts or feelings, the inability to process the traumatic experience (avoidance), and increased arousal, including hyper-vigilance, agitation and disassociation (APA 2012; Herman 1992). PTSD became the central framework for treatment of trauma in psychiatry and psychology, and feminist scholars in the late 1970s capitalised on this model as a way to recognise the deleterious effects of sexual abuse, rape and domestic violence (Burgess and Holmstrom 1974; Herman 1992; Tseris 2019).

The scientific language of trauma and PTSD has provided much-needed validation and recognition of the harms of sexual violence, domestic violence and child abuse, which have been historically denied and minimised (Burgess and Holmstrom 1974; Herman 1992). A PTSD diagnosis or other formal recognition of trauma can be very meaningful for some victim-survivors, and may be necessary for them to access psychological and medical support (see Tseris 2019). However, the trauma discourse has been critiqued by feminist scholars as 'deficit-focused', individualising and medicalising the harms of violence, and viewing victim-survivors' reactions as a collection of 'symptoms' to be 'treated' (Tseris 2016, 38). As Emma Tseris (2016, 39) has argued, this 'can act as a distraction from broader conversations about patterns of gender-based violence, stifling consciousness-raising efforts aimed at empowering individuals and communities to discuss what might be done to reduce and prevent violence'.

The trauma discourse is premised on the 'default presumption that all rape is traumatic' and that the dominant harms of rape are 'psychological and permanently scarring' (Vera-Gray 2020, 59). To be clear, we do not deny the very real harm and trauma that many survivors experience. Rather, we are critical of the tendency within the trauma discourse to construct victim-survivors as inherently damaged, fragile and dysfunctional (Gavey and

Schmidt 2011; Tseris 2019). This can erase victim-survivors' agency and render invisible their resilience and resistance to violence (Tseris 2016, 2019). As Nicola Gavey and Johanna Schmidt (2011, 17) explain, the trauma discourse functions as a 'double-edged' sword: it makes visible the harms of rape that were previously denied or minimised through rape myth discourse, while simultaneously creating another dominant discourse that can function in 'reductive, prescriptive, and depoliticizing' ways.

Despite these critiques, researchers are often guided by a model of trauma in preparing for risks associated with participants who are assumed to be traumatised. The aim is to ensure that researchers put in place measures to avoid *re*traumatising participants, including providing referral pathways to crisis support services, opportunities for breaks throughout the duration of the interview, and reminding participants that responding to questions is optional (Westmarland and Bows 2019). A 'trauma-informed' model also shapes the types of questions that participants are asked during surveys or interviews, premised on the understanding that participants may recount their experiences in particular ways.

Broadly, we support these efforts and have used trauma-informed strategies ourselves in our own research. We also encourage researchers, especially those new to the field of sexual violence, to learn about the diverse impacts that violence and abuse can have (see Campbell et al. 2009). However, we are concerned that the trauma discourse may reproduce problematic assumptions about how victim-survivors 'should' experience the impacts of violence, and therefore how they 'should' behave during research interviews. When victim-survivors are always-already considered traumatised, they may be seen as unreliable, calling into question the veracity of their testimonies (Henry 2010) and their capacity to comprehend and consent to research (Downes, Kelly, and Westmarland 2014; Mulla and Hlavka 2011). For example, one of us (Bianca) was *only* able to recruit individuals who had received counselling in relation to their experiences of sexual violence for her doctoral research, illustrative of the 'default to a presumption of traumatic impact' highlighted by Gavey and Schmidt (2011, 17) and 'the notion that medical and therapeutic solutions are always the most essential responses' to violence, as critiqued by Tseris (2016, 38).

Rather than assuming that talking about sexual violence is always traumatic, it is important to recognise that many survivors *do want* to share their experiences in the context of research, and report benefits from doing so (Campbell et al. 2009, 2010; Downes, Kelly, and Westmarland 2014; Westmarland and Bows 2019). For example, in Rebecca Campbell and colleagues' (2010, 77) study, survivors reported finding the interview process 'helpful, healing, therapeutic, supportive, useful, insightful, and comforting'. The survivors also provided advice about research practices. They recommended that researchers should have an in-depth understanding of the diverse impacts of sexual violence but cautioned that researchers should not make assumptions, judgements or pretend to understand better than the survivors themselves (Campbell et al. 2009). The trauma discourse may encourage researchers to do just that. While working to mitigate the potential for research to cause harm is clearly important, any discursive model that positions survivors of violence as irredeemably broken and traumatised is itself unethical and a form of injustice and misrepresentation (see Burgess-Proctor 2015, 127; Downes, Kelly, and Westmarland 2014; Mulla and Hlavka 2011; Westmarland and Bows 2019).

Although we are critical of the trauma model's construction of victim-survivors, we would similarly caution against researchers operating from the presumption that sexual violence research will necessarily be empowering and beneficial for all survivors. This attitude and intention could also be prescriptive, patronising and reduce participants' agency. Victim-survivors have a multitude of reasons for participating in research and may experience a diverse range of emotions before, during and after an interview about sexual violence, including those that may surprise participants themselves (Fontes 2004). Even when research is conducted with care and preparation, there is still a possibility of harm. While researchers should be prepared for the possibility that research may be harmful or, conversely, empowering, we would do well to avoid making assumptions about how any individual survivor will encounter the research experience.

Expanding the Frame of Sexual Violence Research Ethics

We have argued that both the risk management and trauma models of research ethics tend to focus on the potential for harm or distress at the level of the individual, and often in a way that is disconnected from social context (Halse and Honey 2007; Whelan 2018). While identifying and managing the risk of individual harm is important, this is nonetheless a limited purview of the ethical implications of sexual violence research as our discussion has thus far illustrated. We advocate for a need to open a space for broader understandings of the differential impacts of sexual violence, including the risks for research participants and the (potential) trauma of sexual violence, *alongside* deeper consideration of the broader social and political contexts that makes talking about sexual violence difficult. In the following section, we explore the ethical issues raised by the social context of disclosure, and the impacts of research on marginalised communities, drawing from examples from our own experiences as researchers within the field of sexual violence.

Speaking out in a Victim-blaming World: The Potential Harms of not Being Heard

Victim-survivors of sexual violence navigate complex, often hostile, social and political environments and are all too aware of the risks and consequences of speaking out about violence (Campbell et al. 2009, 2010). It is this context that distinguishes research on sexual violence (and gendered violence more broadly) from other 'sensitive' or 'traumatising' topics. As Lisa Aronson Fontes (2004, 134) notes:

> Unlike participants in a study on the sensitive topic of bereavement ... women who agree to speak about their victimization are speaking out in a societal context of disbelief, fear, and shame. They are speaking out after hearing women who have suffered experiences similar to theirs denigrated in a variety of ways as having 'asked for it' or 'brought it on themselves' in the case of rape, having 'made it all up' in child sexual abuse and sexual harassment, having 'failed to leave' in the case of wife battering, and so on. (citations removed)

Researchers need to be highly sensitive to the socio-political contexts that make disclosures of sexual violence in any public or private context potentially difficult or harmful.

Researchers need to take great care to ensure they do not reproduce blaming, shaming and judgemental dynamics in their interactions with victim-survivor participants. This especially important when working with people who are additionally socially marginalised – as discussed further below. It is not necessarily retelling one's story that causes harm, but rather the unsupportive, insensitive and/or victim-blaming responses that survivors regularly receive when disclosing their experiences (Andrews, Brewin, and Rose 2003; Becker-Blease and Freyd 2007; Campbell et al. 2010; Ullman and Peter-Hagene 2014).

If the researcher is not aware of the social contexts that shape how sexual violence is understood, an interview can quickly feel like an interrogation – the phrasing and tone of questions can make participants feel disbelieved, misunderstood and judged, as they may have been many other times in their lives (Campbell et al. 2009; Fontes 2004). For example, in one of the author's (Shaez) doctoral research, she consulted with sexual violence support workers and LGBTQA+ community workers, several of whom told her about negative experiences their clients had previously had with researchers. One sexual violence survivor had been asked by a researcher, 'So, when did you get over the abuse?' – causing them to feel confused, judged and 'shut down' emotionally for the rest of the interview. The worker who retold this story to Shaez expressed concern that the researcher in question lacked an understanding of the long-lasting effects of abuse and how language like 'get over it' forms part of a social script that dismisses and disbelieves victims.

Researchers can hold significant power in shaping people's understanding of sexual violence. This is an ethical responsibility beyond the risk of causing emotional distress or reactivating trauma, but a broader recognition of the role that researchers might play in shaping how participants make sense of their experiences. For example, all three authors have interviewed survivors who were sharing their story for the first time and expressed worry that they were 'alone', 'abnormal' or to blame for violence. Campbell and colleagues (2009, 612) suggest that researchers can play a role in contextualising survivors' experiences in these moments by explaining the diverse experiences of survivors and reassuring them that violence is never the victim's fault (Campbell et al. 2009, 612). It is therefore important that researchers have a grounding in understanding the social and political contexts of sexual violence, including rape myths and victim blaming, and how this can impact survivors' lives, as well as the skills to facilitate this kind of conversation with care (Campbell et al. 2009, 2010).

Reframing the harm of talking about sexual violence from one of individual trauma to one of social and political contexts and the *responses* these generate to survivors' disclosure has direct implications for how we approach ethical research in this field. Under the first framing, ethical research is typically centred on mitigating the likelihood that an individual survivor will become distressed or upset through their participation. Ethical research in this case may, as discussed above, involve practices such as the provision of crisis support service details and warning participants about the risks of taking part and the potential for distress. In reframing this harm to factor in the broader social/political context and responses to survivors' experience, the ethical imperative shifts from 'managing' the participant to critically reflecting on *the researcher* and *the research environment*. This approach might instead require us to ask: how am I, as a researcher, working to ensure I do not dismiss or invalidate the survivor's experience? Do I have sufficient knowledge of the social and political contexts of sexual violence to undertake research with survivors? What environment am I creating during the interview/research process? (see also Campbell et al. 2009; Mulla and Hlavka 2011).

Beyond the Individual: Marginalised Communities and the Potential Harms of Sexual Violence Research

Both the institutional risk management and trauma frameworks locate the risk of harm of sexual violence research to individual participants. However, marginalised groups such as Indigenous people, people of colour, LGBTIQA+ people, disabled people and sex workers have strongly criticised academic research for causing harm to whole communities, and there are many historical and contemporary examples of research being used as a tool to perpetuate inequality (see e.g. Adams et al. 2017; den Houting et al. 2021; Douglas et al. 2018; Jeffreys 2010; Kim and Jeffreys 2013; Kwaymullina 2016; Smith 2012; Vincent 2018). There is a long legacy of writing by women of colour and Indigenous women about racist practices of research; including, in an Australian context, criticism of white researchers writing about violence in Aboriginal communities, perpetuating harmful stereotypes about Aboriginal people and justifying the continued dominance of the colonial state over Aboriginal lives (see Douglas et al. 2018; Kwaymullina 2016; Moreton Robinson 2000; Smith 2012). Other groups, such as sex workers and LGBTIQA + communities, have also been stereotyped as 'sexually deviant' and are frequently dismissed or blamed when they experience sexual violence (see e.g. Mortimer, Powell, and Sandy 2019; Sprankle et al. 2018). There is, therefore, legitimate concern from these communities about how research about violence might be used to affirm stereotypes, expose communities to media scrutiny, and contribute to further pathologisation and stigma (see e.g. Adams et al. 2017; Jeffreys 2010; Kim and Jeffreys 2013; Roffee and Waling 2017; Vincent 2018).

The identity of a researcher, their values, their relationships and connections to community, and their respect for cultural/community knowledge and practices, are crucial ethical issues for many marginalised groups (Ahrens, Isas, and Viveros 2011; Douglas et al. 2018; Jeffreys 2010; Kim and Jeffreys 2013; Kwaymullina 2016; Smith 2012; Vincent 2018). People from marginalised groups have called for community-led research and for researchers to work in meaningful partnerships with, and be accountable to, communities (den Houting et al. 2021; Douglas et al. 2018; Kim and Jeffreys 2013; Adams et al. 2017). Researchers endeavouring to work with marginalised communities must listen and learn from *them*: understand how research has harmed their communities in the past (Vincent 2018), work with and be led by community and peer advocacy groups (Adams et al. 2017; den Houting et al. 2021; Douglas et al. 2018; Jeffreys 2010; Kim and Jeffreys 2013), be culturally competent and connected to community (Ahrens, Isas, and Viveros 2011), be transparent about how data will be collected, stored and owned (Douglas et al. 2018; Kwaymullina 2016), and finally, be aware of the potential for study results to be misinterpreted and misrepresented by media and other groups (Kim and Jeffreys 2013; Jeffreys 2010; Vincent 2018). Some of these ethical considerations were highlighted in a recent experience by one of the authors (Bianca) when they reached out to a disability support group for assistance in recruiting participants. Bianca was asked by this support group whether members of the research team included people with disabilities, and what engagement they had with disability scholarship and activism. Notably, none of these concerns were raised through the institutional ethics process they had already gone through.

These issues relate to the fundamental questions of *who* is included in our research, who are 'we' to do this work, and the consequences this has for the theoretical and political claims we make. A commitment to ethical research requires us to consider which survivors are within the scope of our projects – this has historically been white, middle class, cisgender, heterosexual women at the expense of other survivors (Crenshaw 1991; Ahrens, Isas, and Viveros 2011; Mortimer, Powell, and Sandy 2019; Phipps 2020). This is not to suggest that researchers must always endeavour to include *all* survivors in their research – there are sound reasons for focusing on the needs of specific subgroups of survivors who may face unique experiences and concerns. Nonetheless, we engage in a form of epistemic injustice if we continue to only prioritise the voices of a select range of survivors. However, as noted above, some marginalised groups have clearly articulated the need for community-led research and for 'outsider' researchers to work in meaningful collaboration with communities (Douglas et al. 2018; Kim and Jeffreys 2013). A broader, reflexive approach to ethical research prompts us to consider what silences we perpetuate through our research – whose experiences of violence are positioned as worthy of our attention? Who are 'we' to make these choices and what positions and privileges shape our understandings of this topic (Mulla and Hlavka 2011; Phipps 2020)? What are the broader implications of this for how sexual violence is framed and responded to (Crenshaw 1991; Phipps 2020)?

Additionally, sexual violence researchers have an ethical imperative to avoid causing harm and perpetuating inequalities in relation to the responses we advocate for and how we call for violence to be addressed. For example, carceral feminist approaches that push for further punitive state intervention in response to sexual violence have been criticised by Indigenous people and people of colour for contributing to the overpolicing and incarceration of men in their communities (Kim 2020). Yet, the politics of abolition can sometimes sit in tension with the expressed desires of survivors, some of whom *do* want a criminal justice response – a tension experienced by one author (Bianca) in her current research on justice responses to street-based harassment.

As feminist researchers who aim to privilege and centre the voices of survivors, how do we proceed when the needs of some survivors are in direct opposition to others, or may otherwise work to perpetuate inequality? The answer to this question is something we are ourselves still grappling with as researchers. As a starting point, Bianca has navigated this complexity in her work by acknowledging the importance placed on a criminal legal response by some survivors and recognising that survivors currently have few other options in seeking justice – an approach influenced by her reading of abolition activists (e.g. Dixon 2020). This approach has enabled Bianca to (attempt to) mount a critique of criminal legal responses, and to advocate for the development of innovative responses, without casting judgement upon the justice needs or decisions of individual survivors. However, this is undoubtedly an ethical tension that requires ongoing discussion, as well as reflexive engagement with questions about whose voices and needs are prioritised and how this impacts marginalised groups for whom calling the police is not a realistic or safe option (Dixon 2020; Phipps 2020). Nonetheless, the ethical complexities of researchers advocating for particular responses to violence are not concerns that human ethics committees typically ask about, neither are they centred in trauma-informed approaches. As such, this discussion serves as an example of how our ethical obligations as feminist researchers must extend beyond institutional approval to include careful reflection on our positionality and political advocacy.

Conclusion

Sexual violence is a complicated and multilayered issue that is deeply personal and political, involving challenging questions of structural power, community beliefs and practices, interpersonal relationships and bodily autonomy. When studying this form of violence, researchers need to be aware of the potential to cause further harm to people and communities who may already be hurting and experiencing marginalisation and inequality. In this article we have provided critical reflections on the dominant models governing sexual violence research ethics and have argued for the need to include a broader set of considerations in undertaking ethical research in this field. We have argued that, while important, institutional and trauma-informed ethical frameworks curtail the parameters of 'ethical' practice. However, we do not suggest that there is a one size-fits-all answer to the question of what constitutes ethical research praxis. Rather, the answer to this question is always emergent, contextual and relational. Additionally, we acknowledge that we cannot do justice to the full scope of ethical issues in sexual violence research in this article. For example, we have not addressed ethical considerations relating to participant recruitment or engagement with gatekeepers. These are issues that require ongoing dialogue and reflection with researchers in the field (Burgess-Proctor 2015).

One key 'take away' from this discussion relates to the need to continue developing communities of practice around sexual violence research, and the need for careful stewardship of practice-based knowledge and mentoring of new researchers (Atkinson and Butler 2012; Westmarland and Bows 2019). Such practices are particularly important in relation to emerging ethical challenges and to ethical concerns that are unlikely to be addressed through institutional ethics processes. We also recommend further research on this topic to understand how sexual violence researchers work through these complex ethical issues, how they conceptualise the potential harms of their research and what models and practices they are using to ensure safety of participants, communities and other researchers.

Another implication from our discussion is the need to recognise the diversity of how survivors may be impacted by their experience(s) of sexual violence. In contrast to the trauma model, which can be essentialising and lead to paternalistic treatment of survivor-participants, we argue that the harm of sexual violence can be better understood utilising Liz Kelly's (1988) continuum model. The continuum model recognises that the meanings assigned to, and impacts of, sexual violence are 'a process' rather than 'a one-off event' (Fileborn and Vera-Gray 2018, 80; drawing on Kelly 1988). Further, this model avoids framing sexual violence as constituted by key 'episodes' or discrete 'incidents', with an assumption that some forms of sexual violence are more harmful or impactful than others. By drawing on a continuum model, we can understand the harms of sexual violence – and, in turn, the impacts of survivors participating in research – as varied, emergent and embedded. This approach suggests we cannot make assumptions about what 'types' of sexual violence will be distressing for participants to talk about or how they 'should' present/behave at a research interview. Rather, we must be prepared for a range of possibilities and make space for participants' autonomy and self-determination.

A spectrum of harm approach also directs us to look beyond the individual to the structural –to consider *why* sexual violence is difficult to talk about and *why* some groups of people may be more willing to do so than others. This calls us to reflect on ourselves as researchers – our identities, positions and privileges – and how this shapes the research we do, as well as the understandings of sexual violence and the 'solutions' we promote. Additionally, a spectrum of harm approach can make visible the impacts that researching sexual violence can have on *researchers* – an area that deserves further discussion and research (e.g. Campbell 2002; Coles et al. 2014). Thinking structurally through a spectrum of harm approach also underscores the need for further conversations about how institutions constrain us in doing ethical research – from bureaucratic ethics forms, to lack of the training, funding, resources and time to do the slow and careful work to be truly led by victim-survivors and their communities.

Acknowledgements

The authors would like to thank the anonymous peer reviewers for their generous and constructive feedback, as well as Professors Maryanne Dever and Lisa Adkins for their editorial support in putting together this special issue. We would also like to thank Roxana Diamond for her insightful feedback on a draft of this article.

Disclosure Statement

No potential conflict of interest was reported by the author(s).

ORCID

Shaez Mortimer http://orcid.org/0000-0002-8058-6384
Bianca Fileborn http://orcid.org/0000-0002-2650-3592
Nicola Henry http://orcid.org/0000-0003-2241-7985

References

Adams, Noah, Ruth Pearce, Jaimie Veale, Asa Radix, Danielle Castro, Amrita Sarkar, and Kai Cheng Thom. 2017. "Guidance and Ethical Considerations for Undertaking Transgender Health Research and Institutional Review Boards Adjudicating This Research." *Transgender Health* 2 (1): 165–175. doi:10.1089/trgh.2017.0012.

Ahrens, Courtney E., Libier Isas, and Monica Viveros. 2011. "Enhancing Latinas' Participation in Research on Sexual Assault: Cultural Considerations in the Design and Implementation of Research in the Latino Community." *Violence Against Women* 17 (2): 177–188. doi:10.1177/1077801210397701.

American Psychiatric Association (APA). 2012. *Diagnostic and Statistical Manual of Mental Disorders*. 5th ed. Washington, DC: American Psychiatric Association.

Andrews, Bernice, Chris R. Brewin, and Suzanna Rose. 2003. "Gender, Social Support, and PTSD in Victims of Violent Crime." *Journal of Traumatic Stress* 16 (4): 421–427. doi:10.1023/A:1024478305142.

Atkinson, Timothy N., and Jesse W. Butler. 2012. "From Regulation to Virtue: A Critique of Ethical Formalism in Research Organisations." *Journal of Research Administration* XLIII (1): 17–32.

Becker-Blease, Kathryn A., and Jennifer J. Freyd. 2007. "The Ethics of Asking About Abuse and the Harm of 'Don't Ask, Don't Tell'." *American Psychologist* 62 (4): 330–332. doi:10.1037/0003-066X.62.4.330.

Burgess-Proctor, Amanda. 2015. "Methodological and Ethical Issues in Feminist Research with Abused Women: Reflections on Participants' Vulnerability and Empowerment." *Women's Studies International Forum* 48: 124–134. doi:10.1016/j.wsif.2014.10.014.

Burgess, Ann W., and Lynda L. Holmstrom. 1974. "Rape Trauma Syndrome." *American Journal of Psychiatry* 131 (9): 981–986. doi:10.1176/ajp.131.9.981.

Campbell, Rebecca. 2002. *Emotionally Involved: The Impact of Researching Rape*. New York: Routledge.

Campbell, Rebecca, Adrienne E. Adams, Sharon M. Wasco, Courtney E. Ahrens, and Tracy Sefl. 2009. "Training Interviewers for Research on Sexual Violence: A Qualitative Study of Rape Survivors' Recommendations for Interview Practice." *Violence Against Women* 15 (5): 595–617. doi:10.1177/1077801208331248.

Campbell, Rebecca, Adrienne E. Adams, Sharon M. Wasco, Courtney E. Ahrens, and Tracy Sefl. 2010. "'What Has It Been Like for You to Talk With Me Today?': The Impact of Participating in Interview Research on Rape Survivors." *Violence Against Women* 16 (1): 60–83. doi:10.1177/1077801209353576.

Coles, Jan, Jill Astbury, Elizabeth Dartnell, and Shazneen Limjerwala. 2014. "A Qualitative Exploration of Researcher Trauma and Researchers' Responses to Investigating Sexual Violence." *Violence Against Women* 20 (1): 95–117. doi:10.1177/1077801213520578.

Crenshaw, Kimberle. 1991. "Mapping the Margins: Intersectionality, Identity Politics, and Violence Against Women of Color." *Stanford Law Review* 43 (6): 1241–1299. doi:10.2307/1229039.

den Houting, Jacquiline, Julianne Higgins, Kathy Isaacs, Joanne Mahony, and Elizabeth Pellicano. 2021. "'I'm Not Just a Guinea Pig': Academic and Community Perceptions of Participatory Autism Research." *Autism* 25 (1): 148–163. doi:10.1177/1362361320951696.

Dixon, Ejeris. 2020. "Building Community Safety: Practical Steps Toward Liberatory Transformation." In *Beyond Survival: Strategies and Stories from the Transformative Justice Movement*, edited by Ejeris Dixon, and Leah Lakshmi Piepzna-Samarasinha, 15–25. Chicago: AK Press.

Douglas, Lorice, Mark Wenitong, Dorinda Cox, Wayne Muir, Maria Martin-Pedersen, Gina Masterton, Ed Mosby, et al. 2018. *Warawarni-gu Guma Statement: Healing Together in Ngurin Ngarluma*. Accessed April 12, 2021. https://www.anrows.org.au/warawarni-gu-guma-statement/.

Downes, Julia, Liz Kelly, and Nicole Westmarland. 2014. "Ethics in Violence and Abuse Research: A Positive Empowerment Approach." *Sociological Research Online* 19 (1): 29–41. doi:10.5153/sro.3140.

Fileborn, Bianca, and Rachel Loney-Howes, eds. 2019. *#MeToo and the Politics of Social Change*. Cham, Switzerland: Palgrave MacMillan.

Fileborn, Bianca, and Fiona Vera-Gray. 2018. ""Recognition and the Harms of "Cheer Up."." *The Philosophical Journal of Conflict and Violence* 2 (1): 78–96.

Fontes, Lisa A. 2004. "Ethics in Violence Against Women Research: The Sensitive, the Dangerous and the Overlooked." *Ethics & Behavior* 14 (2): 141–174. doi:10.1207/s15327019eb1402_4.

Gavey, Nicola, and Johanna Schmidt. 2011. "'Trauma of Rape' Discourse: A Double-Edged Template for Everyday Understandings of the Impact of Rape?" *Violence Against Women* 17 (4): 433–456. doi:10.1177/1077801211404194.

Halse, Christine, and Anne Honey. 2007. "Rethinking Ethics Review as Institutional Discourse." *Qualitative Inquiry* 13 (3): 336–352. doi:10.1177/1077800406297651.

Henry, Nicola. 2010. "The Impossibility of Bearing Witness: Wartime Rape and the Promise of Justice." *Violence Against Women* 16 (10): 1098–1119. doi:10.1177/1077801210382860.

Herman, Judith L. 1992. *Trauma and Recovery: The Aftermath of Violence - from Domestic Abuse to Political Terror*. New York: Basic Books.

Jeffreys, Elena. 2010. "Sex Worker-Driven Research: Best Practice Ethics." *Dialogue e-Journal* 8, p. 1-16, Accessed April 12, 2021. http://www.nswp.org/sites/nswp.org/files/Elena-Jeffreys-Sex-Worker-Driven-Research-1.pdf.

Juritzen, Truls I., Harald Grimen, and Kristin Heggen. 2011. "Protecting Vulnerable Research Participants: A Foucault-Inspired Analysis of Ethics Committees." *Nursing Ethics* 18 (5): 640–650. doi:10.1177/0969733011403807.

Kelly, Liz. 1988. *Surviving Sexual Violence*. Cambridge: Polity Press.

Kim, Mimi E. 2020. "Anti-Carceral Feminism: The Contradictions of Progress and the Possibilities of Counter-Hegemonic Struggle." *Affilia: Journal of Women and Social Work* 35 (3): 309–326. doi:10.1177/0886109919878276.

Kim, Jules, and Elena Jeffreys. 2013. "Migrant Sex Workers and Trafficking: Insider Research for and by Migrant Sex Workers." *Action Learning, Action Research Journal* 19 (1): 62–96.

Kwaymullina, Ambelin. 2016. "Research, Ethics and Indigenous Peoples: An Australian Indigenous Perspective on Three Threshold Considerations for Respectful Engagement." *AlterNative: An International Journal of Indigenous Peoples* 12 (4): 437–449. doi:10.20507/AlterNative.2016.12.4.8.

Laplanche, Jean, and Jean-Bertrand Pontalis. 1988. *The Language of Psychoanalysis*. Translated by D. Nicholson-Smith. London: Karnac.

Moreton Robinson, Aileen. 2000. *Talkin' Up to the White Woman: Aboriginal Women and Feminism*. Brisbane: University of Queensland Press.

Mortimer, Shaez, Anastasia Powell, and Larissa Sandy. 2019. "'Typical Scripts' and Their Silences: Exploring Myths About Sexual Violence and LGBTQ People from the Perspectives of Support Workers." *Current Issues in Criminal Justice* 31 (3): 333–348. doi:10.1080/10345329.2019.1639287.

Mulla, Sameena, and Heather Hlavka. 2011. "Gendered Violence and the Ethics of Social Science Research." *Violence Against Women* 17 (12): 1509–1520. doi:10.1177/1077801211436169.

National Health and Medical Research Council (NHMRC). 2007. *Australian Code for the Responsible Conduct of Research*. Canberra: NHMRC.

National Health and Medical Research Council (NHMRC). 2015. "Frequently Asked Questions about Human Research Ethics Committees. Accessed April 12, 2021. https://www.nhmrc.gov.au/health-ethics/human-research-ethics-committees-hrecs/frequently-asked-questions-faqs-about-human-res/.

Phipps, Alison. 2020. *Me, Not You: The Trouble With Mainstream Feminism*. Manchester: Manchester University Press.

Roffee, James A., and Andrea Waling. 2017. "Resolving Ethical Challenges When Researching with Minority and Vulnerable Populations: LGBTIQ Victims of Violence, Harassment and Bullying." *Research Ethics* 13 (1): 4–22. doi:10.1177/1747016116658693.

Scott, Deborah. 2013. "Demystifying Ethical Review." In *CFCA Resource Sheet*. Melbourne: Australian Institute of Family Studies.

Smith, Linda Tuhiwai. 2012. 2nd Edition). *Decolonizing Methodologies: Research and Indigenous Peoples*. Dunedin: Otago University Press.

Sprankle, Eric, Katie Bloomquist, Cody Butcher, Neil Gleason, and Zoe Schaefer. 2018. "The Role of Sex Work Stigma in Victim Blaming and Empathy of Sexual Assault Survivors." *Sexuality Research and Social Policy* 15 (3): 242–248. doi:10.1007/s13178-017-0282-0.

Tseris, Emma. 2016. "Thinking Critically About 'Mental Health Issues' Affecting Women During/After Violence." *Social Alternatives* 35 (4): 37–42.

Tseris, Emma. 2019. *Trauma, Women's Mental Health, and Social Justice: Pitfalls and Possibilities*. London: Routledge.

Ullman, Sarah E., and Liana Peter-Hagene. 2014. "Social Reactions to Sexual Assault Disclosure, Coping, Perceived Control, and PTSD Symptoms in Sexual Assault Victims." *Journal of Community Psychology* 42 (4): 495–508. doi:10.1002/jcop.21624.

Vera-Gray, Fiona. 2020. "The Whole Place Self: Reflecting on the Original Working Practices of Rape Crisis." *Journal of Gender-Based Violence* 4 (1): 59–72. doi:10.1332/239868019X15682997635986.

Vincent, Benjamin W. 2018. "Studying Trans: Recommendations for Ethical Recruitment and Collaboration with Transgender Participants in Academic Research." *Psychology & Sexuality* 9 (2): 102–116. doi:10.1080/19419899.2018.1434558.

Westmarland, Nicole, and Hannah Bows. 2019. *Researching Gender, Violence and Abuse: Theory, Methods, Action*. London & New York: Routledge.

Whelan, Andrew. 2018. "Ethics are Admin: Australian Human Research Ethics Review Forms as (Un)Ethical Actors." *Social Media + Society* 4 (2): 1–9.

Archives as Spaces of Radical Hospitality

Jamie A. Lee

ABSTRACT
Deploying feminist notions of embodied, relational archival practices, this article critically defines and creatively unites both 'radical' and 'hospitality' as a tool for enacting generosity in archives. Drawing on the complexities of Derrida's *Of Hospitality (Cultural Memory in the Present)* alongside feminist scholarship and, what Cherríe Moraga calls 'theories of the flesh', it elucidates the urgent work of imagining archives as spaces of radical hospitality. The article uses embodied knowledges and storytelling as an archival methodology to propose a set of elements of radical hospitality and what it means and does in and for the community archives. It attends to the creative possibilities that acknowledging the relational complexities of the archives, its collections, and its records as integral to establishing socially just and generative spaces for its records creators and its visitors. Radical hospitality becomes not only a possibility but also the lively, animated, and joyous archival body and all of its parts.

Introduction

I am a queer activist, documentary filmmaker, scholar, and an unlikely archivist who made my way to archives and archival studies through an urgent collecting of the stories of elders in my community who were dying. I am the storytelling receptionist and concierge. I am in the community meeting people – creating the space and taking the time for them to tell their life stories to me and my video camera. I am touched, moved and changed every time. I bear witness to the changes in each of them through our time together. To witness is a sort of with-ness. An embodied exchange and togetherness that leaves its traces. The archives, to me, becomes a space of reception that itself turns into a sacred resting place. I mean 'rest' as active. An action of pause that articulates the lively potential for creating new worlds around what it means to live as lesbian, gay, bisexual, transgender, queer, and intersex, LGBTQI. The new worlds that community archives can help to create are those defined by embodied stories and archival storytelling practices. The archives that I have come to know is a place and a practice for the potential of radical hospitality.

Radical Hospitality

> An act of hospitality can only be poetic.
> – Jacques Derrida, (2000, 2)

Welcome to the archives.

I begin with this gesture of hospitality as entrée into this essay's mediation on what it might mean, look, and feel like for an archives[1] to be hospitable and radically so. I have come to think of this essay as a mediation on the relational aspects of any archival welcoming. The archives is, becomes, and exists in relationships. Always in relation. Traditionally these relations have been undertaken in the service of asymmetrical social relations. That is, they have been created to categorise and contain stories that supported normative societal structuring and hierarchies, or what I like to playfully call *traditional hierarchives* to draw attention to this longstanding relationship that I am working to dismantle in my work. The archival stories possessed structuring power. The archives I am inviting and welcoming you to is a multi-perspectival space of exchange, meaning/s-making, and reservation! Reservations are required as reservations are the critical practice that make room for consistent questioning in a space meant to remain radically open.

I begin my inquiry into hospitality by looking backwards at my family's practices and sideways at my partner's practices and by a return to readings from women of colour kitchen table wisdoms and feminist theory to social movement organising, poetry, and philosophy. I begin this work in the Arizona Queer Archives,[2] AQA, a community-based LGBTQI archives that I founded in 2008 as an oral histories archives with storytelling as its organising principle and practice. For the AQA, storytelling as an archival methodology means that a certain messiness abounds as multiple perspectives (Lee 2017) and an attention to nuance and difference (Lee, 2021) are central to its everyday archival practices. In this essay, I propose a set of elements of radical hospitality as a way to understand community archives as relational and generative.

Using my hands-on work in the AQA, I begin this mediation with a look at the book *Of Hospitality: Anne Dufourmantelle Invites Jacques Derrida To Respond*. It's a small book, long and narrow, with facing pages whose queries and responses are put in conversation one with the other. This intra-text dialogue is expressed as a distinct dance across words, discourses, and meanings. On the left-side pages of the book is French philosopher Anne Dufourmantelle's *Invitation* which deftly summons, clarifies, and teases out Derrida's responses given on the right-side pages. The two philosophers come together in these tight pages that curve into the inner spine of the book separating each philosopher's ideas and words while also forcing them to touch when the book is closed. This dance of coming together and coming apart as pages are turned and as the book is opened and closed bring Derrida's two lectures together with Dufourmantelle's contextualisation of them. It is a movement of imposed distance and imposed touch across italicised and serif[3] fonts that tells of the long lectures and less long contextualisation of those lectures. It is the lyrical movement of poetics that opens space and also centres intimate and relational proximities to reveal what it might mean to be hospitable.

Dufourmantelle begins her *Invitation* invoking Derrida's 'poetic hospitality' through which she navigates what she considers the dark of night and the light of day. In these navigations, she centres the poetic in the seeming disorder of the night. She contrasts this disorder with the 'order of the day, the visible, and memory' as she explores the creative obsession so many have with the theme of hospitality. She acknowledges that hospitality comes slowly through 'drawing the contours of an impossible, illicit geography of proximity' (2000, 2). Proximity and relationality in time and space. Hospitality is contextualised through proximal relationality. In other words, hospitality is expressed through gestures of closeness, even touch. It is also expressed as an opening, as space between. In the archives, this can mean touching materials – those we reach out to hold and those that move us, stir up our emotions. And the space to be moved. This can mean, then, being a visitor to the archives in relationship with archival subjects. It might also mean becoming the archival subject. These are the kinds of interactive exchanges that occur in the archives through stories. The stories that brought something or someone to be and even to become in the archives. I see stories and storytelling as an elemental part of the archives' hospitable gesture. The archives becomes accessible and knowable through imagined and engaged relations with materials, histories, bodies of knowledge, and the senses. The archivist is a part of the archival body – comprised of 'multiple histories, stories, and bodies of knowledge' (Lee, 2021, 9) – as it embodies, animates, and enacts a contextual relationality that ties together feelings, notions of belonging, self-awareness, integrity, imagination, and even curiosity (Lee, 2021, 59). Radical hospitality is there in the archives. Whether accessing the collections physically or virtually or creating collections or telling your stories for the archives or working in the archives – one can feel the *presence* of hospitality. Or not.

Radical hospitality, then, is foundational. An opening. It starts at the roots and is a de/stabilizing force of the community archives as it is attentive and considerate of the human subjects in and through time and space. Such a foundational move into a paradigm of radical hospitality begins with community archives and their work to be the spaces of and for relationships across temporal moments and, especially, according to Michelle Caswell in *Urgent Archives: Enacting Liberatory Memory Work*, in the present (2021). In the presence. I consider what bell hooks writes about radical feminism and the necessity for any movement to resist the co-option of feminist struggle by 'introducing a different feminist perspective – a new theory – one that is *not* informed by the ideology of liberal individualism' (2000, 9). In other words, to be radically hospitable is to be prepared for change – a change in relationship, in perspective, in being. Radical hospitality in archives and archival studies requires the messiness of poetry and serendipitous practices of storytelling that can produce new understandings, new knowledges, new theories. It is imperative that new and emerging theory engage with archival collections and make foundational changes to the traditional archival theory that has continued to perpetuate harm to non-dominant peoples and communities through obscurity, erasure, and fixity. Feminist thought in the archives means that we can resist hegemonic dominance by 'insisting that it is theory in the making, that we must necessarily criticise, question, re-examine, and explore new possibilities' (hooks, 11). Radical hospitality is in flux and always relational but never guaranteed (Licona, 2012).

In my work to build the AQA, I meet strangers at coffee shops, in parking lots, even at a nondescript gay bar that disguises itself as a trucker bar to the outside world. We introduce ourselves. I ask interested archival subjects to tell me a story about what they understand is in their archival collections. I listen. I take notes and ask them what stories their records, their artifacts, their everyday things that have marked their daily practices and minutiae will tell. Derrida asks if hospitality

> 'begins with the question addressed to the newcomer (which seems very human and sometimes loving, assuming that hospitality should be linked to love – an enigma that we will leave in reserve for the moment): what is your name? tell me your name, what should I

call you, I who am calling on. You, I who want to call you by your name? What am I going to call you?' (2000, 27)

Names in the archives are important as are descriptions, metadata, search terms, and the translated and interpreted stories that the archivists have pored over and carefully written out to ensure relevancy and also the tracing, like a map, from the digital database into the finding aid and to the collection of records. Radical hospitality means that getting from point A to B is possible through as many different pathways and directions as possible. Whether one takes a messy or a direct route one can find so many surprises. Remember, this work is a theory in the making. And remaking.

Derrida asks,

'Or does hospitality begin with the unquestioning welcome, in a double effacement, the effacement of the question *and* the name? It is more just and more loving to question or not to question? To call by the name or without the name? to give or to learn a name already given? Does one give hospitality to a subject? To an identifiable subject? Or is hospitality *rendered*, is it *given* to the other before they are identified, even before they are (posited as or supposed to be) a subject, legal subject and subject nameable by their family name, etc.?' (29)

Hospitality is complex as it works to connect a host and a guest; however, power circulates in ways that allow for some guests to be/come hosts while also elucidating the ways that we are not all guests in the same way. As Sara Ahmed argues,

'the notion of "welcoming the strangers" is premised on the mastery as the notion of "expelling them" – in both cases, the encounter with the "the strangers" becomes a means by which the "we" asserts itself as *willing*, even if that "we" is touched differently by the difference that is assumed to belong to "the strangers"' (2000, 190).

She focuses on the power of colonialism that also influences the urgency through which community archives are often created to disrupt dominant colonial and colonising narratives that frame non-dominant and underrepresented peoples and their communities. Ahmed reminds readers that the power to give remains with the national subject, which means that a turn away from what she describes as *multicultural hospitality* and toward what I call *radical hospitality* creates new and imagined worlds for non-dominant peoples.

Again, I say, welcome to the archives. In the digital world, the archives exists online as a website with disembodied archivists and archival labour as well as records creators and narrators. Radical hospitality, as an embodied practice in and through the archival body, is a relational element of what can be understood as human respect, empathy, reciprocity, and ethics of care.[4] Defourtanelle responds to Derrida, bringing the body into their conversations,

'when we enter an unknown place, the emotion experienced is almost always that of an indefinable anxiety. There then begins the slow work of taming the unknowing, and gradually the unease fades away. A new familiarity succeeds the fear provoked in us by the interruption of the "wholly other." If the body's most archaic instinctual reactions are caught up in an encounter with what it does not immediately recognize in the real, how could thought really claim to apprehend the other, the wholly other, without astonishment? Thought is in essence a force of mastery. It is continually bringing the unknown back to the known, breaking up its mystery to possess it, shed light on it. Name it' (26-28).

Defourtanelle centres the ways that humans experience phenomenological connections to the world/s around them to understand and to become at ease. However, her emphasis is about mastery which disrupts the promise of hospitality as poetic and as something messy, complex, unnamable, and unwilling to be mastered. Defourtanelle does not see or foresee the radical potentials of hospitality; her engagements with Derrida critique power in the exchanges with 'strangers' and all parties' relationships to the state in ways that perpetuate the mastery in colonializing and the visibility of the liberal subject. Julietta Singh, in her book *Unthinking Mastery: Dehumanism and Decolonial Entanglements,* argues for scholars to begin thinking about the anticolonial and postcolonial 'not simply to repudiate practices of mastery but, to borrow from Donna Haraway (2016), to "stay with the trouble" that is produced through attention to where, how, between whom, and toward what futures mastery is engaged' (2018, 2). Singh suggests that mastery is not something to overcome but rather is an 'inheritance that we might (yet) survive' (2). The colonised body embodies the histories of its oppression by identifying in significant and visible ways that reveal how it is not free in relation to the world that surrounds it. Singh writes to elucidate a fundamental collective 'we' as one that arises from the 'promises of those subjugated and emergent worldviews that recognise life, feel energy, and hear rhythms where now there appear to be none' (173). For the community archives that are central to my inquiry, radical hospitality becomes the promise for something more than the singular I. Radical hospitality brings forth the personal engagements that can provide generational nourishment. Stories and storytelling are the embodied forces that can animate connections in and across space and time.

My own personal stories pull me into this work and my thinking. In 1970, my parents were teen-agers when they had me. My father finished up his senior year of high school and graduated. He started working, was welcomed as a young mechanic at a gas station in my first tiny hometown. Meanwhile, my mother was kicked out of her inhospitable high school in her senior year once she was showing that she was pregnant. Such an act centres the inhospitable and deeply gendered nature of education and the normative requirements to be credentialed and also to work and generate income. She had me in April and struggled to find jobs that she could do being a 'high school dropout'. She enrolled in night classes and earned her GED (stands for General Educational Development, which is trademarked all over the Internet; I had thought it stood for Graduate Equivalency Degree, but I was wrong). This inhospitable situation influenced my parents' lives and then mine and my siblings' lives as we struggled with accessing education after high school. In so many ways, we inherited the feelings and the material circumstances of unbelonging.

Radical hospitality in my everyday life meant that we always opened our doors to drop-ins. We set a plate at the table and pulled up a chair to make space for an other. Our family – my partner, two daughters, and elder mother-in-law – invited stories and conversation around our differences and similarities. We exchanged our lives even if for only a short time over sobremesa, the part of the meal when the eating is done but the stories go on. Fast forward to the year that my partner and I officially became 'empty nesters', which meant to us that our grown daughters would no longer move back home for any significant lengths of time. Their bedrooms became spaces for other things – an office, a library, a lounge, and then a guest room for us to practice 'radical hospitality'. My partner told friends and colleagues about our guest room that could be a space for queer, QTPOC, BIPOC, scholars, artists, and activists to stay if they needed. Word spread quickly and we had friends and friends of friends stay with us over the years. In turn, some taught us their family recipes, one taught us how to put up sheet rock, one left us an Instant Pot and taught us how to make corn broth from their *Decolonize Your Diet* cookbook, another helped with building raised garden beds in our backyard. I tell you this to emphasise the exchange of radical hospitality. My partner and I created a welcoming space for them; we broke bread, shared meals; we told stories; we listened; we were quiet together; and we taught and learned from one another. Radical hospitality transformed our home and our relationships and gave us new knowledges to live with and by. It taught us new ways of being in the world together.

Manifesto for Radical Hospitality In/For Archives

> A theory in the flesh means one where the physical realities of our lives-our skin color, the land or concrete we grew up on, our sexual longings-all fuse to create a politic born out of necessity. Here, we attempt to bridge the contradictions in our experience.
> We are the colored in a white feminist movement.
> We are the feminists among the people of our culture.
> We are often the lesbians among the straight.
> We do this bridging by naming our selves and by telling our stories in our own words.
> – Cherríe Moraga and Anzaldua (1981, 23)
>
> Our children cannot dream unless they live, they cannot live unless they are nourished, and who else will feed them the real food without which their dreams will be no different from ours?
> – Audre Lorde (1984, 110–14)

Radical hospitality, as an archival ethos and especially in community archives, is a promise for a newly imagined way of being in and with non-dominant peoples, lived and living, dynamic histories, and distinct bodies of knowledge and evolving bodies. Community archives are integral sites for this world-making work, so I propose a set of elements of radical hospitality. I believe that radical hospitality is a practice and a location in the archives. It can be found and practiced in these ways:

- A relational practice requiring that hosts and guests be open to the understanding that they can be changed by (each) interaction in the archives. This requires a nimbleness that traditional archives (*hierarchives*) have not only eschewed but have considered inconceivable. In archival practices, this means careful attention to what it means to become over time. Who one was at first encounter may well be different from who one becomes at a subsequent archival encounter. As a practice, it means gathering input from communities as well as practicing a critical self-awareness of how power works to re-create hierarchies even within the community itself. The community archives working in and with radical hospitality can focus on relational practices and processes that can intervene in structuring forces. This will need to be nurtured and sustained.
- A place touched by disorderliness; one that avoids the order that has functioned traditionally to erase or capture (as in *fix*). In my own experiences, order has worked to assimilate distinct stories into mythical, if powerful, universals while disorder has made the archives more playful and more possible in its nuance. For community

archives and the communities they are intended to represent, a question to ask is: what role does dis/order play in the archives?

- A place touched by generative chaos; consider this a rhythm. For community archives, the rhythm may be something left over from traditional archival thought that is placed upon the collections and records to contain and, well, to constrain. What is understood, then, can only be found within the frame. What is happening outside of the frame influences how and what we recognise and know within the frame. Generative chaos is without frames and the rhythm is something (or some things) that move us and make for surprise and unknowable experiences within the archives. The archival surprise relates back to hooks' ideas around the need for new and emerging theories to make sense of the world and our places in it. What is the rhythm of chaos and what might it accomplish? Who gets to dance when rhythms are re-imagined and re-mixed?
- A place for (un/expected) encounter. What role can the un/expected play in our own growth and connections to oneself and others. I suggest self-reflection as a practice of self-inventory of expectations. If the community archives is a meeting place, who are you in the archives today and who do you want to meet? Whose stories and histories do you want to learn?
- A place to be moved in and by stories and storytellers that help to shape our ideas of connecting within the world and of creating futures that we want to be a part of. Archival collections and records are moving matters – affective and emotional – that offer ways that we might belong to communities and that might call us to act in particular ways in the world beyond the archives.
- A place to/for touch and to be touched by our histories and the promises of our futures. In the archives, touch is transformational and can be affirming. When we are touched, we are connected. What does that connection do in the archives and in the world beyond?
- A kitchen table ethos – a shared space to learn from and to leave lessons. Radical hospitality helps archivists, records collectors, narrators, visitors, and others imagine their places around the kitchen table in ways that elucidate the meaning of being and becoming historic actors in the community archives.

Radical hospitality is a world-making practice that recognises all the ways people and their histories have been oppressed, erased, and denigrated. It is also a space to lift the voices and visions and living histories of those who have experienced the inhospitable. The archives that I continue to co-create with, for, and from these oral histories become the spaces for ongoing education and community participation so that people from our local LGBTQI communities have their hands, heads, and hearts involved in the building of their own ongoing histories of having been, being, and becoming.

Welcome to the archives.

Notes

1. For more on the use of 'archives' versus 'archive' along with the politics of naming in these ways, see Caswell (2016).
2. See www.arizonaqueerarchives.com for more about the Arizona Queer Archives.

3. A serif is a decorative line or taper added to the beginning and/or end of a letter's stem, which creates small horizontal and vertical planes within a word. Serif fonts have those decorative lines or tapers that are commonly referred to as 'tails' or 'feet.' Serif fonts are commonly used for printing in books and signify a sense of being trustworthy, established, and reliable.
4. For these discussions within Library and Information Science and Archival Studies, please see: Cooke, (2019), Cooke, et al. (2020) and Caswell, and Cifor, (2016).

Disclosure Statement

No potential conflict of interest was reported by the author(s).

ORCID

Jamie A. Lee http://orcid.org/0000-0001-6182-2372

References

Ahmed, Sara. 2000. *Strange Encounters: Embodied Others in Post-Coloniality*. London: Routledge.
Caswell, Michelle. 2021. *Urgent Archives: Enacting Liberatory Memory Work*. London: Routledge Press.
Caswell, Michelle. 2016. "'The Archive' Is Not an Archives: Acknowledging the Intellectual Contributions of Archival Studies." *Reconstructions: Studies in Contemporary Culture* 16 (1). https://escholarship.org/uc/item/7bn4v1fk.
Caswell, Michelle, and Marika Cifor,. 2016. "From Human Rights to Feminist Ethics: Radical Empathy in the Archives." *Archivaria* 81 (1): 23–43.
Cooke, Nicole A. 2019. "Leading with Love and Hospitality: Applying a Radical Pedagogy to LIS." *Information and Learning Science* 120 (1/2): 119–132. doi:10.1108/ILS-06-2018-0054.
Cooke, Nicole A., Kellee E. Warren, Molly Brown, and Athena Jackson. 2020. "It Starts at Home: Infusing Radical Empathy Into Graduate Education." Special issue on Radical Empathy in Archival Practice. *Journal of Critical Library and Information Studies* 3. https://journals.litwinbooks.com/index.php/jclis/article/view/123
Derrida, Jacques. 2000. *Of Hospitality: Anne Dufourmantelle Invites Jacques Derrida to Respond*. Stanford, CA: Stanford University Press.
Haraway, Donna. 2016. *Staying with the Trouble: Making Kin in the Chthulucene*. Durham, NC: Duke University Press.
hooks, bell. (1984) 2000. *Feminist Theory: From Margin to Center*. Cambridge, MA: South End Press.
Lee, Jamie A. 2021. *Producing the Archival Body*. London: Routledge Press.
Lee, Jamie A. 2017. "A Queer/ed Archival Methodology: Archival Bodies as Nomadic Subjects." Critical Archival Studies Special Issue. *Journal of Critical Library and Information Studies* 1 (2): 1–27.

Licona, Adela C. 2012. *Zines in Third Space: Radical Cooperation and Borderlands Rhetoric*. New York: SUNY Press.

Lorde, Audre. 1984. "The Master's Tools Can Never Dismantle the Master's House." In *Sister Outsider: Essays and Speeches*. Berkeley, CA: Crossing Press: 103–106.

Moraga, Cherríe, and Gloria Anzaldua. 1981. *This Bridge Called My Back: Writings by Radical Women of Color*. San Francisco: Aunt Lute Press.

Singh, Julietta. 2018. *Unthinking Mastery: Dehumanism and Decolonial Entanglements*. Durham, NC: Duke University Press.

A Screen of One's Own: The Domestic Caregiver as Researcher During Covid-19, and Beyond

Cathy Smith

ABSTRACT
Much has been written about the domestic interior as a site of subjection and containment for women, both literal and metaphoric. This brief essay engages the ethical complexities resulting from the unexpected transformation of the domestic interior from a site of largely non-market exchanges into a work-from-home (WFH) and research base during the Covid-19 pandemic. The consequent enfolding of private and public life, work and family, consumerism and caregiving has been particularly complex for those whose research projects have been forced online. To explore these complexities, and within the methodological frame of 'nomadic research', this essay draws from feminist writings about the domestic interior as well as my own intersectional experiences of the pandemic which, while localised and personal, also resonate with those of others' similarly wrestling work and caring from shared, and often overcrowded homes. It argues that it is from our messy bedrooms that we must confront and reimagine ethical research practices, and the often-hidden role of the domestic interior within them.

Locked Down but not Locked Out? Feminist Research Methodologies and the Pandemic

As I stare blankly at my equally blank screen waiting for the zoom videoconferencing app to load, I am distracted by my neighbour. He motions from the footpath merely metres away from a tiny self-made bench that, since the first Covid-19-pandemic-triggered lockdown of early 2020, has become an impromptu micro-office for my university work (Figure 1). Sandwiched between wardrobes in my equally tiny, shared bedroom, this bench is not the 'Room of One's Own' (Wolf [1929] 2002) in a far-distant snow-covered continent I *was* to be sitting in Canada, to complete my major research project. My neighbourly distractions draw my attention away from what I should be writing to the problem of why I am not writing it. Stranded at home, swamped by the unexpected home-schooling, additional caregiving, and housework that the pandemic silently deposited into our workloads, workspaces, and worlds, I am relieved I work for a supportive employer, but inevitably – like so many others – exhausted. My thoughts wander to the wider career and life barriers still faced by so many women academics stemming from their dual

Figure 1. My WFH desk: feminist space or feminist containment? Source: Author (2021).

roles as caregivers in social, political, and cultural milieus in which 'the social value of caring is not recognized organizationally' (Nash and Churchill 2020, 837).

This article focuses specifically on one of those aforementioned barriers: the WFH spaces from which we work and research particularly since the Covid-19 pandemic-triggered lockdowns. It is written in the hope that the negative disruptions of Covid-19 might be leveraged as another opportunity to radically rethink about how, what, and from where we research. In the context of digital technological advancements that enable many forms of paid professional work to be conducted in and from the home whilst 'in your dressing gown' (Gornall and Salisbury 2012, 151), the binaries that once distinguished domestic, public, and commercial spaces and their attendant subjectivities have been rendered obsolete. As such, this article also builds upon feminist discourses exploring and questioning increasingly blurred distinctions 'between work and family' (Currie and Eveline 2011, 533) and more broadly paid and unpaid labour within the home – positive, negative, or otherwise (Currie and Eveline 2011; Gornall and Salisbury 2012; Adkins and Dever 2014, 2016; Schiller and McMahon 2019). Scholarly in orientation, this article is also a personal reflection upon, and a simultaneous manifesto for cultural change within academic settings. As an interior architect and female-identifying researcher with dependents, I am particularly interested in the relationship between our WFH spaces and feminist research methodologies within university settings whose performance metrics are already known, even before the present pandemic, to disadvantage certain demographics such as women and caregivers (Symonds et al. 2006; Eagly and Miller 2016).

This article is also written to demonstrate the alternative practice-led research methodology which it advances (for to do otherwise would work to undermine the argument). To this end, I engage and contextualise my lived experiences in the present context of the Covid-19 pandemic using two key areas of discourse: those on domestic interior spaces, and feminist practice-led research methodologies. Importantly, both discourses are interwoven with my own direct personal experience as researcher and community of focus. This discursive interweaving, moving from the personal to the scholarly, aligns with what feminist researcher Rosi Braidotti describes as a nomadic research methodology (Braidotti 2014, 2019, 47). The article's approach also resonates with methodologies of Ficto-criticism (Flavell 2009), particularly given that invoking my own experience within a critical research frame arguably constitutes a form of critical storytelling, albeit one intended to counteract and shift dominant epistemological forms (Kjellgren 2021, 66).

In drawing from personal experiences in and of the home, this article is also methodologically framed by feminist discourses which deem the spaces in which we write and produce research an important part of positionality of the researcher in relation to the research subjects (Gandolfo 2012, 62). These feminist methodologies recognise the social-political dimensions of spaces and the 'politics of location' (Braidotti 2012, 13; Loobak and Thapar-Björkert 2014, 47), as well as the lived and corporeal dimensions of research 'in both everyday life and in the work of research and scholarship' (James and Woglam 2015, 116). Ficto-critical methodologies extend this position further, foregrounding the researcher herself as a source of research knowledge; intermixing research writing and criticism with the experiences of the author, and thus unsettling distinctions between the subjects and objects of research (Gandolfo 2012).

Feminist philosopher Rosi Braidotti's nomadic research methodology is of particular interest to this article because of her desire to give voice to those 'missing people' (Braidotti 2019, 41) otherwise precluded from established forms of knowledge production which may undervalue the social, experiential, and corporeal dimensions of research. Inspired by Virginia Woolf's notion of the woman subject as a dynamic and malleable 'flow' (Woolf quoted in Braidotti 2014, 163), she also positions research as an ethical project involving 'deep-seated transformation' (Braidotti 2014, 163). This transformation, both personal and communal is enhanced by alternative, creative, embodied forms of knowledge production that counterbalance established, and thus neoliberal and patriarchal world views. Though writing several years before the Covid-19 global pandemic and the associated precarities it has produced, her argument for a nomadic methodology seems even more pressing today. To this end, this article is one attempt to explore a more ethical, inclusive approach to knowledge production by recognising the home as a space and site of outward-facing knowledge production, particularly for women whose voices are otherwise marginalised or excluded in public life. These 'homes' make take many forms – from those that are precarious and temporal through to those that are supportive (and versions thereof) – but all are the underacknowledged influential sites from which many of us 'write' our knowledge, making them worthy of interrogation.

Considering the pandemic as an opportunity to transform our research approaches is particularly important for women as there is an ongoing tendency to position their academic life and caregiving as distinct domains, as if: 'caring responsibilities are "exceptional" circumstances, rather than what are more far-reaching circumstances affecting all academic workers' (Nash and Churchill 2020, 842). Some recent shifts in academic settings do account for the influence of caring on individual career trajectory, often in the form of 'career disruptions' within a 'Relative to Opportunity' statements (NHMRC 2021, 3), thus with the onus on the applicant to argue their equivalence to those without similar obligations. For caregivers who are researchers operating within a potential research site, a more radical approach to research methodologies may also be needed; one that considers that knowledge is both entangled in, and simultaneously derived from the researcher's immediate milieu (Adams St Pierre 2015, 145).

Such an approach may be found in practice-led research methodologies which question not only the content and process of research, but the role of the researcher, her body, and her practice. In architecture and design, these methodologies similarly insert the personal and the professional within scholarly settings, framing existing knowledge in and through the perspectives of the researcher. Indeed, practice-based research could be seen as the intersection of the agentic, gendered perspective of Braidotti's nomadic methodology and Flavell's fictocriticism, whereby the personal is scaffolded by the scholarly. A notable distinguishing feature of practice-led research is that it also assumes that scholarly research and our embodied lives are intertwined, thereby extending the role of the researcher as 'intimate insider' (Taylor 2011) into the setting of her own lived, corporeal self. In the words of educational academic Elizabeth Adams St Pierre: 'Who told us we could, and should, separate our messy bodies from our pure minds lest they contaminate rational thought? When did we begin to believe our bodies were, indeed, absent from research and scholarship?' (Adams St Pierre 2015, 138).

To this end, the interweaving of the different discourses and my own experiences with published discourses constitutes the methodological limit of this essay, as well as its contribution. The limit relates to the foregrounding of personal experience as a creative practice-led research method, research data, and thus 'knowledge' (Gandolfo 2012, 62). It is written from the position of an academic writer with employment, access to internet and to a home (albeit an overcrowded one) from which to work during the pandemic. The contribution of this article extends from its advocacy for ways of working or thinking in academia that are inextricably linked to family, home, and community space.

As a researcher focused on the social and spatial impacts of phenomena, I am also interested in the agency of the researcher to investigate from the position of an insider, thus speaking in, to and of the communities she researches; specifically, to mitigate the effects of colonising the voices of other. For this reason, I have always initiated research from places and spaces I intimately know, produce, and consume. Thus, in this essay, I also draw from my experiences of practice-led research methods and which, while explicitly informed by my own discipline and circumstances, may also resonate with other researchers silently or secretly juggling work and caregiving outside of the frame of zoom camera lens.

Zoomspace: The Interiors From Which we Write and Speak

Focusing on what I imagine others might wish to see around me during zoom videoconferencing, I position my laptop to selectively edit what is visible through its camera lens – thus excluding passing teenagers, puppies devouring socks, a forgotten wine glass, and misshapen pillows seemingly bobbing above a sea of crinkled bedsheets. One of my

Figure 2. Curating home life for WFH research: futile pillow-fluffing for the zoomspace backdrop. Source: Author (2021).

amused colleagues once catches me on camera clumsily arranging said pillows (Figure 2) as if they belonged to a far more salubrious home than my own. My failed zoom-styling moment causes me to reflect upon the spaces that we see slipping in and behind our videoconferencing camera lens, and what they mean to our academic work, our research, and our presence in what I will term 'zoomspace'.

Much has been written about the effects of the Covid-19 pandemic lockdowns on our work practices and domestic lives due to the rapid shift to online remote working from home (WFH) using videoconferencing platforms like the ubiquitous zoom and the associated 'zoom fatigue' (Sklar 2020; Jiang 2020). Some research has drawn important attention to the socio-economic inequalities influencing people's ability to care for their families whilst working online (Clavijo 2020; O'Connor 2020, 605), and the difficulty of conducting academic teaching and research work online whilst caregiving (Flaherty 2020; Guy and Arthur 2020; Nash and Churchill 2020; Vermeir 2020), otherwise known as 'academic motherhood' (Guy and Arthur 2020, 887). These studies refer to the increase in women's university service roles during the pandemic, thereby reducing their dedicated research time (Dolan and Lawless 2020; Flaherty 2020; Guy and Arthur 2020, 887).

Comparatively little has been written about the spaces in which this rapid shift to telework shift has occurred, which feature as subtle, and sometimes not-so-subtle backdrops to our online meetings (Guy and Arthur 2020; Lerner 2020). These hybrid zoomspaces are also the sites from which we now conduct and write our research work and are typically co-located within homes. Whether selectively filtered or carefully curated, these backdrop interior spaces are constitutive of our work current personas yet communicate far more of our intimate and personal family lives than we might ordinarily wish to disclose in professional settings and which – courtesy of the technology of video meeting recordings – can be documented at the touch of a red recording button. By rendering the relationship of our home spaces to our work visible, these spaces collapse the habitual distinction between work and family life, thus: 'creating a paradox within us' (Guy and Arthur 2020, 897). However uncomfortable they may be, I would also argue that it is also from and within these zoom spaces that we might rethink both what, and how we research as part of a wider feminist agenda.

In her 1929 seminal essay 'A Room of One's Own', Woolf introduced a decidedly economic and spatial dimension to the question of women's writing which continues to inform feminist research methodologies. Woolf suggests that:

> a woman must have money and a room of her own if she is to write fiction; and that, as you will see, leaves the great problem of the true nature of woman and the true nature of fiction unsolved. ([1929] 2002, 2)

As others have observed, Woolf was able to make such claim from the privilege of her British home (Pearson 2016, 436); though her observations remain salient to others because of her still-radical interpretation of a woman's 'room' as 'an unlimited realm, with "infinite space to maneuver"' (Sheikh 2018, 29). If money and space are also practically essential to women's writing as Woolf suggests (fictional or otherwise), then the Covid-19 pandemic has exposed the precarity of women's academic work as secure employment, research funding and access to dedicated research spaces have been compromised. In parallel, many women researchers face increasing demands for their non-market service labour in the form of caring for family, home-schooling, and increased demands for online teaching and administration, all simultaneously delivered from the shared spaces of their homes (Dolan and Lawless 2020; Flaherty 2020; Guy and Arthur 2020; Nash and Churchill 2020).

When considering the impacts of pandemic-triggered lockdowns and WFH scenarios, it is equally important to acknowledge how the domestic spaces in which our work continues have been historically undermined due to their association with women's work. Patriarchal conceptions of housework can transform the home into a space of entrapment. In cultural and architectural discourses, interior spaces and particularly domestic interiors are often negatively associated with enclosure (Grosz 2001, 65), containment (Irigaray [1983] 1999, 96; Hawthorn 2017), and the oppression of women more generally (Wise [2000] 2006, 394). At the same time, interior spaces may also be sites of resistance and positive identification for women and families (Irigaray 1993; Purcell 2017, 14), if they can be made and occupied in ways that challenge 'normative structurations of space' (Wise [2000] 2006, 395). In this vein, feminist researchers Gibson-Graham have questioned the ongoing 'discursive marginalization of the household sector' in these spaces based on the

> output and the numbers of people involved, the household sector can hardly be called marginal. In fact, it can arguably be seen as equivalent to or more important than the capital sector. (Certainly more people are involved in household production than are involved in capitalist production.). ([1996] 2006, 261)

For them, the 'non-market exchanges' (Gibson-Graham [1996] 2006, 261) occurring in and from the home are inseparable from the wider world of work and production. Additionally, the validation of non-market work production inside of domestic interiors has important implications for market-based exchanges that occur alongside them, thereby unsettling binaries of work and home, public and private (Heim LaFrombois 2018, 19).

Accordingly, some scholars have recognised that the occupation and making of residential buildings and their interiors can inflect other domains and thus become 'part of a broad public negotiation over the future of the city' (Kinder 2016, 118). The community-led artistic transformation of vacant buildings in Detroit is one such example of what urban planner Kimberley Kinder describes as 'Domesticating the Counterculture' (2016, 117). She refers to grassroots redeployment and transformation of Detroit's abandoned houses and residential land into community gardens and, in the case of neighbours painting murals on a plywood hoarding, as artworks in themselves (Kinder 2016, 117). Domestic Do It Yourself (DIY) also has a long history of providing women with the tools to augment their homes, albeit within the frame of capitalism (Smith 2014). Its experimental forms unsettle habitual binary relations between production and consumption, container and contained, individual and community, expert and layperson, researcher and researched (Smith 2001, 2004, 2005, 2016).

If DIY practices such as decoration, gardening, non-structural furniture-making, and temporary installations are a form of non-market exchange; they also involve the production of space in a way that is independent of its architectural container, and thus the hegemonies of architectural production and consumption. Moreover, as these DIY practices do not permanently alter building structures, they can be enacted by a wider demographic than homeowners, including women and often using inexpensive materials, found or 'second-hand space' (Heim LaFrombois 2018, 85) and, in some cases, the explicitly non-market and community-based exchanges of sanctioned and unsanctioned squatting (Smith 2019). In such scenarios, the domestic interior may be transformed from a space of pure subjection of gendered-based production to one involving a more inclusive and transformative practice.

Importantly, the unravelling of the binaries of home and work invoked in these discourses resonates with the dissolution of home and work life boundaries amplified by the pandemic lockdown. Just as many of us scramble to self-assemble impromptu desks and spaces from which we can telework within our homes, it is important to recognise the socio-economic and cultural dimensions of our WFH scenarios, and indeed, our research practices within and about them. And as our bedrooms become impromptu broadcast studios for our research and teaching, I would argue it is to these spaces that we must turn as part of a broader examination of feminist research ethics.

Are You Sitting in a Cupboard? Authority, Agency, and Method in Zoomspace

Late one night in early 2020 at the peak of worldwide pandemic-triggered lockdowns, I connect with my U.K.-based colleague using zoom, sitting uncomfortably wedged between my bed and wardrobes away from the family chaos a few metres beyond. 'Are you sitting in a cupboard?', he cheekily inquires. In some ways, I wished this were true: if my wardrobe was emptied of the detritus of family life, perhaps I could occupy it like a private Narnia-esque world, escaping the burdens of the ordinary domestic world as my teenager demonstrated in lockdown humour (Figure 3). Yet I also wondered about the optics of my bedroom in relation to my academic authority and presence in the zoomspace.

I belong to a class of professional worker who can still work-from-home (however painful it may be), and indeed has a home from which to work in the first instance. Despite limitations of budget, space and labour, and with the labour help of a relative, I could apply my professional skillsets to produce what some might see as a glorified shelf, but which to me was world-making, both in process and product. Repurposed timber, offcut leather, copper pipe and laminated flatpacks were assembled to define my place within shared room (Figure 1); and I invested heavily in their 'spatial imaginary' (Ferreri and Dawson 2018, 429). This joinery may be insignificant when compared with the large commissions and wealthy clientele that typically launch the careers of high-profile architects. Yet within the blinkered frame of a computer camera lens, much can be made of very little. As Bachelard himself notes: 'the inner space of an old wardrobe is deep' ([1958] 1994, 78).

Others have wondered about the impacts of our new telework spatial backdrops, without necessarily considering their socio-economic and political carriage in the way I may have hoped. Existing scholarly and industry discourses on videoconferencing spaces often assume they should replicate real-world physical spaces to maintain the authority and influence of those hosting them (Rowden and Wallace 2018; Lerner 2020). In a pre-Covid-19 study of videoconferencing and live broadcasting of courtroom proceedings, law academics Rowden and Wallace drew attention to the impacts of the architectural 'scene' (2018, 515) on the perceived authority of the judge. The judge's capacity to preside over a physical courtroom was seen to be harder within the flatted and heterarchical videoconferencing format (Rowden and Wallace 2018, 514).

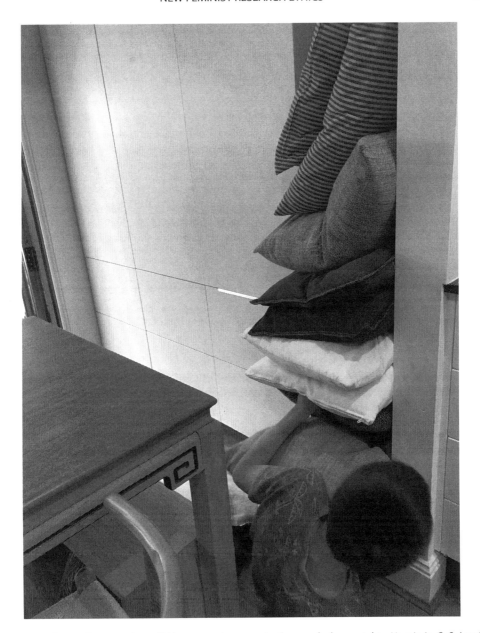

Figure 3. Occupying a cupboard? Humorous homage to the wardrobe portal to Narnia in C. S. Lewis' *The Lion, The Witch and the Wardrobe* (1950). Source: Author (2020).

Highlighting the way that meeting backdrop interiors influence the perceptions of virtual meeting attendees, these discourses reinstate the 'great rooms' (Lerner 2020) of our physical worlds within zoomspace, thereby replicating the spatial structures, the disciplinary norms, and the ideologies they represent. This simulation of real-world extant structures and spaces may be essential to some endeavours, but it could also be antithetical to some feminist-based research projects aiming to explicate, critique and authentically transform phenomenon.

As a young architect and researcher similarly frustrated with disembodied approaches to (in my case) mainstream building design and procurement at the turn of the millennium, I was drawn to then-emergent practice-led research methodologies. Practice-based research provided me with a way of integrating the personal with the professional within an academic setting. For one, I sensed the resonances between the experimental methodologies of practice-led research and the agile, creative design thinking essential for the practicing architect. For another, I wanted to produce research which expanded architectural understandings beyond the privilege and patriarchy often associated with mainstream urban design and development. Despite 'challenges of methodology design and alignment to the often-vexed relationship between practice and writing' (Vaughan 2017, 6), these research methodologies bridged the fluidity of the designer and the criticality of the scholar. This also necessitated exploring architecture from its outside (Grosz 2001, 65), and thus as a woman, mother and building occupant casting aside some of the tools of her trade.

Fascinated by grassroots actions, DIY building, and the non-market exchanges of architecture without architects, I transformed the occupation and maintenance of my own home in a community-minded street into a practice-led research case study intimately tied to caring for my young family, and thus at a time when it was also improbable for me to travel far from the home. Our first family home, Avebury St, was ravaged by termites and disrepair: between babies and work we lovingly repaired its broken interior finishes, fixtures and furnishings using found and salvaged materials (Figure 4). Interrogating its shambolic, upcycled interiors and the lives of the family and community within them

Figure 4. My first home and practice-based research experiment was made in and through the labours of family life, literal and metaphoric. Source: Author (2007).

provided a platform for critiquing mainstream architectural practice. Two subsequent home experiments followed over the last two decades, including the present space from which I write in lockdown. My subsequent understandings of architectural production and consumption, and by extension my scholarly research, can no longer be disentangled from what I once described as the 'chaos of life and bodies, nappies and milk, tears and mortgages' (Smith 2012, 156). Most notably, this earlier practice-led research did not preclude subsequent research methods and projects that continue to this day: rather it provided me with the agency to reach out to and connect with other like-minded communities where I could pursue other, more traditional forms of qualitative, grounded research. Paraphrasing from Braidotti, these encounters in and from the home generated: 'otherwise unlikely encounters and unsuspected sources of interaction, experience and knowledge' (Braidotti 2014, 182).

Given the complexities of pandemic-triggered lockdowns and their long-lasting impact on global societies (O'Connor 2020), we need to consider alternative forms and sites of research, and thus think differently about what constitutes research and its accessibility. Redirecting our research attention and skillset to our locales may also reveal unexpected but worthwhile topics of inquiry. Braidotti observes: 'some of the greatest trips can take place without physically moving from one's habitat. It is the subversion of set conventions and the consciousness-raising that defines the nomadic state, not the literal act of travelling' (2014, 182). As communities of researchers, we can advocate for the value of different sources and forms of research not simply as ways to accommodate career disruptions, but as rich and valid research in themselves.

The Productive Glitch

Writing in and of the twentieth century, Bachelard links domestic furniture to our private inner lives, as if: 'Wardrobes with their shelves, desks with their drawers, and chests with their false bottoms are veritable organs of secret psychological life' ([1958] 1994, 78). With doors thrown open and shelves laid bare to a virtual audience, the WFH furniture of the twenty-first century suffers no such illusions to privacy or intimacy (Figure 5). No longer the storer of secrets, the domestic cupboards and bookshelves starring in so many zoom meetings are virtual portals through which we traverse time zones and borders. At the same time, pandemic lockdowns have thwarted our capacity to travel to, and therefore access research sites beyond our immediate physical locale and /or digital networks. Whether seen as a gift or a curse for our research endeavours (or indeed, both), the wider embrace of remote working requires us to seek out alternative research models that bare witness to the work-life slippages of 'academic motherhood' (Guy and Arthur 2020).

To this end, turning our attention to small-scale research problems within our domestic milieu may enable a productive research life during this, and future pandemics but without excluding subsequent involvement with other more conventional research methods, locations, and topics. On the contrary: lived experiences of a research problem can provide a platform and springboard for other research projects further afield which enrich, diversify, and sometimes coalesce with our own knowledges. Questions surrounding the transformation of one's home and its occupation into a research project are fundamentally ethical questions (as with any form of research): that is,

Figure 5. Cupboards and glitches: a screengrab of a video meeting with colleagues and students in Canada. Source: Author (2020).

questions of study limits, the relationship between the researcher and researched, and indeed, the nature of knowledge itself. In my own case, the new modes of thought, nomadic ethics, methodologies, and knowledges that followed my early practice-led research was possible because I considered my messy domestic life as a potential source of rich data about a phenomenon, rather than a research variable to be bracketed out like my misshapen bedroom pillows in the zoom meeting frame.

Pandemic-triggered lockdowns should prompt a revaluation of academic research norms, particularly in relation to researchers and research topics which sit uncomfortably within established methodologies and output metrics. Embracing these approaches at scale requires institutional support, in the form of our universities, academic publishers, and grant authorities accepting the methodological and epistemological equivalencies of certain research. What is at stake is not only women's and caregivers' career trajectories, but the enrichment and diversification of research knowledge itself.

Disclosure Statement

No potential conflict of interest was reported by the author(s).

References

Adams St Pierre, Elizabeth. 2015. "Afterward: Troubles with Embodiment." In *Methodologies of Embodiment: Inscribing Bodies in Qualitative Research*, edited by Mia Perry and Carmen Liliana Medina, 138–148. London: Routledge, Taylor & Francis Group.

Adkins, Lisa, and Maryanne Dever. 2014. "Gender and Labour in New Times: An Introduction." *Australian Feminist Studies* 29 (79): 1–11. doi:10.1080/08164649.2014.913469.

Adkins, Lisa, and Maryanne Dever. 2016. *The Post-Fordist Sexual Contract: Working and Living in Contingency*. London: Palgrave Macmillan UK.

Bachelard, Gaston. [1958] 1994. *The Poetics of Space*. Translator Maria Jolas. Boston: Beacon Press.

Braidotti, Rosi. 2012. *Nomadic Theory: The Portable Rosi Braidotti*. New York: Cambridge University Press.

Braidotti, Rosi. 2014. "Writing as a Nomadic Subject." *Comparative Critical Studies* 11 (2-3): 63–84. doi: ro.3366/ccs.2014.0122.

Braidotti, Rosi. 2019. "A Theoretical Framework for the Critical Posthumanities." *Theory, Culture & Society* 36 (6): 31–61. doi:10.1177/0263276418771486.

Clavijo, Nathalie. 2020. "Reflecting upon Vulnerable and Dependent Bodies During the COVID-19 Crisis." *Gender, Work, and Organization* 27 (5): 700–704. doi:10.1111/gwao.12460.

Currie, Jan, and Joan Eveline. 2011. "E-Technology and Work/Life Balance for Academics with Young Children." *Higher Education* 62: 533–550. doi:10.1007/s10734-010-9404-9.

Dolan, Kathleen, and Jennifer L. Lawless. 2020. "It Takes a Submission: Gendered Patterns in the Pages of AJPS." *American Journal of Political Science*, editorial blog. https://ajps.org/2020/04/20/it-takes-a-submission-gendered-patterns-in-the-pages-of-ajps/

Eagly, Alice H, and David I. Miller. 2016. "Scientific Eminence: Where Are the Women?" *Perspectives on Psychological Science* 11 (6): 899–904. doi:10.1177/1745691616663918.

Ferreri, Mara, and Gloria Dawson. 2018. "Self precarization and the Spatial Imaginaries of Property Guardianship." *Cultural Geographies* 25 (3): 425–440. doi:10.1177/1474474017724479.

Flaherty, Coleen. 2020. "No Room of One's Own." *Inside Higher Ed* 1–1. https://www.insidehighered.com/news/2020/04/21/early-journal-submission-data-suggest-covid-19-tanking-womens-research-productivity.

Flavell, Helen. 2009. "Who Killed Jeanne Randolph? King, Muecke or "Ficto-Criticism"." *Outskirts: Feminisms Along the Edge* 20: 1–4.

Gandolfo, Enza. 2012. "Constructing Imaginary Narratives: Practice-Led Research and Feminist Practice in Creative Writing." *Qualitative Research Journal* 12 (1): 61–74.

Gibson-Graham, J. K. [1996] 2006. *The End of Capitalism (As We Knew It): A Feminist Critique of Political Economy*. London: University of Minnesota Press.

Gornall, Lynne, and Jane Salisbury. 2012. "Compulsive Working, "Hyperprofessionality" and the Unseen Pleasures of Academic Work." *Higher Education Quarterly* 66 (2): 135–154. doi:10.1111/j.1468-2273.2012.00512.x.

Grosz, Elizabeth. 2001. *Architecture from the Outside: Essays on Virtual and Real Space*. Cambridge, MA: MIT.

Guy, Batsheva, and Brittany Arthur. 2020. "Academic Motherhood During COVID-19: Navigating our Dual Roles as Educators and Mothers." *Gender, Work, and Organization* 27 (5): 887–899. doi:10.1111/gwao.12493.

Hawthorn, Jeremy. 2017. "Conradian Claustrophobia: Gender, Confinement, Emancipation." *Conradiana* 49 (2): 9–26. doi:10.1353/cnd.2017.0008.

Heim LaFrombois, Megan E. 2018. *Reframing the Reclaiming of Urban Space: A Feminist Exploration Into Do-It-Yourself Urbanism in Chicago*. Lanham: Lexington Books.

Irigaray, Luce. 1993. *An Ethics of Sexual Difference*. Translated by Carolyn Burke and Gillian C. Gill. Ithaca, NY: Cornell University Press.

Irigaray, Luce. [1983] 1999. *The Forgetting of Air in Martin Heidegger*. Translated by Mary Beth Mader. Austin: University of Texas Press.

James, Stephanie, and James F. Woglam. 2015. "Behind the Body-Filled Scenes: Methodologies at Work on the Body in Graphica." In *Methodologies of Embodiment: Inscribing Bodies in Qualitative Research*, edited by Mia Perry and Carmen Liliana Medina, 116–137. London: Routledge.

Jiang, Manyu. 2020. "Video Chat is Helping us Stay Employed and Connected. But What Makes it so Tiring - and how can we Reduce 'Zoom fatigue'?" *BBC* online. Accessed 16 March 2021. https://www.bbc.com/worklife/article/20200421-why-zoom-video-chats-are-so-exhausting.

Kinder, Kimberley. 2016. *DIY Detroit: Making Do in a City Without Services*. Minneapolis: University of Minnesota Press.

Kjellgren, Adam. 2021. "Mythmaking as a Feminist Strategy: Rosi Braidotti's Political Myth." *Feminist Theory* 22 (1): 63–79.

Lerner, Adam. 2020, April 28. "Humanizing the Spaces of Video Conferences (Zoom et al.)." In The UX Collective, Online Publication. Accessed 16 March 2021. https://uxdesign.cc/part-two-humanizing-the-spaces-of-video-conferences-zoom-et-al-704497aba2f1.

Loobak, Redi, and Suruchi Thapar-Björkert. 2014. "Writing the Place from Which One Speaks." In *Writing Academic Text Differently: Intersectional Feminist Methodologies and the Playful Art of Writing*, edited by Nina Lykke, 47–61. New York: Routledge.

Nash, Meredith, and Brendan Churchill. 2020. "Caring During COVID-19: A Gendered Analysis of Australian University Responses to Managing Remote Working and Caring Responsibilities." *Gender, Work, and Organization* 27 (5): 833–846. doi:10.1111/gwao.12484.

NHMRC. 2021. *Key Changes - Investigator Grants 2021*. Canberra: Australian Government.

O'Connor, Daryl B, et al. 2020. "Research Priorities for the COVID-19 Pandemic and Beyond: A Call to Action for Psychological Science." *The British Journal of Psychology* 111 (4): 603–629. doi:10.1111/bjop.12468.

Pearson, Nels. 2016. "Woolf's Spatial Aesthetics and Postcolonial Critique." In *A Companion to Virginia Woolf*, edited by Jessica Berman, 1st ed, 427–440. Hoboken: John Wiley & Sons, Ltd. doi:10.1002/9781118457917.ch30

Purcell, Bridget. 2017. "The House Unbound: Refiguring Gender and Domestic Boundaries in Urbanizing Southeast Turkey." *City & Society* 29 (1): 14–34. doi:10.1111/ciso.12110.

Rowden, Emma, and Anne Wallace. 2018. "Remote Judging: The Impact of Video Links on the Image and the Role of the Judge." *International Journal of Law in Context* 14 (4): 504–524. doi:10.1017/S1744552318000216.

Schiller, Amy, and John McMahon. 2019. "Alexa, Alert Me When the Revolution Comes: Gender, Affect, and Labor in the Age of Home-Based Artificial Intelligence." *New Political Science* 41 (2): 173–191. doi:10.1080/07393148.2019.1595288.

Sheikh, Sheheryar B. 2018. "The Walls That Emancipate: Disambiguation of the "Room" in A Room of One's Own." *Journal of Modern Literature* 42 (1): 19–31. Accessed 31 March. https://www.jstor.org/stable/10.2979/jmodelite.42.1.02.

Sklar, Julia. 2020. "'Zoom fatigue' is taxing the brain. Here's why that happens." *National Geographic*, Science-Coronavirus Coverage. Accessed 16 March 2021. https://www.nationalgeographic.com/science/article/coronavirus-zoom-fatigue-is-taxing-the-brain-here-is-why-that-happens.

Smith, Cathy. 2001. "Looking for Liminality in Architectural Space (The Space of Liminality and the Space of Architecture)." *Limen* 1 (December). http://limen.mi2.hr/limen1-2001/catherine_smith.html.

Smith, Cathy. 2004. "Inside-out: Speculating on the Interior." *IDEA Journal*: 93–102. ISSN 1445-5412.

Smith, Cathy. 2005. "Spaces of Architectural Overcoming." *IDEA Journal 2005: Inside-Out* 6 (1): 51–59. Brisbane: Queensland University of Technology. ISSN 1445-5412.

Smith, Cathy. 2012. "Remembering in Red." In *Semi-Detached: Writing, Representation and Criticism in Architecture*, edited by Naomi Stead, 152–159. Melbourne: Uro Media.

Smith, Cathy. 2014. "Handymen, Hippies and Healing: Social Transformation Through the DIY Movement (1940s to 1970s) in North America." *Architectural Histories* 2 (1): 1–10. doi:10.5334/ah.bd.

Smith, Cathy. 2016. "Body-Building-Becomings." *Australian Feminist Studies* 30 (86): 402–417. doi:10.1080/08164649.2016.1158688.

Smith, Cathy. 2019. "Licensing the Radical: From Licensed Squatting to Meanwhile Use in London and Regional Australia." 9th State of Australian Cities National Conference, 30 November–5 December 2019, Perth, Western Australia, edited by Dianne MacCallum and Paul Maginn. Perth, Australia. http://dx.doi.org/10.25916/5eb34fe290d9a.

Symonds, Matthew R.E., Neil J. Gemmell, Tasmin L. Braisher, Kylie L. Gorringe, and Mark A. Elgar. 2006. "Gender Differences in Publication Output: Towards an Unbiased Metric of Research Performance." *PLoS ONE* 1 (1): e127. doi:10.1371/journal.pone.0000127. San Francisco: Public Library of Science.

Taylor, Jodie. 2011. "The Intimate Insider: Negotiating the Ethics of Friendship When Doing Insider Research." *Qualitative Research: QR* 11 (1): 3–22. doi:10.1177/1468794110384447.

Vaughan, Laurene. 2017. "Introducing Practice-Based Design Research." In *Practice Based Design Research*, edited by Laurene Vaughan, 1–6. London: Bloomsbury Academic.

Vermeir, Koen. 2020. "Editorial: Doing History in the Time of COVID-19." *Centaurus; International Magazine of the History of Science and Medicine* 62 (2): 219–222. doi:10.1111/1600-0498.12319.

Wise, J. Macgregor. 2000. "Home: Territory and Identity." In *Intimus: Interior Design Theory Reader*, edited by Mark Taylor, and Preston Julieanna, 391–396. Chichester: John Wiley & Sons Ltd.

Woolf, Virginia. [1929] 2002. *A Room of One's Own*. Ebook: Project Guttenberg. Accessed 29 March 2021. http://gutenberg.net.au/ebooks02/0200791h.html.

ə OPEN ACCESS

Towards an Inventive Ethics of Carefull Risk: Unsettling Research Through DIY Academic Archiving

Niamh Moore, Nikki Dunne, Martina Karels and Mary Hanlon

ABSTRACT
In this article, we call for an inventive ethics of care-full risk for qualitative research. While methodological experimentation is widely welcomed across the social sciences, there is little talk of innovation in ethical principles and practice. We argue that research ethics is an 'invented tradition' (Hobsbawm 2012), which has become unquestioned convention. We take up the archiving and reuse of qualitative research data as a challenging, yet compelling, site of methodological innovation, where ethical considerations often appear as an insurmountable barrier. Ethical concerns about informed consent and anonymity, given unknown future use of data, and commitments to destroying data to protect research participants, appear undone by calls to share data. We take up the work of community archives, feminist and queer archivists and archival theory, as generative sites for developing an archival imaginary for researchers. We recount how we came to unsettle ethical practice through creating a 'DIY academic archive', a digital open access research archive, *Clayoquot Lives: An Ecofeminist Story Web* (https://clayoquotlives.sps.ed.ac.uk/). Against a paternalistic research culture of risk avoidance, we argue that care always involves risk. An inventive feminist ethic of care-full risk can resource new ethical research, reimagining research by embracing the risk of caring for data.

Introduction: Reinventing Research Ethics

In this article, we call for an inventive ethics of care-full risk for qualitative research in the social sciences. We argue that research ethics can be understood as an 'invented tradition' (Hobsbawm 2012) which has rapidly become unquestioned convention. While commitment to methodological experimentation, to 'live methods' (Back and Puwar 2012) and 'inventive methods' (Lury and Wakeford 2013), is widely welcomed and rewarded, we note there is little talk of innovation in ethical principles and practice.

We take up the archiving and reuse of qualitative research data as a particularly challenging, yet compelling, site of methodological innovation, where ethical considerations have appeared as an insurmountable barrier to its development. The commitment to informed consent seems compromised because the future use of data remains unknown. Seeking informed consent from research participants for reuse in perpetuity, by other researchers addressing different research questions, can seem impossible. The commitment to anonymisation means that important contextual details are likely to be redacted, leaving data compromised for future researchers. Most obviously, the commitment to enacting safety for participants through destroying their data at the end of projects is utterly undone by the idea of retaining this data for future use. Thus the archiving and reuse of qualitative data appears to threaten established ethical practice in qualitative research (Broom, Cheshire and Emmison 2009; Cheshire, Broom, Emmison 2009; Hughes and Tarrant 2020; McLeod and O'Connor 2020).

Here we recount how our project to create our own 'DIY academic archive', an open access, online archive of research interviews, *Clayoquot Lives: An Ecofeminist Story Web* (https://clayoquotlives.sps.ed.ac.uk/), necessarily involved an 'inventive' approach to research ethics. We name this practice 'DIY academic archiving' to point to different genealogies and orientations to our work. Against the extractivist data harvesting of corporate interests and moving away from the automated data-mining of large scale computational research and big data, we turn to the creative work of archiving and sharing stories of ecofeminist activism to inform a radical data-sharing and archival practice for researchers. We draw on the practices of feminist and queer history-making, the work of community and independent archives, and crucially, to archivists and archival theory, as generative sites for developing an archival imaginary and archival ethics for researchers (Moore 2017).

Crucially, we are extending archival practices to propose the possibility of researchers building open and publicly-accessible digital archives. In making this leap, we are working with a feminist ethic of care. Against a culture of risk avoidance, we argue that research, and care, always involve risk. We suggest that an inventive feminist ethic of care-full risk, understood as responsible action (Welch 2000), allows us to take seriously matters of accountability and that creating archives for sharing our research data can offer an ethical practice of 'world-making' (Haraway 2016).

Research Ethics as an 'Invented Tradition'

We argue that research ethics can be understood as an 'invented tradition':

> a set of practices, normally governed by overtly or tacitly accepted rules and of a ritual or symbolic nature, which seek to inculcate certain values and norms of behaviour by repetition, which automatically implies continuity with the past. (Hobsbawm 2012, 1)

Commitments to informed consent, anonymity, confidentiality, the use of information sheets and the destruction of data, have all become research tradition very quickly. However, the institutionalisation of ethical review has come much more recently, and arguably in a more ad hoc way than many researchers appreciate, involving a mixture of guidelines and governance from professional bodies, funder-led frameworks as well as, more recently, university-based ethical review committees. Here, our attention is less on these more formal processes of ethical review, which have been the focus of significant criticism, and more on ethical practice throughout the research process, where we are suggesting that 'invented traditions' are also readily invoked.

We have found it particularly curious that while claims to novelty and innovation abound in relation to methodology, claims to innovation do not usually extend to research ethics. Hobsbawm remains instructive, observing that '[i] t is the contrast between the constant change and innovation of the modern world and the attempt to structure at least some parts of social life within it as unchanging and invariant that makes the 'invention of tradition' so interesting' (2012, 2). Ethical commitments emerge as the part of the research process which is stabilised, arguably serving to legitimise methodological innovations.

In an insightful article, Nind and colleagues (see Nind et al. 2013) take up the question of methodological innovation and ethics through a study of research innovators. They found a strong orientation to responsible practice amongst researchers, suggesting that the relationship between innovation and ethics can be one of reciprocity, rather than tension. This separation between creative approaches to research and concern about ethical matters is also identified by McLeod and O'Connor (2020) in their recent reflection on archiving qualitative data, where they name these as two distinct trends in the literature. Research ethics do not have to be stabilised to vouch for innovation, rather creativity and innovation *needs* to extend to ethical practice.

We argue that it is the unexamined persistence of key commitments of research ethics that enables research ethics to be so effectively mobilised as a damning argument against the possibility of archiving qualitative data. Paying attention to the questions which emerge in a move to archiving and reuse of qualitative data exposes some limitations of the assumptions of research ethics. Noting that attention to 'invented traditions' has led to a fruitless search for the 'origins' of traditions and examination of how much of a tradition is fictitious, Palmisano and Pannofino (2016) instead approach tradition as a site of ongoing cultural creativity. Drawing on their concept of '*inventive* traditions' (Palmisano and Pannofino 2016) we draw attention to a tradition of creativity in ethical research practice. If we are engaged with inventive methods, we may benefit from an inventive approach to ethics too. Inventiveness does not mean fabricating ethics out of nowhere; it means building on ongoing interventions – this is where we turn to histories of feminist and other critical approaches to an ethics of care.

Towards an 'Inventive Ethics': Feminist and Other Critical Approaches to Care

There has already been reinvention of ethical tradition, largely led by feminist and other critical researchers. Feminists have challenged the application of abstract ethical principles to research encounters. They have insisted on the need to attend to the specificity of lived experience, to reflect on the importance of research relationships, to attend to the complexities of building rapport and to power differences in research encounters. A key feminist intervention was to understand research encounters as co-created (see for example Edwards and Mauthner 2002; Haraway 1988).

Feminist researchers have argued that it is a *paternalistic* ethic of care which has informed practice to date – one which assumes a hierarchy between researcher and researched: that the researcher is the knower and the researched is to be known; that research participants are vulnerable and in need of protection. In this model, the researcher is both the potential source of harm and also the one entrusted with avoiding harm. This approach to research has produced strategies of risk avoidance intended to ensure participants come to no harm. This functions more to protect researchers through assuming asymmetrical relationships with research participants, where the researcher is always powerful, rather than approaching research encounters as much more fraught relationships where multiple inequalities and differences define and shape the research encounter. Feminists have rejected this protectionist, risk-averse ethic, which denies research participants a stake in their own story.

This kind of protectionist ethic has also been traced by Uma Narayan who identified a 'colonialist care discourse', noting that colonialism was rarely presented as being about 'crude self-interest' (1995, 134) but rather was also justified 'as being in the interests of, for the good of, and as promoting the welfare of the colonized' (Narayan 1995, 133). For Narayan, this means that calls for a turn from a rhetoric of individual rights to an ethic of care, and attention to relationships of interdependence, is not sufficient (1995). Rather she argues the need to also 'worry about who defines terms, such as rights and relationships', as these accounts of interdependence will differ for the coloniser and the colonised (1995, 133).

Against beneficent accounts of research, many communities have insisted on naming damage, and have called for more attention to the ethics of research practice. Linda Tuhiwai Smith continues to bear repeating in - *Decolonising Methodologies* she damningly names research as 'probably one of the dirtiest words in the indigenous world's vocabulary' (Smith 1999, 1). Smith opens up a transformative indigenous research imaginary, offering a range of interventions which reimagine research practice. Disability activists have refused decades of objectifying research *on* disabled people, often without informed consent, calling for an inclusive research ethos of 'nothing about us without us' (Charlton 2000; see also Nind 2014). Researchers in Childhood Studies have also identified paternalism in research and have produced a rich literature engaging with children and young people participating in and leading research (e.g. Davidson 2017; Cuevas-Parra and Tisdall 2019). The growth of participatory, collaborative, and inclusive research is one response to these challenges. The history of research ethics is a history of creative intervention.

Sharon Welch has identified an ethic of control in protectionist ethics of care, which leads 'to a paralysis of will when faced with complex problems' (2000, 17), constraining the radical possibilities of social justice. Like Narayan (1995), she is attuned to the matter of who gets to define terms, and who can assume that 'the aim of one's action will be carried out' (Welch 2000, 17). Drawing on Black feminist theorists and writers, she calls for an ethic of risk which, for her, opens up the possibilities for action. We take up this invitation to undermine the opposition between care and risk, and the assumption that to take risks is necessary to be care-less. Rather a 'care-less' approach might be one which substitutes proceduralism for working through dynamics of power. For us, a feminist ethic of care-full risk calls for an inventive approach to ethical practice which can become a resource for supporting creative interventions and 'responsible action' in research.

Attending to Data as 'Neglected Things'

A feminist ethic of care continues to find new resonances – including with those working in Science and Technology Studies, data ethics and archival theory and practice. Maria

Puig de la Bellacasa (2017) calls for research to be a matter of care – supporting the 'relational, material and affective webs that are vital for collective flourishing' (Lindén and Singleton 2021, 2). She notes how some things are proper objects of care, whereas others are cast aside and devalued, and calls for a feminist attention to 'neglected things', to generate better ways of caring. We argue that data are neglected things in research. Against commitments to care for research participants, the traces of research – interview transcripts, audio files, video, images, or material objects, and so on – which are also the traces of participants, appear as some of the 'neglected things' of research projects. Commonly, there has been a benign, or not so benign, neglect, where data accumulates in chaotic disorder in filing cabinets, on office floors, or on computer drives and clouds, where it might languish, eventually discarded through office moves, and the technological obsolescence of new computers and multiple clouds. This practice of discarding data, and the invocation of research ethics as a reason not to save or share data, demonstrates the non-innocence of paternalistic, protectionist 'care'. To create an archive of research data is a matter of care (see also Baker and Karasti 2018). Like Puig de la Bellacasa, we are also building on the work of Haraway and others who understand feminist knowledge projects as matters of world-making (Puig de la Bellacasa 2017; Haraway 2016; Murphy 2015; Lindén and Singleton 2021; Lapp 2020).

To care for the neglected things of research is not an easy or simple task. Michelle Murphy (2015) reminds us of the need to separate care from feeling good or happy, pointing out that one meaning of care is to be concerned, and that to be concerned might also mean to be unsettled. To archive and share research data is to unsettle existing practice and researchers schooled in these conventions. It is to concern others, to take the risk of unsettling other researchers (perhaps more than research participants), and it is to the risk of unsettling taken for granted professional practice. To archive in the context of histories of data destruction requires us to be inventive about ethical practice. To unsettle research conventions certainly requires care-full risk.

Yet there are precedents for sharing research data – with quantitative data the common reference point. Critics argue the unsuitability of the comparison, insisting on the importance of qualitative data as co-created in the context of a relationship and encounter between a researcher and a research participant, against a fantasy of quantitative data as 'abstracted from the conditions of its production' (McLeod and O'Connor 2020, 1). The relational nature of qualitative data is crucial and goes against the assumptions of decontextualised quantitative data. While we want to resist reductive approaches to research materials and the relationships through which these materials have been generated, we also want to refuse any simplistic binaries between data and stories, or data and people. Here, the Feminist Data Manifest-No's (Cifor et al. 2019) commitment to refusal as feminist strategy appeals. Notably, the point of how refusal of existing data regimes opens up possibilities for the emergence of new data futures through making new ethical commitments – and these are futures which are not overdetermined by colonial *or* liberal ethics (see also Hoffmann 2021; Sutherland 2019). In continuing to use the terms data *and* stories, we understand data as always embodied, relational, and affective (Cifor et al. 2019). Against the model of disembodied data often offered up by corporate big data, feminist qualitative research has always been about relations. Against extractivist models, with dubious approaches to consent, feminist social science insists on the co-production of stories, offering participants a more engaged process in creating the stories/data which might go on the record. Drawing on the recent take up of an ethics of care in feminist data science (Cifor et al. 2019; D'Ignazio and Klein 2020), we refuse data neglect, automatic data destruction, as well as extractivism, and call for care in the production, sharing and archiving of data and stories. The question then becomes how to maintain, multiply, proliferate and document relations - and we suggest a more thorough engagement with the productive affordances of archival theory and practice can help.

The Missing Archival Turn in the Social Sciences: Archiving as Care for Neglected Data

One way we can care for research participants is to archive otherwise neglected research data – archivists have long understood the archive is a site of value (Caswell 2016). Through the affordances of metadata, and the connections that archived data can make, concerns that data will be extracted from its context can be assuaged – archival practices can allow us to build webs of relations, to refuse transactional approaches, to multiply relations, to name contexts.

Despite a wide-ranging 'archival turn' across the humanities and social sciences, this turn has rarely extended to a meaningful engagement with actual archivists or archival theory. Michelle Caswell (2016) has written a searing critique of humanities academics who turn to the archive as a metaphor only, remaining largely oblivious to an established body of archival theory, a long history of professional practice, and a site of lively contemporary debate. When discussions about the reuse of qualitative data emerged in the UK in the early 1990s, there was little appreciation of the affordances of archival theory or practice. Discussion, such as it was, was about depositing 'clean' data into a repository, or database, understood as a time-consuming administrative task. Yet archival theory and practice arguably provides much more useful insight for qualitative researchers than, for instance, the continuing turn to, and then away from, quantitative data.

Interestingly, a feminist ethics of care has also appeared in archival studies. In a widely taken up article, Caswell and Cifor (2016; 2021) have called for the practice of 'radical empathy', which they describe as attending to 'theoretical and observed relationships between people, the self and others' (2016, 30). They map out a relational ethic of care for archivists, identifying four key relationships to attend to – the relationships between archivist and (i) record creator, (ii) record subject, (iii) archive user and (iv) larger communities. Crucially for them, these relationships are affective and embodied (Caswell and Cifor 2016; see also Douglas et al. 2019). While social scientists are familiar with the challenges of care for research participants, and generally also think about communities of interest and wider publics, we suggest that relationships with data, with research materials and with records, remain the neglected things of research. Taking up the insights of archival theory offers a way to extend our ethic of care to research data.

The Community Archive Turn: Creating Open Archives

We turn specifically to the overlapping fields of community archiving, activist archiving, independent and autonomous archives, and feminist, queer and anti-racist archival theory and practice as fruitful sites for building what we term 'DIY academic archiving' practices. We are not alone in finding insight here. Leading archival theorist, Terry Cook (2013), offered an alternative archival genealogy, naming not just one archival turn, but four archival paradigms, where community archives are positioned as the cutting edge of contemporary archival theory and practice. Community archives are often understood as focused on community ownership and control of materials, with a commitment to retrieving histories which would otherwise be ignored, discarded, hidden from history (Flinn et al. 2009; Flinn 2011; Bastian and Flinn 2020). In this way, they challenge the centrality of formal institutions, calling for post-custodial arrangements for data and records. Interventions aiming to decolonise archives are calling for 'slow archives' which take care with the relationships at stake in archival processes (Christen and Anderson 2019). What we find most interesting and powerful about community archives is their inventive reworking of archival practices and processes, crafting these so they are fit for purpose. Despite, or perhaps because of, this, these 'DIY archivists' get to grips with archival terms and practices – and work to make them fit local practice (Star 2010). Community archives emerge as inventive with methods and ethics.

A key insight for academic researchers is the question of who gets *access* to these materials. Discussions of open research data often only extend to making data 'open' to other researchers – not to participants, or related communities, or even wider publics. With Jamie Lee (2021) in this issue, we want to imagine archives as 'spaces of radical hospitality'. Tonia Sutherland (2019) argues that carceral logics can pervade even social justice-oriented approaches to data storage and reuse. Behind the gatekeeping of licencing arrangements of research data repositories, research participants likely do not have access to their own transcripts, their own stories, their own words. How ethical is this?

DIY Academic Archiving: *Clayoquot Lives: An Ecofeminist Story Web*

We turn now to our experience working together to create a digital archive of research data – an accessible, structured, searchable online archive of interviews generated in an earlier research project in the mid 1990s. Subsequently, we have also engaged in writing and teaching on DIY academic archiving (see Moore et al. forthcoming, and our project website *DIY Academic Archiving*: www.diyacademicarchiving.org). The interviews consisted of a set of 30 oral histories and originated from Niamh's Ph.D. research on activists at an ecofeminist peace camp. The camp was based on land which is the traditional territory of the Nuu-chah-nulth First Nations (Native Land Digital, n.d.), never ceded to the Candian state, though known as Clayoquot Sound (pronounced 'klak-wat'), the West Coast of Vancouver Island, in British Columbia, Canada. In the summer of 1993, thousands of people came to Clayoquot Sound to protest against the clear-cut logging of temperate rainforest. A local environmental organisation, the Friends of Clayoquot Sound (n.d.), set up a peace camp with daily workshops teaching consensus decision-making and the practice of nonviolent direct action, which was described as based on ecofeminist principles. More than 800 people were arrested while blockading a logging road in one of the largest acts of nonviolent civil disobedience in Canadian history. The online archive, *Clayoquot Lives: An Ecofeminist Story Web* (https://clayoquotlives.sps.ed.ac.uk/), is predominantly a collection of oral history interviews, while also containing a selection of photos and other documents related to the campaign.

Niamh's desire to create a digital archive to share these stories came from a visceral sense of responsibility, compounded every time she moved job, packing up her box of cassettes carefully, always making sure she had the originals in her possession, and not just relegated to the back of a removal van. This sensibility intensified through subsequent work with feminist, queer and other community archival projects (e.g. Moore 2017; 2020) which brought new knowledge of archival practices, and a deeper dive into archival literature (see for example Ashton 2017a; 2017b; Bly and Wooten 2012; Henningham, Evans and Morgan 2017; Lee 2020; McKinney 2020; Sheffield 2020). Importantly this work drew attention to the ways in which feminist activism, feminist sociology and feminist archival practices are in ongoing conversation and traverse the boundaries of academia, politics and archives.

In naming our practice 'DIY academic archiving' we seek to gesture to the ethos of community archival practices. The decision was not whether to offer the interviews to a university data archive or repository *or* to put them online – rather the interviews can be hosted in many places. We are keen to multiply the sites where materials can be found and accessed. We also intend to deposit the interviews with the University repository as it offers more support for longer-term preservation, while also creating a digital archive, which supports wider access to the stories.[1]

In creating our digital archive, we turned to Omeka (https://omeka.org/), an open source, free, web-based publishing platform designed specifically for publishing accessible digital collections and using these collections to create digital exhibitions. Omeka originally emerged from the concerns of public historians interested in the potential of new media to reimagine history and was developed with the support of the Roy Rosenzweig Centre for New Media and Public History at George Mason University in the US. While Omeka does not explicitly describe itself as an archival platform, embedded in Omeka's infrastructure are useful features, such as Dublin Core Metadata which offers a standardised way of describing data, or items, in collections, documenting some of the context of the data, and at the same time, optimising relationality, enabling the data to be located and reused through systematic categorisation of data in digital collections. While we recognise Omeka's modest description of itself as a web publishing platform for 'digital collections', as well as appreciating Caswell's critique of the use of archive as metaphor, nevertheless we persist with our description of *Clayoquot Lives* as DIY academic *archiving* (rather than more precisely a digital collection). In this, we want to signal recognition of archival theory and ethics which inform our practice, even as DIY archivists we inevitably have much more to learn from archivist colleagues and scholars. Our ambition is for more take up of archival theory and practice across the social sciences to inform the sharing and reuse of qualitative data.

How to Build an Archival Web: Standardisation as Weaving Connections

The affordances of archiving became apparent to us in the early stages of the project, even in the mundane and invisible work of 'cleaning' data. We grasped that the process of standardisation enables the creation of a web of relationships between research materials (Star 2010). The practical work of making the *Clayoquot Lives* archive involved first retrieving cassettes and CDs from Niamh's filing cabinet. Since doing the interviews, Niamh had had the interviews digitised and the files copied to CDs. Now, the initial tasks were to complete full transcription of all interviews and to standardise the format of the transcripts, the digital audio files and file names.

As Martina, Mary and Nikki worked on standardising the transcripts and audio files, the interviews came to life again. Approaching the archive with an ethics of care in mind, and aware that we were preparing the interviews for reuse, it became obvious that we were ourselves reusing the interview data, seeking out context and creating new contexts. By re-encountering the interviews through careful, embodied, listening, the technical work of standardisation emerged as a physical, mental, emotional and relational process. What became obvious to us really quickly once the work was underway – and we acknowledge should of course have been obvious to us as social scientists – is that technical work is always social. The usually invisible work of archiving (Oke 2020; Star 2010; Caswell 2016) became very apparent and we gained an appreciation of the affordances of archival thoery and practice. Reading a transcript or listening to audio can offer a way into building a relationship with an interviewee and caring about that person. Making the archive was a project where we learned through the process of doing, opening up a valuable space between doing a qualitative research project and 'depositing' cleaned up data into an existing repository. We argue that a stronger appreciation of the work that archivists do can help to address some of the understandable, but limiting, concerns of social scientists about the challenges of archiving and reusing qualitative data.

A Feminist Practice of Care as a Resource for Archiving Research Data

Feminist ethical practice is often a collective achievement. Crucially for us, the work of ethical decision-making became a collaborative process. There was a value to not making what felt at times weighty decisions alone. We recognised ourselves in Edwards and Ribbens' (1998, 6) account of their research meetings 'as a space in which to express doubt and admit the possibility of unanswerable questions, rather than falling prey to the certainty of academic rhetoric' (cited in Birch et al. 2002, 3). Although research ethics is often treated as the responsibility of an individual researcher, we want to acknowledge research teams, other colleagues and interlocutors as important resources for working through the unanswerable questions which research can throw up. Our collaborative approach involved the co-creation of practices of care (including care for each other). At points, we also recognised the value of drawing in other expertise into our discussions[2].

These ongoing and collaborative conversations were essential for working through the many dilemmas the archive project raised. As well as creating standard formats, we also needed to revisit the content of the interviews. Previous publications in articles, chapters in edited collections, and the book, *The Changing Nature of Eco/feminism: Telling Stories from Clayoquot Sound* (Moore 2015), meant that extracts could be carefully curated, and ethical issues addressed through a selective choice of materials. Now, however, whole interviews would be available. A key question which emerged for us was how to deal with references to other people mentioned in interviews, who might not be aware of being named, and clearly had not given any consent to be included in an archive. These questions about naming or anonymisation of 'third parties' mentioned in interviews, and whether to redact small extracts related to them, were – and continue to be – ongoing conversations.

The requirement for informed consent and the practice of producing consent forms is now taken for granted but, in keeping with our argument that research ethics is an invented tradition, this was not yet the case in 1996, when Niamh carried out most of the interviews. That she did use a consent form at that time is perhaps the surprise. The reason Niamh had a consent form was less because of research ethics, and rather because of a conversation with a Ph.D. student, who had just returned from fieldwork in Canada, and who urged the use of consent forms because North America had such a culture of litigation, a reminder of how research ethics can sometimes be used as a cloak for self-protection.

Presciently, the consent form included permission to 'broadcast' interviews, asking participants if they were willing to approve the following statement:

> I agree that the contents of the interview may be used throughout Niamh Moore's research, in her thesis, teaching, in any ensuing presentations, publications or broadcasts. (https://clayoquotlives.sps.ed.ac.uk/ethics)

Realistically, at the time the distant possibility of a radio programme based on oral histories was in mind, but much has changed in 'broadcasting' since the early 1990s – developments in digital technologies have enabled new ways of 'broadcasting' research. In theory, we had consent to broadcast the interviews on the internet. Nonetheless, legal is not the same as ethical nor do legal frameworks offer an understanding of ethics as a process, ongoing throughout the duration of a project. Despite having nominal consent from the 1990s, we took a further step, contacting original interviewees to tell them about the archive project, notifying them about the planned launch of the digital archive, and providing them with a few weeks' window to view the archive and request any changes or removals before the site was publicly launched. Crucially, rather than sending participants their own individual transcripts to review, we wanted them to be able to see their own contributions as part of a larger digital collection and to be able to view the website as it would look online to any visitor to the archive.

Also important was that many of the interviewees in Clayoquot explicitly understood themselves to have been involved in a historic moment. For many, the experience of being arrested at the camp was a transformative experience they wanted to be documented and shared. As feminists, many easily understood the importance of creating archives of stories of activism. Some explicitly approached the interview as a conversation with future listeners – for example, Sile Simpson finished the interview and then asked for the recorder to be switched on again and she added an address to imagined future listeners. In fact, the dilemma for many researchers is that we understand that many research participants anticipate wider audiences and that we know that not enough people are going to hear the stories that we are entrusted with. Research encounters can be valuable and generative spaces which open up opportunities for participants to decide what story it is that they want to put on the record and to be supported and listened to in telling that story. This generous capacity of research encounters stands in stark contrast with data regimes which obscure the extraction of data, demand consent and seal data forever behind locked doors. An online archive makes the data more accessible to wider audiences.

Through reading and listening, it is possible for a researcher to be thinking about ethics and care. Landsberg's 'prosthetic memory' may be a useful starting point as 'memories of events through which one did not live, memories that, despite their mediated quality, [have] the capacity to transform one's subjectivity, politics, and ethical engagements' (2009, 221–222). For us, thinking about, and engaging with, the memories recorded in these interviews, was less about a prosthetic adoption of these lived experiences as our own, but rather about the archive offering opportunities of emotional encounter and connection, of care and investment via the data.

Building a Relationship with Irene Abbey

When preparing the audio files and transcripts, we divided them up to format and to flag any potential issues which would need collective consideration. We initially approached this as a somewhat mechanical task, yet it became clear that this process also involved a re-encountering of the interview, and as such, an opening for relationship building between interviewee and researcher through the engagement with the transcript. For example, Irene Abbey who was well into her 80s when she was arrested at Clayoquot, and has since died, was alive for Martina, who encountered Irene through listening to the audio files. In the process of careful listening and formatting of the transcript, Martina became invested in her story. The embodied experiencing of the data (reading, listening, typing) and the subsequent emotional investment in Irene's story came to the fore in the team's discussion about redacting specific sections in the transcripts and audio recordings. In one particular instance in the recording, Irene spoke somewhat dismissively about someone else, and this prompted the team to (re)consider questions of consent and redaction. Martina raised the question of removing this particular section so as to not 'taint' Irene's legacy and her own relationship with a woman now deceased. Indeed, she felt fiercely engaged with Irene, not with the data, but with Irene the person, or rather the memory of the person she had gotten to 'meet', and subsequently care for, again highlighting our relational understanding of data. Not wanting to reproduce a paternalistic care in an attempt to protect the integrity of her character, we revisited what it means to care in this case, given Niamh's knowledge of the context of the interview and Irene's own awareness of matters of consent at the time. The outcome was to leave in the material. The discussion highlighted, however, how the embodied relationship with Irene's archival material enabled the capacity of relationship building, and the consideration of an ethic of care towards Irene. This is a profound reminder for social scientists that connections and rapport can and do emerge through engagement with archival materials, that it is not always necessary to have been 'there' to care, and to reflect on the ethical implications of research. Rather the 'there' has moved – it is possible to be there in the archive and build connections that are meaningful and real, to echo Caswell and Cifor's (2016; 2021) emphasis on affective connections and radical empathy with the subjects of archival records.

Anonymisation and the Ethics of Names

Throughout the process of preparing the data for publication in the archive, consent was a key consideration. From the beginning of Niamh's research, decisions were made which sometimes ran counter to certain taken for granted assumptions in much social science research. Specifically, and drawing on the ethical conventions of oral history, a decision had been taken to offer participants the opportunity to choose for their real names to be used in any publications and other research outputs (see also Moore 2012). This was consistent with the original consent forms and how use of interviewees' real names had been addressed in publications (see https://clayoquotlives.sps.ed.ac.uk/ethics). With the creation of the digital archive, we continued with this intention to use participants' real names and not to anonymise the interviews. Rather, we note that blanket anonymisation as a universal practice actually forecloses ethical consideration (see Moore 2012). The practice denies participants, and researchers, the opportunity to reflect on whether they want real names used, what the implications of naming, or anonymising might be, and to consider these questions as part of the process of informed consent (see Moore 2012; 2007; Grinyer 2002).

At the same time, in attending to the details of each story, we determined it would not be appropriate to upload all the interviews. By carefully listening to each interview in preparation for publication, we decided not to publish one interview. In the original research, one interviewee was anonymised, as the person wanted a pseudonym used in any publications (Moore 2015). In the case of this interview, making an anonymised transcript available did not feel in keeping with their original desire for a pseudonym; not least, it would have been very difficult to thoroughly anonymise the interview, removing not just names and locations, but places of work and family details. This case demonstrates how a blanket approach to using real names would also not be in line with the spirit of the feminist ethic of care we aimed to practice.

Extending the Web of Care to 'Third Parties'

As we worked through our approach to informed consent, we had to consider 'third parties' – the friends, families, other activists and people mentioned in the interviews, who would likely not know they had been named, and who had therefore not given any consent to be included in an archive. We initially considered a blanket approach to anonymising third parties mentioned in the interviews. However, a careful reading made us appreciate the need for attention to the specificity of each case here too. Some of the names were public figures – we did not seriously consider anonymising references to politicians or other well-known individuals. This also extended to some of the very public faces of Clayoquot Summer, such as Valerie Langer or Tzeporah Berman, or others who were named as supporting and facilitating activism, or merely named in passing with reference to the campaign. We did give further attention to references to participants' children or grandchildren, and to other children mentioned, and who would now be adults. References varied from mentioning children's own activism, to children's support (or lack of) for parents' activism, to the need for childcare while engaging in the court process, or mundane references to daily life. While we did reflect on possible impact on adult lives, for example, on employment possibilities if involvement in activism was being made public, in the end we decided to keep in children's names. We recognised, especially with reference to interviewees' own children, that they could easily be identified, and so anonymisation was relatively meaningless in this case. In other interviews, the nature of the stories required careful attention with respect to details surrounding the experience of being arrested. We removed one disclosure of medical information about someone mentioned in passing in an interview. We removed a short section that one interviewee had asked at the time to be deleted from the record. This latter example is important because it shows that what is considered significant for participants, and their relationships with others can appear relatively innocuous to us as researchers, and we would not have considered redacting this text otherwise. This was not the only occasion when interviewees explicitly demonstrated that they were aware of and thinking through matters of public record and future audiences. Throughout the interviews, a number of participants were at times explicitly reflecting on ethical issues themselves. Sometimes interviewees did their own anonymising, by saying 'a friend', rather than giving a name; other times, having named someone, they paused and reflected aloud about whether it was okay to identify that person.

Particular challenges came when women mentioned their own ex-partners or others who had been abusive or violent to them. We realised that anonymisation of third parties, in this case, meant that we would in effect silence women's stories of violence and abuse, which seemed quite counter to our feminist approach. We were running the risk of sanitising the data and of distorting women's accounts. We went back and forth over what it meant to remove women's references to their own relationships where the abuse happened, but in the end, we left these in. However, we did redact names or identifying details when interviewees mentioned other women with experience of domestic abuse or violence.

It should not come as a surprise that participants, especially those involved in ecofeminist activism, should have a finely attuned attention to ethical matters. In this case, some had also become familiar with talking to the media and paying attention to matters of public record. This does not absolve us as researchers from responsibility. For instance, when participants refer to each other implicitly, they may nonetheless be identifiable to those in the know, when this was not their intention. It is a reminder that if we understand interviews as co-created, we can also extend this thinking to ethical matters, appreciating that an ethic of care in interviews is also co-created.

Ongoing Consent: Using a 'Take Down' Approach

While pressing the button and going live might create an impression of finality, this would be to perpetuate assumptions about the stability of the archive. With respect to consent, it became clear when preparing the interview audio files and transcripts for publication that we needed to institute an approach which reflected our understanding of consent as an ongoing process. This approach is particularly important in relation to the decision not to anonymise the data. To extend the negotiation of consent beyond the moment of the launch of the archive, we instituted a 'take down' policy, where interviewees (or indeed any user of the archive) can contact the project to discuss any content they would like to be edited or removed; and we remain mindful of the 'right to be forgotten' (General Data Protection Regulation, n.d.) In publishing the archive, material is not necessarily online forever.

As we worked through the practical challenges we encountered in preparing the data for publication, a feminist ethic of care motivated us to (re)consider informed consent as interactive, contextual, not without limits, and ongoing; building the online archive was a technological, relational and emotional process. While risk is always at work when it comes to ethics, the different examples given in this article demonstrate how blanket approaches of standardisation and anonymisation fail to sufficiently enact care. Working as a team, it was necessary to collectively, and creatively, to take care-full risks, to find ways to move beyond sociological convention.

Pressing the Button and Taking Care-full Risks: The Ongoing Time of Ethics

We poured so much work into preparing the digital archive. Perhaps pressing the button to publish it should have been a celebration, that the data 'cleaning' was done, and that we could move on from our ethical angsting – but this moment was excruciating, at least for Niamh, who could hardly bear to press the button, and insisted that someone else did this, and Mary took on the responsibility for this. Despite, or rather *because* of, all the care, we were also profoundly aware of the risks. Here the risks were not only to the interviewees, and the people they talk about, but also to ourselves, and the work we had done. In the context of social science research, publishing interviews, publishing *non-anonymised* interviews, with participants' real names, online, for anyone to find and read, felt like the most outrageous act. Yet, at the same time, for Niamh, as a feminist, it felt like the most right thing to do, both for the interviews and as an intervention in conventional practice. People have been doing this for so long – but not social scientists. From a feminist ethic of care, from oral history, from political activism, from a desire to change the world, from a sense of commitment to participants, it felt like: what had taken so long to make these interviews available and to share these stories of activism with others? To destroy the 'data', these stories of incredible activism, incredible lives, would have been such an act of violence. We wanted others to read, hear these interviews – other Clayoquot activists, other activists, feminists and ecofeminists. But wanting other sociologists and social scientists to know about our project is a more ambivalent feeling. We also took a risk with the amount of work we did upfront, before recontacting interviewees. It was possible that we would have been faced with many requests for edits or changes that we would have to do so much more work or have to go back to the beginning, or even that the whole project would fall apart if too many wanted their transcripts removed, but this did not happen.

Pressing the button felt both huge and also small. All that work for thirty interviews. More than 800 people were arrested that summer and more than 12,000 people passed through the peace camp. These interviews represent only a fragment of stories of the camp – there are many more stories to be told. And indeed, even of the thirty interviews, it was clear that many stories were carefully constructed and that there was much yet to be said. In a place where the politics of 'race', class, gender and histories of colonialism are spectacularly visible, not all the stories can yet be told. At the time the interviews were carried out, Clayoquot was a place with an environmental movement that had many women leaders. It was a place where government processes had been led by mainly male politicians. The logging industry was dominated by male industry leaders and predominantly employed male loggers in highly paid jobs, which were rapidly disappearing as technological 'innovations' replaced labour. It was a place where local Indigenous communities were caught up in complex negotiations over land, over jobs and employment, and over matters of governance and participation in local political processes. We hope the archive continues to change, and indeed, understand this is unavoidable, as even if the archive itself remains the same, contexts for understanding and interpreting the material will change.

The archive has a 'contribute' button - it is possible for people to contribute new stories to the archive, and we remain hopeful as the thirtieth anniversary of the peace camp approaches in 2023 that there will be renewed interest. Perhaps we can pursue further funding to develop the archive with new stories. The digital archive is now live, but the archive also lives. We have not stopped caring, having conversations about the archive, revisiting decisions, living with the response-ability for what we have created.

What became obvious from making *Clayoquot Lives* is that the archive is not the end of a project - a further reminder of the importance of research that takes temporality seriously (McLeod and Thomson 2009). The archive now opens up new research possibilities, for us, and not only for other potential users. The archive, and the access to data afforded by Omeka, provides Niamh new possibilities of engaging with the data originally generated in the 1990s. How can we share the archive – with academics, students, and other publics; how can we demonstrate creative ways of using the data; how can we bring this data into contact with new stories – of feminism, ecofeminism, climate crisis, indigenous politics, what it means to engage in nonviolent action, amongst others.

What new imaginaries of research can serious attention to archival possibilities bring into being? Thomson and Berriman (2021) offer a creative demonstration of what is possible when we start research with the archive in mind. They involved children and their families in the creation of an open access public archive documenting everyday childhoods, and included children, parents and researchers writing postcards to future users of the research data. In another project, *Reanimating Data: Experiments with People, Places and Archives* (http://reanimatingdata.co.uk/), Niamh is working with colleagues from the University of Sussex, UK (including Thomson, who was one of the original researchers), to archive data from a flagship social science project from the late 1980s, frank and compelling interviews with young women about sexual practices, sexual health and everyday relationships in the immediate aftermath of the emergence of HIV/AIDS (see the *Feminist Approaches to Youth Sexualities* archive https://archives.reanimatingdata.co.uk/s/fays/). We have worked not only to create a digital archive but also to 'rematriate' data back to communities, building new relationships with contemporary youth groups (Moore et al. 2021), through a series of creative experiments with data (https://archives.reanimatingdata.co.uk/s/fays/page/experiments). DIY academic archiving promises new research futures, and an ongoing need for an inventive feminist ethic of care-full risk.

Conclusion: Towards an Inventive Ethics of Care-full Risk

Research ethics are inventive and always have been. Moves to archive, share and reuse qualitative data do unsettle existing research practice. Yet continuing to rely on conventional ethical commitments in the social sciences does not provide the resources necessary to work through the challenges of archiving and reusing research data. Archiving and reusing does require ongoing transformation and inventive ethics.

In creating an open archive of qualitative research data, we resisted so-called 'ethical' injunctions to destroy data, calling this out as a paternalistic ethic of 'protection'. Against this single-use, disposable research culture of data destruction, we propose a risky ethos of sharing data as a way of caring for and valuing research participants, and the stories, memories and accounts of the world they craft with researchers. What becomes curious as we worked through a feminist ethic of care, is why an *a priori* commitment to destroying data is considered the ethical standard.

Arguably a failure to innovate in research ethics leaves archiving and reuse more open to being framed by other drivers. These include increasing audit regimes under neoliberal governance and the take up of extractivist corporate data harvesting practices, which are also permeating universities, as well as the apparently more liberal ambitions of the open data movement. There are other genealogies we can turn to – feminist, queer and decolonial approaches to archival theory and community archiving practices – to inform archiving and reuse of qualitative data.

A feminist ethic of care-full risk can resource new ethical research practices. Care and risk can appear to be in opposition – a researcher cares by avoiding risks, by engaging in mitigating actions. We suggest that care always involves risk. Rather than approaching ethics as an inviolable, unchanging tradition, we approach ethics as an inventive tradition. Ethics can be a resource which supports taking new leaps in research, instead of a barrier which blocks creative interventions into existing research practice. It is precisely our commitment to ethics as researchers that can distinguish good academic practice from the sometimes more questionable practices of organisations who harvest data in return for services, who obscure matters of consent, and who abnegate the importance of simple, straightforward takedown policies and a right to be forgotten.

Ethical questions continue to arise in discussions of archiving and reuse. They appear as barriers when in fact they can be signs of the limitations and flaws of current ethical thinking. Archiving and reusing does not threaten to undermine the discipline and its ethical commitments, but to revitalise it. A feminist ethic of care-full risk is not just for archiving and reuse – it is for all research. A feminist ethic of care offers an inventive approach to the responsibility of research. A feminist ethic of care-full risk allows us to work towards 'responsible action' while taking seriously matters of accountability. A feminist ethic of risk is collaborative, refusing the individualising and privatising of ethical decision-making. And a feminist ethic of care opens to a commitment to re-making relations, to flourishing and re-making the world.

Notes

1. University libraries have been developing capacities for archiving research materials through creating data repositories, with the University of Edinburgh being a leader with its DataShare repository and its successful online research data management training, called MANTRA (Mantra, n.d.; Rice 2014).
2. We were fortunate to be able to discuss ethics, consent and open research data with Robin Rice, Data Librarian and Head of Research Data Support at the University of Edinburgh (see also Rice 2014; Rice and Southall 2016), and her colleagues.

Acknowledgements

We appreciate the generous engagement of the reviewers of this article and are grateful for their suggestions to improve the article. We would also like to thank some early readers, Joan Haran, and the members of the *Theorising our Work* seminar in Sociology at the University of Edinburgh, including Thalia Assan, Isabelle Darmon, Mary Holmes, Steve Kemp, Angélica Thumala, Sophia Woodman and others – for comments, feedback and encouragement on previous drafts. Thanks to Sacha Alfonzo Villafuerte for assistance with preparation for publication.

Disclosure statement

No potential conflict of interest was reported by the author(s).

ORCID

Niamh Moore http://orcid.org/0000-0002-5372-7428

References

Ashton, Jenna. 2017a. "The Feminists Are Cackling in the Archive … ." *Feminist Review* 115 (1): 155–164. doi:10.1057%2Fs41305-017-0024-4.
Ashton, Jenna. 2017b. "Feminist Archiving [a Manifesto Continued]: Skilling for Activism and Organising." *Australian Feminist Studies* 32 (1): 126–149. doi:10.1080/08164649.2017.1357010.
Back, Les, and Nirmal Puwar. 2012. *Live Methods*. Oxford: Wiley-Blackwell.
Baker, Karen S., and Helena Karasti. 2018. "Data Care and Its Politics: Designing for Local Collective Data Management as a Neglected Thing." In *Proceedings of the 15th Participatory Design Conference: Full Papers* 1 (10): 1–12. doi:10.1145/3210586.3210587.
Bastian, Jeanette A., and Andrew Flinn. 2020. *Community Archives, Community Spaces: Heritage, Memory and Identity*. London: Facet Publishing.
Birch, Maxine, Tina Miller, Melanie Mauthner, and Julie Jessop. 2002. "Introduction." In *Ethics in Qualitative Research*, edited by Melanie Mauthner, Maxine Birch, Julie Jessop, and Tina Miller, 1–13. London: SAGE Publishing.
Bly, Lyz, and Kelly Wooten. 2012. *Make Your Own History: Documenting Feminist & Queer Activism in the 21st Century*. Los Angeles: Litwin Books.

Broom, Alex, Lynda Cheshire, and Michael Emmison. 2009. "Qualitative Researchers' Understandings of Their Practice and the Implications for Data Archiving and Sharing." *Sociology* 43 (6): 1163–1180. doi:10.1177%2F0038038509345704.

Caswell, Michelle. 2016. "'The Archive' Is Not an Archives: On Acknowledging the Intellectual Contributions of Archival Studies." *Reconstruction* 16 (1): 3–22. https://escholarship.org/uc/item/7bn4v1fk.

Caswell, Michelle, and Marika Cifor. 2016. "From Human Rights to Feminist Ethics: Radical Empathy in the Archives." *Archivaria* 81 (Spring): 23–43. https://muse.jhu.edu/article/687705.

Caswell, Michelle, and Marika Cifor. 2021. "Revisiting A Feminist Ethics of Care in Archives: An Introductory Note." *Journal of Critical Library and Information Studies* 3: 1–6.

Charlton, James I. 2000. *Nothing About Us Without Us: Disability, Oppression and Empowerment*. Berkeley: University of California Press.

Cheshire, Lynda, Alex Broom, and Michael Emmison. 2009. "Archiving Qualitative Data in Australia: An Introduction." *Australian Journal of Social Issues* 44 (3): 239–254. doi:10.1002/j.1839-4655.2009.tb00144.x.

Christen, Kimberly, and Jane Anderson. 2019. "Toward Slow Archives." *Archival Science* 19 (2): 87–116. doi:10.1007/s10502-019-09307-x.

Cifor, Marika, Patricia Garcia, T. L. Cowan, Jasmine Rault, Tonia Sutherland, Anita Say Chan, Jennifer Rode, Anna Lauren Hoffmann, Niloufar Salehi, and Lisa Nakamura. 2019. "Feminist Data Manifest-No." Feminist Data Manifest-No. Accessed October 14, 2021. https://www.manifestno.com.

Clayoquot Lives. n.d. Clayoquot Lives: An Ecofeminist Story Web. Accessed October 14, 2021. https://clayoquotlives.sps.ed.ac.uk/.

Cook, Terry. 2013. "Evidence, Memory, Identity, and Community: Four Shifting Archival Paradigms." *Archival Science* 13 (2): 95–120. doi:10.1007/s10502-012-9180-7.

Cuevas-Parra, Patricio, and Kay Tisdall. 2019. "Child-led Research: Questioning Knowledge." *Social Sciences* 8 (2): 1–15. doi:10.3390/socsci8020044.

Davidson, Emma. 2017. "Saying it Like it is? Power, Participation and Research Involving Young People." *Social Inclusion* 5 (3): 228–239. doi:10.17645/si.v5i3.967.

D'Ignazio, Catherine, and Lauren F. Klein. 2020. *Data Feminism*. Cambridge: MIT Press.

DIY Academic Archiving. n.d. Accessed Oct 14, 2021. http://www.diyacademicarchiving.org/.

Douglas, Jennifer, Alexandra Alisauskas, and Devon Mordell. 2019. "'Treat Them with the Reverence of Archivists': Records Work, Grief Work, and Relationship Work in the Archives." *Archivaria* 88 (2019): 84–120.

Edwards, Rosalind, and Melanie Mauthner. 2002. "Ethics and Feminist Research: Theory and Practice." In *Ethics in Qualitative Research*, edited by Melanie Mauthner, Maxine Birch, Julie Jessop, and Tina Miller, 14–31. London: SAGE Publications.

Edwards, Rosalind, and Jane Ribbens. 1998. "Living on the Edges: Public Knowledge, Private Lives, Personal Experience." In *Feminist Dilemmas in Qualitative Research*, edited by Rosalind Edwards, and Jane Ribbens, 2–23. London: SAGE Publications. doi:10.4135/9781849209137.

Feminist Approaches to Youth Sexualities Archive (FAYS). n.d. Accessed October 14 2021. https://archives.reanimatingdata.co.uk/s/fays/.

Flinn, Andrew. 2011. "The Impact of Independent and Community Archives on Professional Archival Thinking and Practice." In *The Future of Archives and Recordkeeping: A Reader*, edited by Jennie Hill, 145–170. London: Facet.

Flinn, Andrew, Mary Stevens, and Elizabeth Shepherd. 2009. "Whose Memories, Whose Archives? Independent Community Archives, Autonomy and the Mainstream." *Archival Science* 9 (1): 71–86. doi:10.1007/s10502-009-9105-2.

Friends Of Clayoquot Sound. n.d. Accessed April 19, 2021. http://focs.ca/.

General Data Protection Regulation. n.d. "Everything you need to know about the 'Right to be forgotten.'" GDPR.eu. Accessed October 14, 2021. https://gdpr.eu/right-to-be-forgotten/.

Grinyer, Anne. 2002. "Social Research Update 36: The Anonymity of Research Participants." *Social Research Update* 36 (1). https://sru.soc.surrey.ac.uk/SRU36.html

Haraway, Donna. 1988. "Situated Knowledges: The Science Question in Feminism and the Privilege of Partial Perspective." *Feminist Studies* 14 (3): 575–599. doi:10.2307/3178066.

Haraway, Donna. 2016. *Staying with the Trouble: Making Kin in the Chthulucene.* Durham: Duke University Press.

Henningham, Nikki, Joanne Evans, and Helen Morgan. 2017. "The Australian Women's Archives Project: Creating and Co-Curating Community Feminist Archives in a Post-Custodial Age." *Australian Feminist Studies* 32 (91-92): 91–107. doi:10.1080/08164649.2017.1357015.

Hobsbawm, Eric. 2012. "Introduction: Inventing Traditions." In *The Invention of Tradition,* Edited by Eric Hobsbawm and Terence Ranger, 1–14. Canto Classics. Cambridge: Cambridge University Press.

Hoffmann, Anna Lauren. 2021. "Even When You Are a Solution You Are a Problem: An Uncomfortable Reflection on Feminist Data Ethics." *Global Perspectives* 2 (1): 1–5. doi:10.1525/gp.2021.21335.

Hughes, Kahryn, and Anna Tarrant. 2020. *Qualitative Secondary Analysis.* London: SAGE Publications.

Landsberg, Alison. 2009. "Memory, Empathy, and the Politics of Identification." *International Journal of Politics, Culture, and Society* 22 (2): 221–229. doi:10.1007/s10767-009-9056-x.

Lapp, Jessica. 2020. The Provenance of Protest: Conceptualizing Records Creation in Archives of Feminist Materials. Ph.D. diss., University of Toronto (Canada), https://www.proquest.com/dissertations-theses/provenance-protest-conceptualizing-records/docview/2466327785/se-2?accountid = 10673 (accessed October 17, 2021).

Lee, Jamie A. 2020. *Producing the Archival Body.* London: Routledge.

Lee, Jamie A. 2021. "Archives as Spaces of Radical Hospitality." *Australian Feminist Studies,* doi:10.1080/08164649.2021.1969520.

Lindén, Lisa, and Vicky Singleton. 2021. "Unsettling Descriptions: Attending to the Potential of Things That Threaten to Undermine Care." *Qualitative Research* 21 (3): 426–441. doi:10.1177/1468794120976919.

Lury, Celia, and Nina Wakeford. 2013. *Inventive Methods: The Happening of the Social.* Abingdon: Routledge.

Mantra. n.d. Mantra: Research Data Management Training. The University of Edinburgh. Accessed October 14, 2021. https://mantra.ed.ac.uk/.

McKinney, Cait. 2020. *Information Activism: A Queer History of Lesbian Media Technologies.* Durham: Duke University Press.

McLeod, Julie, and Kate O'Connor. 2020. "Ethics, Archives and Data Sharing in Qualitative Research." *Educational Philosophy and Theory* 53 (5): 523–535. doi:10.1080/00131857.2020.1805310.

McLeod, Julie, and Rachel Thomson. 2009. *Researching Social Change: Qualitative Approaches.* London: SAGE Publications.

Moore, Niamh. 2007. "(Re)Using Qualitative Data?" *Sociological Research Online* 12 (3): 1–13. doi:10.5153%2Fsro.1496.

Moore, Niamh. 2012. "The Politics and Ethics of Naming: Questioning Anonymisation in (Archival) Research." *International Journal of Social Research Methodology* 15 (4): 331–340. doi:10.1080/13645579.2012.688330.

Moore, Niamh. 2015. *The Changing Nature of Eco/Feminism: Telling Stories from Clayoquot Sound.* Vancouver: UBC Press.

Moore, Niamh. 2017. "Weaving Archival Imagines: Researching Community Archives." In *The Archive Project: Archival Research in the Social Sciences,* edited by Niamh Moore, Andrea Salter, Liz Stanley, and Maria Tamboukou, 129–152. London: Routledge.

Moore, Niamh. 2020. "'Wibbly-Wobbly Timey-Wimey' LGBT Histories: Community Archives As Boundary Objects." In *Communities, Archives and New Collaborative Practices,* edited by Simon Popple, Andrew Prescott, and Daniel Mutibwa, 195–206. Bristol: Policy Press. doi:10.1332/policypress/9781447341895.003.0014.

Moore, Niamh, Nikki Dunne, Mary Hanlon, and Martina Karels. forthcoming. *DIY Academic Archiving: Sharing Data and Curating Research Materials.* London: Palgrave MacMillan.

Moore, Niamh, Rachel Thomson, and Ester McGeeney. 2021. "Putting Place Back Into the Patriarchy Through Rematriating Feminist Research: The WRAP Project, Feminist Webs and Reanimating Data." In *Temporality and Place in Educational Research: Looking Beyond a Local/Global Binary,* edited by McLeod Julie, and Kate O'Connor. London & New York: Routledge.

Murphy, Michelle. 2015. "Unsettling Care: Troubling Transnational Itineraries of Care in Feminist Health Practices." *Social Studies of Science* 45 (5): 717–737. doi:10.1177/0306312715589136.

Narayan, Uma. 1995. "Colonialism and Its Others: Considerations on Rights and Care Discourses." *Hypatia* 10 (2): 133–140. http://www.jstor.org/stable/3810285.

Native Land Digital. n.d. "Nuučaan̓uuɫʔatḥ Nism̓a (Nuu-Chah-Nulth)." Last modified September 2, 2020. https://native-land.ca/maps/territories/nuu-chah-nulth-tribal-council/.

Nind, Melanie. 2014. *What Is Inclusive Research?* London: Bloomsbury. doi:10.5040/9781849668149.

Nind, Melanie, Rose Wiles, Andrew Bengry-Howell, and Graham Crow. 2013. "Methodological Innovation and Research Ethics: Forces in Tension or Forces in Harmony?" *Qualitative Research* 13 (6): 650–667. doi:10.1177%2F1468794112455042.

Oke, Arike. 2020. "The Civic Archivist." Filmed November 2020 at London School of Economics Library (online), London. Video, 1:14:39. https://www.lse.ac.uk/library/events/general/the-civic-archivist.

Omeka. n.d. Digital Scholar. Accessed October 14, 2021. https://omeka.org/.

Palmisano, Stefania, and Nicola Pannofino. 2016. "Inventive Traditions: Sacred Creativity in the Spirituality of The Secret." *Alternative Spirituality and Religion Review* 7 (1): 3–21. doi:10.5840/asrr201652519.

Puig de la Bellacasa, Maria. 2017. *Matters of Care: Speculative Ethics in More Than Human Worlds.* Posthumanities, Minnesota: University of Minnesota Press.

Reanimating Data: Experiments with People, Places and Archives. n.d. Accessed October 14 2021. http://reanimatingdata.co.uk/.

Rice, Robin. 2014. "Research Data MANTRA: A Labour of Love." *Journal of EScience Librarianship* 3 (1). doi:10.7191/jeslib.2014.1056.

Rice, Robin, and John Southall. 2016. *The Data Librarian's Handbook.* London: Facet.

Sheffield, Rebecka Taves. 2020. *Documenting Rebellions: A Study of Four Lesbian and Gay Archives in Queer Times.* Sacramento: Litwin Books.

Smith, Linda Tuhiwai. 1999. *Decolonizing Methodologies:Research and Indigenous Peoples*. London: Zed Books.

Star, Susan Leigh. 2010. "This Is Not a Boundary Object: Reflections on the Origin of a Concept." *Science, Technology, & Human Values* 35 (5): 601–617. doi:10.1177%2F0162243910377624.

Sutherland, Tonia. 2019. "The Carceral Archive: Documentary Records, Narrative Construction, and Predictive Risk Assessment." *Journal of Cultural Analytics* 4 (1): 1–22. doi:10.22148/16.039.

Thomson, Rachel, and Liam Berriman. 2021. "Starting with the Archive: Principles for Prospective Collaborative Research." *Qualitative Research*, 1–18. doi:10.1177/14687941211023037.

Welch, Sharon D. 2000. *A Feminist Ethic of Risk*. Minneapolis: Fortress.

Learning to Stand with Gyack: A Practice of Thinking with Non-Innocent Care

Lisa Slater

ABSTRACT
Settler colonialism attempts to make invisible the labours of care that Indigenous peoples have been doing for millennia. Notably, the imposition of settler colonial ontologies-epistemologies disrupt and compromise Indigenous people's obligations to land and ancestors (Kwaymullina, Ambelin. 2020. *Living on Stolen Land*. Broome: Magabala Books, 7). Kim Tallbear calls upon settler scholars to think more expansively about what counts as the benefits and risks of research (2014. "Standing With and Speaking as Faith: A Feminist-Indigenous Approach to Inquiry." *Journal of Research Practice* 10 (2): 1–7. http://jrp.icaap.org/index.php/jrp/article/view/405/371, 2). She asks settler scholars to learn to 'stand with' a community and be willing to be altered and revise one's stake in knowledge production (Tallbear, Kim. 2014. "Standing With and Speaking as Faith: A Feminist-Indigenous Approach to Inquiry." *Journal of Research Practice* 10 (2): 1–7. http://jrp.icaap.org/index.php/jrp/article/view/405/371, 2). What does my feminist ethics of care, which strives to unsettle my settler colonial logic of knowledge production, look like? To respond, I will reflect upon a collaborative cultural revitalisation project with Wolgalu and Wiradjuri First Nations community in Brungle-Tumut (New South Wales, Australia). The social world I am imbedded in is different from that of Wolgalu/Wiradjuri colleagues. How is meaning negotiated in the encounter between settler colonial and Aboriginal practices of care and knowledge production? It's a methodological conundrum, which requires thinking with care. Maria Puig de la Bellacasa conceptualises thinking with care as a thick, non-innocent obligation of living in interdependent worlds (2017. *Matters of Care: Speculative Ethics in More than Human Worlds*. Minneapolis: University of Minnesota Press, 19). I want to practice non-innocent care.

Gyack's call sounds like a creaky door: 'creeeee-ek'. You might know this tiny frog, regal in its yellow/green and black markings, as the corroboree frog. The people of the Wolgalu nation call it Gyack (Williams, Connolly, and Williams 2019, 268).[1] I am listening out for Gyack at Micalong Swamp, on Wolgalu country, in Buccleuch State Forest, east of Tumut. According to the NSW Forestry Corporation (2021), 'Micalong Swamp is a unique montane peatland and one of the largest remaining swamps on the south-western slopes of New South Wales' (NSW), Australia. Our newly formed research team are visiting Micalong because it is home to the threatened northern corroboree frog (*Pseudophryne pengilleyi*). Initially I could not tune in to Gyack's call; they sounded like, well, frogs. Not the green trees frogs that are familiar to me from growing up in northern NSW, on Bundjalung country. If I slow down and listen carefully, I hear different calls, like instruments in a small band, but initially I couldn't discern one species from another. After some time and guided by finely tuned ears, I learn to hear Gyack's call. But not their song.

Although the project is a few hundred kilometres from my home, I am culturally, politically and ecologically in another country. I'm settler colonial Australian, born and raised on Bundjalung country on the far north coast of NSW, now living on the Dharawal country, in Wollongong, NSW. Our project is a collaboration with Wolgalu and Wiradjuri First Nations community members, Brungle Tumut Local Land Council, scientists from Department of Planning, Industry and Environment (DPIE) and two settler colonial and one Bundjalung and Wonnarua social scientists from the University of Wollongong.[2] The project is designed to reconnect the Wolgalu/Wiradjuri community of Brungle Tumut to a species of ecological and cultural importance. Significantly, the northern corroboree frog was connected to Wolgalu/Wiradjuri annual ceremonies in the NSW High Country (Alpine region) (Williams, Connolly, and Williams 2019, 268). Thus, ours is a cultural revitalisation project. In the words of trawlwulwuy countrywoman Emma Lee (quoted in Tynan 2021, 601), to protect the corroboree frog the project aims to reclaim Wolgalu/Wiradjuri's web of relationships that are mediated through country.[3] Notably, it is a cross-disciplinary project, but more so it works across different cultural and knowledge practices.

We are in the early stages of the project: relationship-building and learning our responsibilities and obligations to community, Country, frog and each other. Thus, it is not appropriate to discuss the research in detail. Instead, I want to address a central question: what does my feminist ethics of care, which strives to unsettle my settler colonial logics of knowledge production, look like? Kim Tallbear (2014, 2) asks scholars to think more expansively about what counts as the benefits and risks of research. For Indigenous people ontological harm is a significant risk. She identifies a key problem in knowledge production as the imagined distinction between those who have the 'resources' for knowledge production – researcher – and the 'raw materials' that are extracted for knowledge production – the researched. After all, scholars are dependent on the knowledge, expertise and experiences of the 'researched'. She cautions researchers to soften these boundaries and conceive of research as a process of relationship-building. More so, learn to 'stand with' a community of subjects and be willing to be altered and revise one's stake in knowledge production (Tallbear 2014, 2). She calls this her Feminist-Indigenous approach to inquiry. She provokes me in several ways. One, as a feminist, critical Indigenous studies scholar, what is my approach? The second, and more importantly, is the risk of ontological harm. The ongoing imposition of settler colonial ontologies-epistemologies disrupt and compromise Indigenous people's obligations to land and ancestors (Kwaymullina 2020, 7). The social world I am imbedded in is different from that of Wolgalu/Wiradjuri colleagues. Gyack is not a frog in the same way a 'frog' is a frog to me. How can I care for the corroboree frog/Gyack, when we are not caring for the same thing? Therefore, as a settler colonial scholar how do I practice care for Wolgalu/Wiradjuri cultural revitalisation?

Settler colonialism attempts to make invisible the labours of care that Indigenous peoples have been doing for millennia.[4] Indeed, it threatens Indigenous practices of care for the human and more-than-human world. By attempting to destroy Indigenous legal-political and social orders, colonialism forces Indigenous people to violate their principles of reciprocity and responsibility to self, community, country and the past and future (Watson 2015). Indigenous knowledges, as Zoe Todd (2016, 18) explains, are not simply stories or a well-spring of abstract ideas to draw upon. As numerous Indigenous scholars and activists have argued, Indigenous epistemologies and ontologies are alive and embody legal obligations though which Indigenous people are fighting for self-determination, sovereignty and cultural-political existence (see for e.g. Watson 2015; Watts 2013; Kwaymullina 2020; A. Simpson 2014; L. Simpson 2014; Graham 2014). Much has been spoken, written, sung, danced, painted, and more, about why and how settlers continue to sanction violence, ignorance and erasure (Sundberg 2013, 41). Ontological violence plays out in research in numerous ways: simplification, appropriation, distortion, or even a cursory nod, quick citation, to Indigenous scholars. Another is the conviction that settlers have knowledge, whilst Indigenous peoples have culture. Thus, I understand Indigenous scholars and activists to be appealing for a serious engagement with Indigenous epistemologies and ontologies as socio-political orders, with the proviso of accepting difference, and acknowledging the history and continuation of colonialism.

However, does a serious engagement require legibility? Genuinely encountering difference does not mean 'knowing' difference. Arguably, it requires recognising my epistemic limits, thus not understanding. In this light, Tallbear's challenge to be altered and revise one's stake in knowledge production by reimaging where expertise lies raises a methodological conundrum. How is meaning negotiated in the encounter between settler colonial and Indigenous practices of care and knowledge production?[5] To respond to my own question, I want to think with care. Maria Puig de la Bellacasa (2017) conceptualises thinking with care as coming to know and reveal one's ethico-political commitments and alliances. She theorises care as an analytic, a provocation that potentially disrupts, what Tallbear might call, one's stake in knowledge production. Thinking with care is a thick, non-innocent obligation of living in interdependent worlds (Puig de la Bellacasa 2017, 19). In this article, I want to consider what non-innocent care is in practice?

Decolonising Methodologies

Feminist scholarship has long argued that cultural politics and power relations are embedded in everyday life and social relations, and produce our subjectivity, indeed our world. In Australia 'we' are embedded in settler colonial authority, so normalised it appears as common sense (Rifkin 2014). Aboriginal and Torres Strait Islander sovereignty was denied through, what Irene Watson (2002, para. 21) calls, the 'legal fiction' of Terra Nullius: colonisers regarded the land as empty, thus existing 'for their invasion and settlement'. Settler colonialism asserts sovereignty through the violent dispossession and legal domination of Indigenous peoples, justified by narratives of European progress and supremacy. Drawing upon Patrick Wolfe's work, Audra Simpson (2011, 205) posits that '[i]n this model of colonialism, "the settler never leaves", so the possession of territory requires the disappearance of "the native"'. To do so, settler colonialism renders Indigenous people out of place: temporally and spatially. It is both a project of elimination and replacement, the persistent need to disavow the presence of the Indigenous other; what Veracini (2010) calls the settler colonial non-encounter. Significantly, as Simpson (2011) diagnoses, a form of disappearance, or non-encounter, is the evasion and destruction of political independence and sovereignty. Thus, settlers imagine themselves as in possession of all resources: land, knowledge, authority, expertise, human and more-than-human bodies. In contemporary Australia white possessive logic continues: the nation is figured as a belonging to white settlers (Moreton-Robinson 2005, 22). Under the spell of settler colonial authority, there are so many ways to escape an encounter and exclude difference; to make a people (appear) to disappear through the well-oiled apparatuses of assimilation.

The colonial project of elimination and replacement has always relied on 'research'. It is a truism that Indigenous people were and are highly 'studied'. The poking, prodding, measuring and testing and comparison of Indigenous peoples, as Lester Rigney (1999, 109) writes, continues. Although the 'studying' is often concealed by discourses of care, concern and remedialism. Arguably, researching about – rather than with – Indigenous peoples has proliferated with the technological capacity for data collection, heightened surveillance and 'consultation and inclusion'. Think of Closing the Gap (CtG), the national strategy to reduce statistical disadvantage among Aboriginal and Torres Strait Islander people in regard to life expectancy, child mortality, access to early childhood education, educational achievement, and employment outcomes (Australian Government 2021). CtG is an epistemological practice through which Indigeneity comes to be 'known' in comparison with an idealised healthy population. Statistics supply the 'facts' needed to demonstrate the extent of the problems. Thus, they create the artifice of reasoned knowledge and progress and foreclose on other epistemologies. The dominant way of 'knowing' Aboriginal and Torres Strait Islander peoples becomes the dominant mode of care, what I call the management of care (Slater 2019). CtG is a naturalisation of colonial authority over Aboriginal and Torres Strait Islander lands and life and assumes political incorporation. To be clear, statistics matter; they highlight inequality. However, government policies are arguably the most ubiquitous and influential representations of Indigeneity and thus overly determine how settler Australians understand and relate to Indigenous people (Slater 2019; Strakosch 2015). Statistics are part of the arsenal: reproducing the colonial relation of knowing and known, the problem and solution. Maggie Walters (2018) identifies that data is often collected using lines of inquiry that are valid for non-Indigenous contexts, but not for Indigenous circumstances. Indigenous driven data paucity results in a dearth of data that is relevant and accurate from the perspective of Indigenous peoples. Hence why Walter (and other Indigenous scholars) calls for political and ethical considerations of Indigenous data management, use and collection: data sovereignty.[6] Evidence based social policy can be a cunning form of colonialism: by excluding difference, care becomes a form of epistemic and ontological violence.

There is a long history of Indigenous scholars advocating for research that is driven by, in the words of Karen Martin (2003), Aboriginal Ways of Knowing, Ways of Being and Ways of Doing. The earlier work of Rigney and Smith (1999) demonstrates how colonialism informs research practices and was foundational in calling for the decolonisation of research and establishing Indigenist methodologies. Indigenist methodologies demand not only a recognition of Indigenous epistemologies and ontologies, but also an emphasis on the social, historical and political contexts which shape and overly determine

Indigenous lives and lands, and the recognition of distinct cultural, political and legal orders, which are vital for the existence and survival of Indigenous peoples and lands (see for e.g. Kwaymullina 2020; Watson 2015). Thus, it has never been a matter of inclusion of Indigenous peoples; 'simply adding Indigenous researchers to the academy of research and stirring', to borrow from Rigney (1999, 114). But rather, as he and many maintain, Indigenous perspectives must infiltrate, and therefore challenge and transform, academic structures and research methods. In the face of the endurance of colonialism there is now a diverse and dynamic body of Indigenous scholarship, defined and driven by Indigenous realities. Rigney and Smith illustrated the significance of Indigenist research to self-determination and liberation struggles. In his earlier work, Rigney (1999) noted the clear alignment with feminist research methodologies, notwithstanding many white feminists' ongoing allegiance to colonialism.

Thinking with Care

Feminist scholarship is committed to making visible neglected, marginalised and undervalued experiences: the everyday labours of the maintenance of life (Harding 1991; see Puig de la Bellacasa 2010). One of which is care. Feminist ethicists of care have long insisted that care is vital, ubiquitous and indispensable to the everyday sustainability of life (Puig de la Bellacasa 2010, 55, quoting Carrasco 2001). Despite that autonomy, independence and self-sufficiency continue to be privileged, they insist that dependency – weakness and vulnerability – is central to what it is to be human (Tronto 1993; Vaittinen 2015). In this formulation, the social is conceptualised as a weave of interdependencies and interconnections. The political theorist of care Joan Tronto (1993, 5) has long argued for care being conceived as a part of the work of citizens, and that we need to take seriously a collective commitment to care. Yet, because care has been historically associated with women and the marginalised, the labour of social reproduction, it is associated with the private and individual. Notably, practices of care provide a source of moral thinking and social belonging, and thus central to reproducing moral-political orders, social worlds and citizens, which have powerful material and personal consequences (Vaittinen 2015; Berlant 2004; Puig de la Bellacasa 2017). Social norms are perpetuated through caring practices. Building upon Tronto's work, Puig de la Bellacasa (2012, 198) notes, we need to insist on this 'interweaving' in order to be able to think about how care holds together the world as we know it and how it perpetuates, and negates, power relationships. If care holds the world together as we know it, then what or whose world are *'we' holding together*? What other worlds are possible?

Care is often conflated with good feelings, affection and nurturing (Murphy 2015). The ethics in the ethics of care, Puig de la Bellacasa (2017) insists, is not about normative moral dispositions, rather it is a transformative ethos. She is committed to care's potential to disrupt hierarchies of value; however, she wants to dislodge the notion that care is something that only humans do ('and some surrogate persons such as nonhumans deemed capable of intentional agency and emotion'). Therefore, she extends feminist ethics of care beyond the usual focus – social worlds – to reorientate the meaning of care to knowing and thinking with more-than-human worlds (2017, 12). She does so in conversation with Bruno Latour's (2004) 'matters of concern'. Latour drew attention to the knowledge politics – the ethico-political affects – of constructivist accounts of science and technologies: how things are re-presented matters. It is not enough to critique matters of fact or interests, he argues, interests, concern and care are entangled in the ongoing remaking – re-presentation of the world. Thus, he appeals for studying 'objects', to borrow from Murphy (2015, 721), as 'extensive, contestable and dynamic social, technical, and political assemblages', which he calls 'matters of concern'. Puig de la Bellacasa (2017, 40) emphasises that not only does Latour's concept represent a way of comprehending knowledge politics in technoscience, but it also suggests the need to care in particular ways. Her concern is that the democratisation of 'matters of concern' also potentially hides power relations. If ways of studying and representing things have world-making effects, then scholars' ethico-political commitments and obligations are a fundamental part of creating knowledge. Despite feminists' insistence on situating the self, largely scholars' loyalties and allegiances remain hidden.

Thus thinking with non-innocent care calls upon researchers, in the words of Sundberg (2013), to become accountable for their epistemological and ontological habits. For some time, postcolonial, critical Indigenous and race scholars have demonstrated how race, class, gender and sexuality determine what and whose caring work is valued and whose labour goes unrecognised, as it maintains and supports the prosperity of some (Murphy 2015, 725). Care, rescue and liberation are not innocent but rather entangled in histories of racisms, class privilege, colonialism and capitalism (Arvin, Tuck, and Morrill 2013; Morgensen 2011; Murphy 2015; Tuck and Yang 2012; Slater 2019). In solidarity with scholars and activists of decolonisation, Michelle Murphy (2015, 722) appeals for unsettling care: a project that 'responsibilizes settlers to histories, entanglements, and complications that come from the historical and current structural violence of colonialism'. I share Murphy's (2015) commitment to the purposeful undoing and troubling of particular arrangements of value.

Furthermore, like Murphy I am troubled by post-humanist and feminist ethics of care enmeshment in the logics of settler colonialism. The persistent omission of Indigenous knowledge practices reproduces settler common sense (Rifkin 2014). However, as Rigney (1999) insists, inclusion is not enough. Indigenist research is a challenge to the academy; it strives to intervene in and transform settler colonial knowledge production. To unsettle my fledgling practice of 'non-innocent ethics of care', I will reflect upon Todd's critique of the Ontological turn. Todd examines Latour's exclusion of Indigenous knowledge, writing:

> It is easier for Euro-Western people to tangle with a symbolic polar bear on a Greenpeace website or in a tweet than it is to acknowledge arctic Indigenous peoples and their knowledge systems and legal-political realities. (2016, 6)

Todd's (2016, 7) assessment is that the Ontological turn is another Euro-Western academic narrative 'spinning of the backs of non-Europeans thinkers'.[7] In her account Latour is applauded and credited, indeed many Euro-Western scholars, for their astonishing insights into the sentience and agency of the more-than-human, with little to no recognition of and engagement with Indigenous people's ways of knowing and being with the more-than-human. These erasures are made easy, she argues, within the academy because disciplines continue to be practiced in ways that erase Indigenous bodies, intellectuals and political-legal orders (2016, 7). The academy is under the spell of white possessive logic (Moreton-Robinson 2015). However, Latour (and Puig de la Bellacasa) is explicitly engaging with 'modern' knowledges and not Indigenous social worlds and knowledge practices; principally to not risk appropriation. Afterall, assimilation, misrepresentation or erasure are a threat to Indigenous self-determination and existence (Watts 2013, 31). Thus, Latour's (2013) position is that one needs to understand one's own world before entering a dialogue with and learning to listen to others.[8] In contrast, I have chosen to understand settler colonialism, including the ongoing effects of colonialism and to encounter – take seriously – Indigenous ontologies, epistemologies, and practices of care. I might be able to become accountable, but that is no guarantee I can listen, let alone hear.

Like those before and after, Todd (2016) appeals for an enactment of our duties of reciprocity as citizens of shared territories. I understand her concept of shared territories as not only geographical situatedness – Australia, Wollongong, northern NSW of my upbringing – but rather that 'we' are closely woven together by colonialism and inter-relations with the human and more-than-human world. Thus, 'we' are always, already, in inter-dependent relations. But not in a feel-good, innocent, forgetful, ignorant, negating difference, get-out-of-colonialism kind a way. 'We' need to learn how 'I' and 'we' are situated in relation to one another (human and more-than-human), whilst never forgetting how history, experiences, realities and socio-legal orders differently position 'us' (Todd 2016, 18). It is an obligation, Todd (2016, 19) cautions, to pay attention to who else is speaking alongside 'us'. Who else is speaking, labouring and caring, and for too long gone unheard? More recent appeals echo the earlier work that began the long road to decolonise scholarship. Leanne Betasamosake Simpson adds another challenge when she writes of the need to rebel:

> against the permanence of settler colonial reality and not just 'dream alternative realities' but to create them on the ground in the physical world, in spite of being occupied. If we accept colonial permanence, then our rebellion can only take place within settler colonial thought and reality … . (2014, 8)

We are all citizens of shared territories, but not of shared social worlds. The rebellion Simpson advocates for is beyond my epistemic limits. To stand with Gyack and Wolgalu/Wiradjuri – to learn how to support their socio-political, legal and cultural goals of decolonisation – requires learning to listen not to know, but to learn otherwise.

Practicing Non-Innocent Care

How do we enact our duties of reciprocity as citizens of shared territories if we don't share the same social worlds? When Puig de la Bellacasa cautions that we must disrupt the notion that care is something that only humans do, she is referring to a particular we (of which she is aware). She is gesturing toward other social worlds; human and more-than-human. There are divergences in how humans conceptualise social worlds – who and what are kin, for example – and thus practices of care. Thinking with care is a transformative ethos; it unsettles hierarchies of value (Puig de la Bellacasa 2017). Notably, Indigenous knowledge practices are sub-ordinated through the imposition of settler ontology-epistemologies (Blaser and de la Cadena 2017). This occurs, Mario Blaser and Marisol de la Cadena (2017) argue, through practices of equivalence. Take their example of the 'naturalisation' of the distinction between human and non-humans which Indigenous peoples don't necessarily make themselves. An equivalence – nature/culture – is proclaimed, Blaser and de la Cadena reason, where a divergence is operating. A consequence of ongoing colonialism is that dominant practices can eventually operate as if the subordinate ones were irrelevant to the constitution of the common (Blaser and de la Cadena 2017, 189). Despite declaring equivalence, much exists which exceeds colonial distinctions (Blaser and de la Cadena 2017, 186). Thus, to fail to understand that 'we' are using the same terms but referring to different things, is to make divergence disappear (Blaser and de la Cadena 2017, 189, quoting Viveiros de Castro). For example, let's take the shared word, but divergent concept, Country. To do so, I'll listen to trawlwulwuy scholar Lauren Tynan:

> Country inhabits all relationality and is used widely across Australia to describe how all land is Aboriginal land, Aboriginal Country; Country is agentic and encompasses everything from ants, memories, humans, fire, tides and research. Country sits at the heart of coming to know and understand relationality as it is the web that connects humans to a system of Lore/Law and knowledge that can never be human-centric. (2021, 597)

Many would agree that there are inter-dependent relations between the human and more-than-human, but this does not make for an equivalence. Tynan proposes a different social world than mine; one in which she has an obligation and responsibility toward other-than-human as kin. Quoting Daniel Wildcat, Tynan posits:

> Can you imagine a world where nature is understood as full of relatives not resources, where inalienable rights are balanced with inalienable responsibilities and where wealth itself is measured not by resource ownership and control, but by the number of good relationships we maintain in the complex and diverse life-systems of this blue green planet? I can. (2021, 603)

She responds, I can too. I can't. Not because I don't want to: I am politically, ethically, emotionally aligned with a world full of relatives not resources. It's not that the ideas are unfamiliar to me. As an Australian, let alone a critical, Indigenous studies scholar they are familiar to me. However, as a lived experience the more-than-human as relative is uncommon to me.[9] I have a sense of responsibility and obligation to Country. When I slow down, take the time, I feel how the bush, the ocean, the trees that wave in the wind just beyond my balcony, are a source of nurturance, wisdom and wonder. I know I am not separate, but I do not know Country as kin. It is not the same. To assume equivalence is a form of innocent care.

Again, I would argue that taking Indigenous epistemologies-ontologies seriously does not require legibility. Afterall settlers need to keep a check on our desire for possessive logic. However, how do I de-centre my knowledge practices and become 'aware of different social worlds when all at one's disposal is terms which belong to one's own?' (Strathern et al. 1987, quoted, Blaser and de la Cadena 2017, 191). This is the classic anthropological methodological challenge of how best to make sense of concepts that do not make sense within one's own conceptual schema (Heywood 2017). The settler ethnographer is confronted with things that are uncommon and the challenge is, usually, to render them comprehensible in the terms available to them (Blaser and de la Cadena 2017, 191). However, entangled within the common world is an excess to modern, colonial epistemic practices. This entangled excess, Blaser and de la Cadena (2017, 186) call 'the uncommons': 'a condition that disrupts (yet does not replace) the idea of "the world" as shared ground'. They propose that the uncommons is the very condition of the possibility of the common. However, colonialism renders divergence the same by 'subordinating one set of practices to the other' and claiming equivalence (Blaser and de la Cadena 2017, 189).

> Uncommoning runs counter to this possibility, not simply emphasising that practices taken as common are different (that is, the contrarily of the same) but rather by stressing that they are divergent, a concept Isabelle Stengers (2005) uses to explain what she calls an 'ecology of practices.' Accordingly, the practices that interest us are constituted by their own positive divergence as they symbiotically come together – like in an ecological system – while also remaining distinct: what brings them together is an interest in common that is not the same interest. The point of uncommoning, then, is not to preclude the possibility of commoning but rather, whenever possible, to seek ways to base the latter on the more solid grounds of recognised productive divergences. (Blaser and de la Cadena 2017, 189–190)

Thus, the practice is not to lose sight of that which is not shared. To paraphrase Heywood (2017, np), the recursive anthropologist instead would ask what sort of adjustments to my conceptual schema must be made for it to make sense to think of the frog as kin. The challenge is not so much to know the frog as kin – to somehow make the adjustments, despite my epistemic limits – but for Indigenous concepts of relationality to unsettle my naturalised distinctions of nature-culture.

If thinking with care is a non-innocent obligation of living in interdependent worlds (Puig de la Bellacasa 2017, 19), then it requires refusing the colonising reduction to shared categories (Blaser and de la Cadena 2017, 191). A recognition that one's analytic tools are insufficient, and thus, to borrow from de la Cadena (Taguchi and de la Cadena 2019), working from not understanding. Importantly de la Cadena's methodology was inspired by Stenger's (2005) conceptual figure of the idiot: a practice of slowing down thought and action and decision-making when engaging with radical uncertainties and alterity. Not a striving for understanding but rather to suspend 'knowingness' to allow the emergence of different arrangements of relationships and value (Taguchi and de la Cadena 2019, np). In an interview, de la Cadena recalls a particular teaching ethnographic moment in which her interlocutor, Mariano, dismissed one of her foundational ideas. She came to understand that:

> he was telling me something like 'If you want to meet me' – in the sense of encountering him at a crossroads built with both his terms and my terms affecting each other – 'we' have to talk about *something else*. (Taguchi and de la Cadena 2019, np)

Her (modern epistemic) knowledge didn't allow her to understand Mariano's practices. To continue the conversation and meet him at the crossroads, she needed another methodology, for which she drew upon Marilyn Strathern's (2004) partial connections. Partial connections is not simply an awareness that one doesn't understand, it is a form of slowing down which pays attention to the translation process. Gyack (and many other entities) makes present a world that is different from 'my' world. My terms are inadequate for understanding the frog as kin. I can only 'know' Wolgalu/Wiradjuri concepts, practices, knowledges in translation – partial connection. Thus, I do not understand but rather am puzzled, productively confused (Taguchi and de la Cadena 2019, np). The practice is not to make sense out of my uncertainty – disconcertment – by digging around in my analytical toolbox to find the answer, but instead recognising the limits of my knowing. Instead, my translation, which is not the same as Wolgalu/Wiradjuri concepts, challenges and alters my categories (Taguchi and de la Cadena 2019, np).

To think with care is a practice of disrupting, in my case, settlers' ethico-political commitments, alliances – knowledge politics – that largely remain invisible to me. What Rifkin (2014) might refer to exposing settler common sense. My practice of non-innocent care is one of productive confusion, which not only reveals the limits of my 'knowing', but importantly therefore the limits of what worlds I can perceive, know. Social worlds that none-the-less can move me. Thus, I understand my research partnerships as relationship building, a co-labour in which we work carefully and slowly to create connections built on different terms. I think of non-innocent care as tending to the connection between entities. In this sense, it might be likened to Shawn Wilson's research as ceremony. He writes, '[t]he purpose of any ceremony is to build stronger relationships or bridge the distance between our cosmos and us' (2008, 137). However, the cosmos, worlds, are not necessarily shared. Thus, in our corroboree frog project, it is unlikely that my Wolgalu/Wiradjuri colleagues and I will have shared understandings of cultural revitalisation and practices of care. Yet, we continue the conversation. One in which I need to pay careful attention to my translation processes. Non-innocent care is a different relation with knowledge production. One in which I want to tend to the connections between 'things', without making them the same. Thus, being affected by a world that is beyond my knowing. Non-innocent care might be hearing the call, being moved by the song and learning to think otherwise with Gyack.

Notes

1. In Wolgalu there are two names that describe frogs. Gyack – because of its call – best describes the corroboree frog (Shane Herrington, personal communication, September 21, 2021).
2. I wish to acknowledge and thank the project team: Country, Gyack, Brungle-Tumut Wolgalu/Wiradjuri, Aunty Sue Bulger, Shane Herrington, Vanessa Cavanagh, Geoff Simpson, Kat Haynes, Mal Ridges and Dave Hunter.
3. Tynan notes, 'trawlwulwuy, tebrakunna sometimes do not use capitalisation' (2021, footnote 5, 608).
4. Throughout this article I use the term 'Indigenous' to refer to diverse peoples, from around the world, with ancestral connections and claims to specific lands prior to colonisation, and who remain subjected to all different forms of colonialism. When referring to Australia, I use Aboriginal and Torres Strait Islander or the particular nation. The risk of making a distinct between Indigenous and settler epistemes is to suggest there are not ongoing interactions and inter-relationships. There are, rather I am making an analytical separation, despite the inter-relations and commonalities (see Sundberg 2013, 34).
5. I want to thank the anonymous reviewer for pointing me to this question.
6. I wish to thank Vanessa Cavanagh for her insights and reflections on Walter's work.
7. Todd writes the 'trendy and dominant Ontological Turn (and/or post-humanism, and/or cosmo-politics – all three of which share tangled roots, and can be mobilised distinctly or collectively, depending on who you ask), and discourses of how to organise ourselves around and communicate with the constituents of complex and contested world(s) … ' (2016, 7).
8. I wish to thank and acknowledge the anonymous reviewer who reminded me of these crucial points.
9. By which I mean all more-than-humans, not simply domesticated species.

Acknowledgements

I wish to acknowledge Dharawal Country, on which I live and much of this article was written, and Wolgalu and Wiradjuri Country – Brungle-Tumut – on the lands on which this project is taking place. I wish to acknowledge and thank the project team: Country, Gyack, Brungle-Tumut Wolgalu/

Wiradjuri, Aunty Sue Bulger, Shane Herrington, Vanessa Cavanagh, Geoff Simpson, Kat Haynes, Mal Ridges and Dave Hunter.

Disclosure Statement

No potential conflict of interest was reported by the author(s).

Funding

This project is funded by a Global Challenges grant, Buidling Resilient Communities, University of Wollongong.

References

Arvin, Maile, Eve Tuck, and Angie Morrill. 2013. "Decolonizing Feminism: Challenging Connections Between Settler Colonialism and Heteropatriarchy." *Feminist Formations* 25 (1): 8–34.
Australian Government. 2021. *Closing the Gap*. Canberra: Department of the Prime Minister and Cabinet. https://www.closingthegap.gov.au.
Berlant, Lauren, ed. 2004. *Compassion: The Culture and Politics of an Emotion*. New York: Routledge.
Blaser, Mario, and Marisol de la Cadena. 2017. "The Uncommons: An Introduction." *Anthropologica* 59 (2): 185–193.
Graham, Mary. 2014. "Aboriginal Notions of Relationality and Positionalism: A Reply to Weber." *Global Discourse: An Interdisciplinary Journal of Current Affairs and Applied Contemporary Thought* 4 (1): 17–22.
Harding, Sandra. 1991. *Whose Science? Whose Knowledge? Thinking from Women's Lives*. Ithaca, NY: Cornell University Press.
Heywood, Paolo. 2017. "The Ontological Turn." *The Cambridge Encyclopia of Anthropology*. https://www.anthroencyclopedia.com/entry/ontological-turn.
Kwaymullina, Ambelin. 2020. *Living on Stolen Land*. Broome: Magabala Books.
Latour, Bruno. 2004. "How to Talk About the Body? The Normative Dimension of Science Studies." *Body & Society* 10 (2-3): 205–229.
Latour, Bruno. 2013. *An Inquiry into Modes of Existence: An Anthropology of the Moderns*. Cambridge, MA: Harvard University Press.
Martin, Karen. 2003. "Ways of Knowing, Ways of Being and Ways of Doing: A Theoretical Framework and Methods." *Journal of Australian Studies* 27 (76): 203–214.
Moreton-Robinson, Aileen. 2005. "The House that Jack Built: Britishness and White Possession." *Australian Critical Race and Whiteness Studies Association Journal* 1: 21–29.
Moreton-Robinson, Aileen. 2015. *The White Possessive: Property, Power, and Indigenous Sovereignty*. Minneapolis: University of Minnesota Press.
Morgensen, Scott. 2011. "The Biopolitics of Settler Colonialism." *Settler Colonial Studies* 1 (1): 52–76.
Murphy, Michelle. 2015. "Unsettling Care: Troubling Transnational Itineraries of Care in Feminist Health Practices." *Social Studies of Science* 45 (5): 717–737.
NSW Forestry Corporation. 2021. "Micalong State Forest." *State of NSW*. Accessed 25 March 2021. https://www.forestrycorporation.com.au/visit/forests/micalong.

Puig de la Bellacasa, María. 2010. "Ethical Doings in Naturecultures, Ethics." *Place & Environment: A Journal of Philosophy & Geography* 13 (2): 151–169.
Puig de la Bellacasa, María. 2012. "'Nothing Comes Without its World': Thinking with Care." *The Sociological Review* 60 (2): 197–216.
Puig de la Bellacasa, María. 2017. *Matters of Care: Speculative Ethics in More than Human Worlds*. Minneapolis: University of Minnesota Press.
Rifkin, Mark. 2014. *Settler Common Sense: Queerness and Everyday Colonialism in the American Renaissance*. Minnesota: University of Minnesota Press.
Rigney, Lester. 1999. "Internationalization of an Indigenous Anticolonial Cultural Critique of Research Methodologies: A Guide to Indigenist Research Methodology and It's Principles." *Wicazo Sa Review* 14 (2): 109–121.
Simpson, Audra. 2011. "Settlement's Secret." *Cultural Anthropology* 26 (2): 205–217.
Simpson, Audra. 2014. *Mohawk Interruptus: Political Life Across the Borders of Settler States*. Durham: Duke University Press.
Simspon, Leanne Betasamosake. 2014. "Land as Pedagogy." *Decolonization: Indigeneity, Education & Society* 3 (3): 1–25.
Slater, Lisa. 2019. *Anxieties of Belonging in Settler Colonialism: Australia, Race & Place*. New York: Routledge.
Smith, Tuhiwai Linda. 1999. *Decolonizing Methodologies: Research and Indigenous Peoples*. Dunedin, NZ: University of Otago Press.
Stengers, Isabelle. 2005. "A Cosmopolitical Proposal." In *Making Things Public: Atmospheres of Democracy*, edited by B. Latour and P. Weibel, 994–1003. Cambridge: The MIT Press.
Strakosch, Elizabeth. 2015. *Neoliberal Indigenous Policy*. London: Palgrave.
Strathern, Marilyn. 2004. *Partial Connections*. Walnut Creek: AltaMira Press.
Sundberg, Juanita. 2013. "Decolonizing Posthumanist Geographies." *Cultural Geographies* 21 (1): 33–47.
Taguchi, Yoko, and Marisol de la Cadena. 2019. "An Interview with Marisol de la Cadena." https://www.natcult.net/interviews/an-interview-with-marisol-de-la-cadena/.
Tallbear, Kim. 2014. "Standing with and Speaking as Faith: A Feminist-Indigenous Approach to Inquiry." *Journal of Research Practice* 10 (2): 1–7. http://jrp.icaap.org/index.php/jrp/article/view/405/371.
Todd, Zoe. 2016. "An Indigenous Feminist's Take on the Ontological Turn: 'Ontology' is Just Another Word For Colonialism." *Journal of Historical Sociology* 29 (1): 4–22.
Tronto, Joan. 1993. *Moral Boundaries: A Political Argument for an Ethic of Care*. New York: Routledge.
Tuck, Eve, and Wayne Yang. 2012. "Decolonization is not a Metaphor." *Decolonization: Indigeneity, Education & Society* 1 (1): 1–40.
Tynan, Lauren. 2021. "What Is Relationality? Indigenous Knowledges, Practices and Responsibilities with Kin." *Cultural Geographies* 28 (4): 597–610.
Vaittinen, Tiina. 2015. "The Power of the Vulnerable Body: A New Political Understanding of Care." *International Feminist Journal of Politics* 17 (1): 100–118.
Veracini, Lorenzo. 2010. *Settler Colonialism: A Theoretical Overview*. New York: Palgrave Macmillan.
Walters, Maggie. 2018. "The Voice of Indigenous Data: Beyond the Markers of Disadvantage." *Griffith Review* 60: 256–263.
Watson, Irene. 2002. "Aboriginal Laws and the Sovereignty of Terra Nullius." *Borderlands* 1 (2): np.
Watson, Irene. 2015. *Aboriginal Peoples, Colonialism and International Law: Raw Law*. New York: Routledge.
Watts, Vanessa. 2013. "Indigenous Place-Thought and Agency Amongst Humans and Non-Humans (First Woman and Sky Woman go on a European Tour!)." *Decolonization, Indigeneity, Education and Society* 2 (1): 20–34.
Williams, Simon, Dianne Connolly, and Alice Williams. 2019. "The Recognition of Cultural Water Requirements in the Montane Rivers of the Snowy Mountains, Australia." *Australasian Journal of Environmental Management* 26 (3): 255–272.
Wilson, Shawn. 2008. *Research is Ceremony: Indigenous Research Methods*. Black Point, Nova Scotia: Fernwood Publishing.

⑧ OPEN ACCESS

The Use/Less Citations in Feminist Research

Xin Liu

ABSTRACT
This article points to the paradox in feminist citation practices. It provides a brief overview of the key issues at stake in feminist citational practices. By highlighting the ways in which the logic of territoriality, authority and property continues to inform the mood and mode of moralistic repair, it cautions again the reification of certain racialised and gendered bodies as the remedy, ground and supplement for feminist research ethics. Thinking through the figure of the (bio)degradable, this article asks whether it is possible to consider feminist citation as use/less.

'Why Don't You Cite Any Decolonial Scholars?'

During the Q&A session after my presentation at a symposium in Finland, which concerned the issue of air pollution in China, I received the following question: 'Why don't you cite any decolonial scholars?'. The aim of the symposium was to engage with decolonial theory and to rethink the practices of feminist knowledge production. It did so not only by inviting keynote speakers whose work is located in the field of decolonial studies, that draw on the 'work of diasporic scholars from South America' (Bhambra 2014, 115), but also through seating arrangements that encouraged a collective mode of knowledge production. For example, the organisers placed round tables in the conference room, so that participants could sit in circles facing each other. The organisers also placed a big sheet of paper on each table and encouraged participants to take notes on the paper. The sheets of paper were kept on the tables throughout the symposium so that participants could walk around the room and read others' notes. This symposium seating arrangement materialised a decolonial approach to knowledge production which challenges the logic of coloniality that undergirds the notion of knowledge as '*located* in the individual, the "knowing subject" in front of a detached object (society, nature, the cosmos, other persons), isolated from the community of knowers (Mignolo and Walsh 2018, 200; emphasis in original).

In contrast to the typical forms of notes that are written within the confines of a notebook and/or a screen that is a property of an individual, the note-taking practice at the symposium was open, messy and collective. Each sheet of paper was covered with

---

This is an Open Access article distributed under the terms of the Creative Commons Attribution-NonCommercial-NoDerivatives License (http://creativecommons.org/licenses/by-nc-nd/4.0/), which permits non-commercial re-use, distribution, and reproduction in any medium, provided the original work is properly cited, and is not altered, transformed, or built upon in any way.

words and scribbles, whose contents might be coherent, overlapping or difficult to interpret. There were not any signatures identifying the author(s) of the notes. And since participants sat in different places during the symposium, it was impossible to tell who wrote which words, draw which lines or mark which sections. The uncoordinated note-taking practice also made felt the sociality of writing and knowledge production. As Fred Moten writes, to say the text is a social space 'is to say that stuff is going on: people, things, are meeting there and interacting, rubbing off one another, brushing against one another' (2013, 108). I not only saw the visually different handwritings – different colours and shapes, but I also heard and bodily felt the frictions between the tips of the marker pens and the surface of the paper, with different speed, weight and intensity. Such an open, messy and collective form of knowledge production made visible and challenged the sense of privacy and ownership of the typical note-taking practice.

Interestingly, this invitation to participate in the collective social space of knowledge production that called into question the logic of ownership and property was contradicted by the demand of citing decolonial scholars, which in many ways should also be considered as a decolonising practice. My presentation drew on Gayatri C. Spivak's observation of the 'denegation of the natural and rational inscription of the possibility of surplus-value' (1993, 121) to make an argument that humanism cannot be simply abandoned but must be incessantly negotiated with. I also took inspiration from Trinh's (2016) theorisation of lovecidal to rethink the discourse of war on smog in China. Spivak and Trinh have engaged with various modes of coloniality in their respective work and have contributed to feminist research on questions of difference and otherness. However, the question 'why don't you cite any decolonial scholars' suggests that neither Spivak's nor Trinh's work falls in the category of decolonial scholarship. The question was posed by the keynote speaker, who noted that I only cited postcolonial scholars located in the Anglo-American context in my presentation. While a detailed account on the relation between postcolonial and decolonial studies is beyond the scope of this text (see, for example, Mendoza 2016; Bhambra 2014), it is important to briefly explain their received difference to contextualise the comment I received.

According to Madina Tlostanova, postcolonial studies 'tend to interpret the other through the concepts of the same and seldom the other way round, and in this fundamental sense they remain loyal to and inadvertently reproduce the coloniality of knowledge' (2010, 25). In contrast, the decolonial turn starts 'not from Lacan but from Gloria Anzaldúa or from the Zapatistas, from Caucasus cosmology or from Sufism' (2010, 25), and in so doing calling into question 'the essence, logic, and methodology of the existing system of knowledge and disciplinary spheres' (2010, 24). Along these lines, despite their critique of modes of colonialism, Spivak's and Trinh's works are not radical and decolonialising enough, as they are mired within the epistemic structure of modernity.

In view of this, the question 'why don't you cite decolonial scholars' could be read as a demand for citing certain bodies of/and work that are considered *properly* decolonial, and as a critique of the reproduction of the logic of coloniality that my presentation risks producing. Interestingly, although my presentation concerned the Chinese context, the lack of reference to Chinese scholars working on the issue of air pollution or the 'ecological civilization' in China was not pointed out or criticised (see, for example, Chang 2019). The demand for better – more radical because properly decolonial – citations of the work that *belongs* to decolonial scholars contradicts the open, messy, collective and social process of knowledge production that the symposium tried to facilitate. Interestingly, *both* practices could be considered as following decolonial ethos. Whereas the note-taking practice could be considered as in line with the decolonial approach that rejects 'the all-authoritative, definitive, and individualized property-related tenets of Western academic knowledge' (Mignolo and Walsh 2018, 248), the citation of decolonial scholars contests the history of and ongoing silencing, appropriation and marginalisation of their intellectual labour. And yet, the demand for certain citational practices reinstalls the logic of proper(ty) and author(ity) at the centre of the decolonial project.

My point is not that one form of decolonialising practice should be privileged over the other. Rather, I am interested in the paradox in feminist citational practices that this opening scene is symptomatic of. In what follows, I first provide a brief review of the key issues that concern feminist citational practices, which is considered one of the most important components of feminist research ethics. Feminist research is a diverse field with various citational practices. Factors such as the specific institutional, disciplinary settings and the preferences of the journal communities – 'editors, boards, peer reviewers, and responses to publishing conventions and expectations' (Hemmings 2011, 21) – shape whom and what is cited and how. My aim here is however not to reason nor to justify the citational choices of individual authors but to identify and foreground some of the repeated and shared patterns of (critiquing) citational practices across the field of feminist research. I take inspiration from Clare Hemmings' citation tactics that 'shift priority away from who said what' (2011, 21) to focus on shared knowledge practices. I then zoom in on the logic of territoriality, authority and property. As I will show, this logic continues to inform the mood and mode of 'moralistic repair' (Chow 2021), the form of suspicious critique and the reification of certain racialised and gendered bodies as the remedy, ground and supplement for feminist research ethics. Thinking through the figure of the (bio)degradable, I end this article by asking about the use/lessness of feminist citational practices.

'Why Do You Cite Dead White Men?'

'Why do you cite dead white men?', a professor asked me when reading the draft of my doctoral manuscript, which rethinks the question of race through engaging with Ferdinand de Saussure's theorisation of sign. The practices of citation – whom and how to cite – are central to feminist research ethics. A citation provides the material, evidence and support for an analysis or argumentation. It concerns the question of the subject of knowledge production – who speaks – that orients feminist ethical and political practices. Citations are performative in the sense that whom and what is cited and how constitute the 'political grammar' (Hemmings 2011) of a particular feminist narrative. For example, as a contestation and refusal of the historical and continued exclusion of women from the subject position of knowledge, feminist archives centre on feminists, especially those that Robyn Wiegman calls 'the namer' who become 'both the referent and agency for the analytic tradition she is taken to inaugurate and represent' (2012, 244). As Wiegman writes,

> Think here of Judith Butler's figural status in poststructuralist feminist theory or Gayatri Spivak's signatory representation of postcolonial deconstruction or Donna Haraway's canonical designation as the originator of cyborgian feminism or even Nancy Hartsock's textual centrality to feminist standpoint epistemologies. In these instances, the feminist archive has

elaborated a conversation through ongoing argument, contestation, and critical dissection about the analytic capacities and political utilities of each author's work *and* the texts that found of extend the tradition they represent. (2012, 244–245; emphasis in original)

As words such as 'figural', 'signatory', 'canonical' and 'originator' indicate, the citation of the work of feminist thinkers positions them as the authors, authorities and originators of feminist theory. In so doing, feminist citational practices re-member the landscape and genealogy of knowledge by claiming the specificity of feminist knowledge production. As Sara Ahmed writes, 'Citation is a feminist memory. Citation is how we acknowledge our debt to those who came before; those who helped us find our way when the way was obscured because we deviated from the paths we were told to follow' (2017, 15–16). In her book *Living a Feminist Life*, Ahmed states explicitly her citation policy, which is not citing any white men, is understood as the racialised and gendered structure of the academic institution. The insistence on citing feminist and anti-racist scholars is then a refusal to reproduce the institutional violence.

The positioning of feminist thinkers as the originators and signatories of knowledge has effectively challenged the routine exclusion and denigration of women as object, rather than subject, of knowledge. Nevertheless, critics have called into question the construction of feminist archive through citing and centring the work of white feminists located within West-European and Anglo-American contexts, which is seen to reproduce the whiteness of academic feminism. For example, Terese Jonsson observes the techniques that construct 'British feminism as a story that belongs to white women' that include '(1) the erasure of the work of British feminists of colour; (2) white feminist co-option of work by feminists of colour; and (3) the narration of feminist theory and politics as having "moved on" from racism' (2016, 50).

In an attempt to make visible and challenge the whiteness of academic feminism, feminist researchers have urged more inclusive citational practices. For example, Eve Tuck, K. Wayne Yang and Rubén Gaztambide-Fernández initiated the 'Citation Practices Challenge' (2015). As they write 'We often cite those who are more famous, even if their contributions appropriate subaltern ways of knowing. We also often cite those who frame problems in ways that speak against us. ... We aim to stop erasing Indigenous, Black, brown, trans*, disabled POC, QT*POC, feminist, activist, and disability/crip contributions from our intellectual genealogies'. Similarly, the continued absence of Sámi and Inuit contributions in the Nordic feminist archive (see, for example, Svendsen 2021; Dankersten 2021) has been criticised as attesting to the 'epistemic ignorance' (Kuokkanen 2007) in the Nordic region. As Rauna Kuokkanen notes, in a response to the question of whether there is any resistance within feminist academia to Sámi perspectives, 'I think the dismissiveness of white liberal feminism takes shape in the form of non-recognition, indifference, or plain ignorance. Nordic feminists don't openly resist Sámi perspectives on feminism, but they don't engage with them either. In fact, I am not sure if they even know that such things may exist' (Knobblock and Kuokkanen 2015, 278).

In view of this, the citation of the work of the marginalised is an important feminist ethical and critical practice that challenges the whiteness of feminist knowledge production. And yet, the inclusive citation practice may result in forms of appropriation and reification that re-centres whiteness, despite 'good intentions'.[1] For example, Ulrika Dahl shows the ways in which the displacement and absorption of the concept and analytical framework of intersectionality function to reproduce the whiteness of '(hegemonic) Nordic Academic feminism' (2021, 118). According to Dahl, the rhetorical movements include, for example, the broadening of intersectionality's genealogy that displaces its origin from black feminism (see also Bilge 2013). In other words, instead of conferring on the namer, the citational status and the original and authoritative signature of the theory as is often the case in feminist citational practices, Kimberle Crenshaw's theorisation of intersectionality is considered internal to and inheriting/extending from feminist collective and political endeavour to critically engage with the problem of difference. For example, it is argued that in so far Marxist feminism and queer theory concerns more than one categorical difference, they are performing 'intersectionality',[2] without using the term as such. The significance and specificity of intersectionality, and relatedly black feminist intellectual work, are thus flattened out.

Moreover, intersectionality, along with black feminism and postcolonial theory, is seen as 'useful additions' and elements of diversity to be included in the Nordic Academic feminism. More specifically, as Dahl makes clear, the usefulness of intersectionality is said to lie not so much in its attention to categorical differences and multiple forms of marginalisation, as in its foundation in questions of race and racism. In other words, intersectionality introduces the problem of race and whiteness that supplements and, hence, remains secondary concerns of the scholarly field of Nordic feminism whose primary concerns are questions of gender equality and sexual rights, and whose whiteness remains hegemonic and invisible.

As I see it, the inclusive citation practice performs and is shaped by the logic of remedy, and relatedly, the politics of completion, which inform the citation of intersectionality, and the work of feminists of colour have also been observed in the US context. For example, as Jennifer Nash notes, intersectionality is called upon to 'remedy feminism's histories of racism and exclusion … and imagined as the flip side of "white feminism," the kind of ethical, inclusive, and complex feminism required for feminists to revive – and to complete – their political project' (2018, 13). Citation as a form of remedial inclusion reifies the figure of black woman (and other feminists of colour) as 'the literal and epistemological bodies' that come to stand in and as race, on the one hand, and the figure of (hegemonic) feminism whose primary focus on gender excludes concerns of race, on the other hand. It is as if race can be simply present or absent – included or excluded – from feminist research. For Rey Chow, the remedial logic needs to be understood in its embeddedness in the 'corporate university milieu' (2021, 19). As Chow makes explicit,

> Contrary to the basis of disinterestedness that underpins classical humanistic inquiry, area-based and identity-based knowledge (and their representatives) are, within the corporate university milieu, thus aligned with an implicit solution to the problems that supposedly beset the conventional pursuits of Western knowledge. This problem-solving and, I would add, reparative logic whereby some kinds of knowledge carry the service function of delivering (or at least bringing us closet to) social justice and whose presence supposedly attests to a neoliberal academy's compassion, atonement, and capacity for 'self-culpabilization' mean that a certain kind of purpose … is systematically yoked to a part of humanistic inquiry in an attempt to rescue all of it. (2021, 19; emphasis in original)

It follows then that the remedial logic does not reconfigure relations of power in the process of knowledge production. Instead, it reinforces the predetermined relation between the norm, the hegemonic and its 'outside' that is filled by the bodies and/of knowledge of its geopolitical, disciplinary and identitarian other. And yet, this logic of remedy precisely necessitates the separation of different realms of knowledge and the continued subordination and marginalisation of the other/ed bodies and/of knowledge, for it is this predetermined difference – lack and excess – that carries the promise of progress and completion (see, for example, Hemmings 2011). This predetermined separation and hierarchical differentiation between forms of knowledge that are often seen to belong to certain bodies give rise to the following inter-related issues.

First, given that the visibility and recognition of marginalised others' intellectual labour often hinge on and produce a certain other/ed identity, the demand for inclusive citation goes hand in hand with forms of territorialisation and exclusion (through, for example, the absence of citation) of feminist work that is deemed difference epistemologically and politically. This investment in the ownership of knowledge is tellingly manifested in the demand for not simply citing, but correct citation – circulation – of intersectionality (by, for example, telling its correct origin story), and the rejection of its integration into the genealogy of hegemonic feminist thought (understood as white and indifferent to questions of race). By the same token, it informs the critique of the absence of reference to decolonial scholarly work in my presentation, which is considered distinct from postcolonial feminist theorisation. In other words, to do decolonial work requires a singular correct form of citing the decolonial text and their truthful and rightful owners.[3]

The simultaneous demand for inclusion and claim of ownership are often felt as defensiveness, which, as Nash asserts, in the context of debates on intersectionality, should be interpreted as an affective response to histories of institutional violence that has and, in many cases, continues to devalue and extract from black women's intellectual labour. Nevertheless, Nash is critical of the assertion of ownership over intersectionality, for it recuperates the logic of captivity and property. As Nash notes, this is ironic, for black feminist theory has been committed to reveal and challenge 'the racialized and gendered underpinnings of property – from theorizing "whiteness as property" to radically exposing how conceptions of property make possible forms of racially violent vigilantism' (2018, 136). Moreover, in so far as the citation of concepts such as intersectionality and decoloniality across various boarders – linguistic, disciplinary, geopolitical and epistemic – often results in their re-interpretation and translation, it is unclear how to draw the line between circulation and appropriation, or how to guard the identifying outline of these concepts against corruption and erosion by processes of interpretation and translation.

Second, the logic of property, ownership and territoriality that undergird the predetermined differentiation and separation of bodies and/of knowledge also informs the antagonism and suspicion which are the dominant modes and moods of critique in feminist research. This is not only manifested in the policing of citational practices and the demarcation between various forms of feminist knowledge, but also in the unequal distribution of critical attention on research objects, or what Chow observes as an implicit selection process. As Chow notes, one example is that 'a text by a white author is subject to dispute because it is, by default, considered symptomatic of Western imperialism and exploitation' (2021, 22). In contrast, 'the non-Western X is often preassigned a politicized status and fixed in an externally imposed role – as the witting or unwitting harbinger of repair and purification' (Chow 2021, 22). Although not new, this form of suspicious and antagonistic critique is currently encountered with heightened tension, anxiety and fatigue in the field of feminist studies, in particular, and in the globalised and corporatised university in general.

Despite their challenge to essentialist conceptions of difference, these modes of critique are often informed by the conflation of 'bodies of knowledge and the racially marked bodies of the scholars' (Nash 2018, 14). This predetermined fixation of the subject and *its* object of knowledge also takes form in the various policing of who can cite as and for whom. For example, in her response to Barbara Tomlinson's (2013) critique of the appropriation of intersectionality by European intersectionality scholars, Kathy Davis writes, 'Tomlinson makes no reference to her own racialised position as a white woman who, wittingly or not, is invariably complicit in the histories of racism and imperialism of her own country. She neither acknowledges her own location as a tenured academic in the neoliberal university might shape the way she frames her arguments … Rather she unreflexively situates herself, along with other "true" US intersectionality scholars, as gatekeepers in need of protecting "their" (whose*) theory from "unauthorized" interlopers' (2020, 120).

Here, the predetermined ownership and property that fixes the relation between the subject and object of knowledge, in the sense that each defines and identifies the other, informs *both* the critique of appropriation and its counter-argument. For Davis, Tomlinson's argument is itself appropriating in so far as she cannot speak *as*, but *for*, '"ruue" US intersectionality scholars'. This is because Tomlinson is privileged both as a 'white woman' and as a 'tenured academic in a neoliberal university'. It seems then that reification and separation of different bodies of/and knowledge, and their social relations conceived of as defined by indebtedness, trespassing and appropriation, function as the starting point and conclusion of feminist ethics of citation and its critique. The question that remains is how the demand for correct and inclusive citation sits together with feminist commitment against the logic of coloniality and essentialised notions of hierarchical differences.

The Use/Less Citation

Citation is useful. As the foregoing discussion has hopefully shown, to cite a particular body and/of work can be used to distinguish the different strands of feminist thoughts and to perform a specific feminist narrative. For example, the citation of decolonial scholarship, *rather than* feminist postcolonial theories, signals the promise of transcending the limit of postcolonial thinking (its embeddedness in and loyalty to the epistemic system of modernity). Citation is also useful, as it can be a confirmation and reproduction of the authority of the namer. For example, the repeated citation of certain feminist scholars as originators of feminist thoughts, often abstracted from the collective intellectual labour that informs them, supports the claim on the legitimacy and specificity of feminist knowledge. Citing certain bodies and/of knowledge that are considered valuable can also affirm the value of the citation, and the work that the citation is part of.

Citation is also a technique that promotes diversity and inclusivity. The citation of the work by subjects whose voice and intellectual labour have been erased and appropriated is an important technique for making them visible and recognised. And yet, it could also be the case that the citation of the other/ed work functions as a non-performative apology that signals the overcoming of the limits of the field without actually critically engaging with the other/ed work in a way that would radically reconfigure the relations of power in the process of research and knowledge production. In this sense, citation functions to solicit the other, whose existence is supplementary, and hence disposable, to provide the service of remedy and repair. Citation could also be used as an affective resistance to being incorporated and appropriated. For example, the insistence on correct citation of intersectionality as black feminist property can be read as a refusal of double erasure – black women are reduced to object rather than the subject of knowledge, *and* their intellectual labour is appropriated in being subsumed in the genealogy of white feminism.

In view of this, it could be said the use of citation centres on the logic of ownership and its corollary assumptions about property and debt. My point here is not to announce citation's uselessness and suggest its abandonment so as to radically destabilise the hold of – affective attachment in – the logic of ownership. To do this would be to project, and rush to fill in, an outside of citation and the form of feminist knowledge it produces, that promises to amend its ills, transcend its limits, as if the demarcation between inside and outside, and the narrative of overcoming, are not themselves forms of territoriality. Moreover, to refuse to cite might conveniently erase the voice of those who have struggled and are struggling to be listened to and engaged with. I contend that the problem is not so much citation itself, but how it is used, or how certain rather than other uses become valued.

Rethinking citation thus requires reconsidering its use. To cite also means to 'set in motion, to call, invite, to move to and fro'.[4] Citation then is inter-subjective. It produces the addressed and the solicitor. It is also the irreducible movement that *is* their dynamic relationality. It follows then that citation not simply concerns who cites whom, what and how, but also whom is invited/solicited/cited to cite, and what structures of circulation – the motion of to and fro – that conditions this specific relationality of citation. I think here of the figure of (bio)degradable that Jacques Derrida contemplated in the essay 'Biodegradables Seven Diary Fragments', in which Derrida responded to the critique of Paul de Man as well as deconstruction by insisting on the need to read and engage. The history of Paul de Man's war is beyond the scope of this article. What interests me is the ways in which the figure of (bio)degradable assists a rethinking of citation and its use/lessness. As Derrida mulls,

> [A] text must be da(bio)degradable' in order to nourish the 'living' culture, memory, tradition. To the extent to which it has some sense, make sense, then its 'content' irrigates the milieu of this tradition and its 'formal' identity is dissolved. And by formal identity, one may understand here all the 'signifiers,' including the title and the name of one or more presumed signatories. And yet, to enrich the 'organic' soil of the said culture, it must also resist it, contest it, question and criticize it enough … and thus it must not be assimilable ([bio]degradable, if you like). (1989, 845)

The figure of the (bio)degradable for Derrida sheds light on the strange kinship between waste, which is dissolved, assimilated, circulated and whose identity is broken open and apart, and the masterpiece, which precisely resists the process of assimilation and decomposition. Interestingly, the use of the text – *its* contribution to the culture/memory/tradition that also conditions its intelligibility and significance – necessitates its dissolution and assimilation. However, in order to nourish the culture, to animate its metabolic process, the immediate assimilation and disappearance must be resisted through forms of engagement – 'contest it, question and criticize it enough'. The use of text – its citation and circulation – is thus displaced from the logic of ownership to the dynamic ecological relationality, the to and fro of assimilation and resistance.

What resists? In her recent book *What's the use: On the use of use*, Ahmed reflects on her own citation practices:

> In living a feminist Life (2017), I had a rather blunt citation policy, which was not to cite any white men. In this book, I have not been able to have such a policy: following use has meant engaging with the history of utilitarianism, which is a history of books written mainly by white men. Even if I have been critical of this history, use as reuse, I kept it alive. A reuse is still a use, damn it! If I have their names, I am not writing to them, or for them. I write to, for, those who are missing, whose names are not known, whose names cannot be used: those who are faint, becoming faint, fainter still. (2019, 213; emphasis in original)

Ahmed's reflection alludes to the possibility of use/less citation. Despite the citation of the work by white men, the cited – the reader, the cited names that are not known and that are not visibly cited, the solicitor herself – is read, heard and felt as a resistance that disrupts the logic of ownership that undergirds the authoritative designation of the namer. Rather than focusing on who cites, whom, what and how, I suggest shifting attention to the to and fro movement that is the use/less citation of feminist research.

Notes

1. Dahl associates whiteness as an epistemic habit with 'innocence' and 'good intentions' (2021, 118).
2. As Dahl writes, 'Marxist feminism is an "intersection" of class and gender, and "queer theory" of gender and sexuality. A range of texts addressing the subject of feminism, from the sexual difference theory of Rosi Braidotti and Luce Irigaray to Trinh T. Minh-ha's and Donna Haraway's in/appropriated other(s) are thus presented as examples of intersectionality and of "difference"' (2021, 119).
3. It is important to note that Mignolo has warned against the commodification of decoloniality as property. As Mignolo cautions, 'Another danger is the commodification of decoloniality as the property of a group of individuals (i.e., the modernity/[de]coloniality project) and as a new *canon* of sorts, both of which erase and shroud decoloniality's terrain of political project, praxis, and struggle.' (2018, 82; emphasis in original).
4. Accessed 5 March 2021. https://www.etymonline.com/word/cite.

Disclosure Statement

No potential conflict of interest was reported by the author(s).

References

Ahmed, Sara. 2017. *Living a Feminist Life*. Durham: Duke University Press.
Ahmed, Sara. 2019. *What's the Use: On the Uses of Use*. Durham: Duke University Press.
Bhambra, Gurminder K. 2014. "Postcolonial and Decolonial Dialogue." *Postcolonial Studies* 17 (2): 115–121. doi:10.1080/13688790.2014.966414.
Bilge, Sirma. 2013. "Intersectionality Undone: Saving Intersectionality from Feminist Intersectionality Studies." *Du Bois Review* 10 (2): 405–424. doi:10.1017/S1742058X13000283.
Chang, Chia-ju, ed. 2019. *Chinese Environmental Humanities: Practices of Environing at the Margins*. Cham: Palgrave Macmillan.
Chow, Rey. 2021. *A Face Drawn in Sand: Humanistic Inquiry and Foucault in the Present*. New York: Columbia University Press.
Dahl, Ulrika. 2021. "Nordic Academic Feminism and Whiteness as Epistemic Habit." In *Feminisms in the Nordic Region: Neoliberalism, Nationalism and Decolonial Critique*, edited by Suvi Keskinen, Pauline Stoltz, and Diana Mulinari, 113–134. Cham: Palgrave Macmillan.
Dankersten, Astri. 2021. "Indigenising Nordic Feminism – A Sámi Decolonial Critique." In *Feminisms in the Nordic Region: Neoliberalism, Nationalism and Decolonial Critique*, edited by Suvi Keskinen, Pauline Stoltz, and Diana Mulinari, 135–154. Cham: Palgrave Macmillan.
Davis, Kathy. 2020. "Who Owns Intersectionality? Some Reflections on Feminist Debates on How Theories Travel." *European Journal of Women's Studies* 27 (2): 113–127. doi:10.1177/1350506819892659.
Derrida, Jacques, and Peggy Kamuf. 1989. "Biodegradables Seven Diary Fragments." *Critical Inquiry* 15: 812–873. doi:10.1086/448522.
Gaztambide-Fernández, Rubén, Eve Tuck, and K. Wayne Yang. 2015. "Citation Practice Challenge." *Critical Ethnic Studies* (Blog), April 2015. Accessed 5 March 2021. http://www.criticalethnicstudiesjournal.org/citation-practices
Harney, Stefano, and Fred Moten. 2013. *The Undercommons: Fugitive Planning & Black Study*. Wivehoe: Minor Compositions.
Hemmings, Clare. 2011. *Why Stories Matter: The Political Grammar of Feminist Theory*. Durham: Duke University Press.
Jonsson, Terese. 2016. "The Narrative Reproduction of White Feminist Racism." *Feminist Review* 113: 50–67. doi:10.1057/fr.2016.2.
Knobblock, Ina, and Rauna Kuokkanen. 2015. "Decolonizing Feminism in the North: A Conversation with Rauna Kuokkanen." *Nora: Nordic Journal of Feminist and Gender Research* 23 (4): 275–281. doi:10.1080/08038740.2015.1090480.
Kuokkanen, Rauna. 2007. *Reshaping the University: Responsibility, Indigenous Espistemes, and the Logic of the Gift*. Vancouver: UBC Press.
Mendoza, Breny. 2016. "Coloniality of Gender and Power: From Postcoloniality to Decoloniality." In *The Oxford Handbook of Feminist Theory*, edited by Lisa Disch and Mary Hawkesworth, 100–121. New York: Oxford University Press.
Mignolo, Walter, and Catherine E. Walsh. 2018. *On Decoloniality: Concepts, Analytics, Praxsis*. Durham: Duke University Press.
Nash, Jennifer C. 2018. *Black Feminism Reimagined: After Intersectionality*. Durham: Duke University Press.
Spivak, Gayatri C. 1993. *Outside in the Teaching Machine*. New York: Routledge.
Svendsen, Stine H. Bang. 2021. "Saami Women at the Threshold of Disappearance: Elsa Laula Renberg (1877–1931) and Karin Stenberg's (1884–1969) Challenges to Nordic Feminism." In *Feminisms in the Nordic Region: Neoliberalism, Nationalism and Decolonial Critique*, edited by Suvi Keskinen, Pauline Stoltz, and Diana Mulinari, 155–176. Cham: Palgrave Macmillan.
Tlostanova, Madina. 2010. *Gender Epistemologies and Eurasian Borderlands*. New York: Palgrave Macmillan.
Tomlinson, Barbara. 2013. "Colonizing Intersectionality: Replicating Racial Hierarchy in Feminist Academic Arguments." *Social Identities* 19 (2): 254–272. doi:10.1080/13504630.2013.789613 .
Trinh, Minh-ha T. 2016. *Lovecidal: Walking with the Disappeared*. New York: Fordham University Press.
Wiegman, Robyn. 2012. *Object Lessons*. Durham: Duke University Press.

Embracing Amateurs: Four Practices to Subvert Academic Gatekeeping

Michelle Moravec

ABSTRACT
Citational practices function as a form of academic gatekeeping. To create a more inclusive scholarship, authors must consciously commit to embracing the contributions of all researchers, including amateurs. I base my case on Mildred Crowl Martin's biography of Donaldina Cameron, a New Zealand-born moral reformer in San Francisco's Chinatown. Martin undertook extensive original research during the late 1960s, and materials she compiled form the basis for an archival collection at Stanford University that researchers still consult today. However, Martin also admitted to incorporating a 'few fictionalized scenes' into her biography, and because she wrote for a popular audience, Martin omitted references in her texts. These two decisions left her vulnerable to charges of amateurism. Nonetheless, more than fifty monographs, book chapters, and journal articles from the 1980s to the present cited her biography. This success makes a fascinating case study for deriving research practices that fulfil our intellectual debts to all predecessors.

Feminist academics have challenged scholars to think harder about who we reference in our work. As Sara Ahmed argues, citations are a form of 'feminist memory' through which we 'acknowledge our debt to those who came before' and credit 'those who helped us find our way when the way was obscured because we deviated from the paths we were told to follow' (2017, 15–16). In selecting who to cite, we have the opportunity to legitimize past scholarship and accord it greater status. Feminist geographers observe that citational practices are also key to a more inclusive future, as 'a tool for either the reification of or resistance to, unethical hierarchies of knowledge production' (Mott and Cockayne 2017, 954). By incorporating work produced beyond academia, we help to subvert academic gatekeeping. As feminist scholars noted in the 1970s, gatekeepers 'set the standards, produce the social knowledge, monitor what is admitted to the systems of distribution, and decree the innovations in thought, or knowledge, or values' (D. E. Smith 1978 quoted in Spender and Spender 1983). Academic gatekeeping often thwarts a fundamental premise of feminist research 'to seek out the perspectives of those who have historically been marginalized from active inclusion in the knowledge-building process' (Leavy and Harris 2018, 104). We function as gatekeepers, whether we wish to or not, but this position means we have the power to undermine scholarly hierarchies and to broaden the range of work circulated via academic publications. To create this more inclusive scholarship, authors must consciously commit to embracing the contributions of all researchers.

While most reflections on citational practices focus on authors within the academy, this essay joins other recent calls for greater attentiveness to the contribution of amateurs. I base my case for embracing amateurs based on the unlikely success of Mildred Crowl Martin's biography of Donaldina Cameron, *Chinatown's Angry Angel* (1977). Cameron, born in New Zealand in 1869, immigrated to California as a child. In 1895 she volunteered at the San Francisco Presbyterian Mission Home, a shelter for Chinese women who had escaped prostitution. While initially intending to devote a year to teaching needlework, Cameron worked closely with the superintendent, who she eventually replaced. Throughout her career, Cameron authored many articles for the popular and religious press, entertained a president, and became a subject of a biography before she had even retired (Wilson 1931). Martin became a journalist and then biographer relatively late in life after some years as a teacher. Although not formally educated as a historian, Martin drew on skills developed in her prior occupations to conduct original research about her subject. The reports and articles authored by Cameron provided ample details about her work, but she left a diary for only one year, leading Martin to conducted interviews with Cameron's peers and friends to gain further insights into her personal life. Martin also studied under historical novelist Dorothy James Roberts and incorporated a 'few fictionalized scenes' into her 'story' of Cameron's life (1977, 7). Since its publication in 1977, more than fifty authors of monographs, book chapters, and journal articles have cited *Chinatown's Angry Angel* as an authoritative source. That total does not include the many works of fiction that incorporate Cameron based on Martin's book.

Analysis of the process by which Cameron's biography became accepted by academic authors provides insights into research practices that subvert academic gatekeeping – cite, acknowledge, discuss and contextualize the work of all researchers. While the case study presented here derives from the discipline of history, the argument applies to all fields of scholarly inquiry. Similarly, while I view these recommendations as part of feminist research practices, they also pertain to researchers who do not consider themselves feminists. Finally, I frame my suggestions within existing professional guidelines and augment them with additional examples to illustrate that my argument is not as far-fetched as it might initially appear.

What is an Amateur?

Resistance to my proposal may come simply from invoking a fraught term – amateur. The definition of amateur proves frustratingly slippery. The label has been applied to individuals who research without receiving remuneration (Arnold 2000, 57). Amateurs are also said to be identifiable by their method, deviating from the disciplinary-specific practices that came to dominate within the academy (King 2011, 16). Another definition consigns anyone without advanced degrees to the realm of amateurism (Tuchman 2011, 57). Vocation has also been used to identify amateurs; professionals occupy positions in the academy, amateurs follow an avocation (Bell and Whitfield 1996, 22). How amateur is defined may ultimately be of less significance than its function in establishing hierarchies of value within academia, whose work is acknowledged and whose is marginalized

(Cronon 2012; Kammen 2014; Townsend 2014)? In the case of history, as in so many disciplines, the distinction between amateur and professional occurred in the process of credentialing researchers. In the late nineteenth century, trained historians distanced themselves from their untrained contemporaries as part of a series of strategic moves to gain greater status and legitimacy (Hamerow 1990; Wright 2005; Tyrrell 2005; Tuchman 2011). By the twentieth century, the role of historian came to be synonymous with a professor of history. Local historians have been at the forefront of objections to this arbitrary dividing line. As the editors of the *Encyclopedia of Local History* note, 'there has been some recent discomfort with the word as amateur came to mean the opposite of 'professional' or 'academic'" (Wilson 2017, 25). Local historians also pointedly challenge the notion that credentials ensure quality scholarship by observing that 'academic history = professional = good' falsely implies all other work is unprofessional and bad (Dymond 2011, 25). Independent scholar or researcher could well replace the term amateur; they appear instead in the remainder of this essay.

Gender and Amateurism in Academia

The process of professionalizing history in the nineteenth century excluded most women. Although Kate Everest earned the first doctorate granted to a woman in history by an American university in 1893, few women followed (Des Jardins 2003, 34). Doubly excluded by sex and race, African American women functioned as historians without 'portfolio,' even as Anna Julia Cooper became the first black woman to earn a doctorate in history in 1924 (Dagbovie 2010, 100–103). Independent researchers continued to participate in historical endeavours in the first half of the twentieth century, but most authors wrote from the margins of academia or as outright outsiders (DuBois 1991a, 1991b; Scott 1988; Parfait 2020). As historian became defined as a male-occupation, topics considered worthy of scholarly significance centred on white men's political activities alone, and deviation risked relegating an author to the realm of amateurism (Offen, Pierson, and Rendall 1991; Smith 2000; Spongberg 2002; Smith 2007; Dagbovie 2007; White 2009; Dagbovie 2010; Alberti 2014; Parfait, Dantec-Lowry, and Bourhis-Mariotti 2016; Spongberg, Curthoys, and Caine 2005; Snyder 2018). The tendency to dismiss the work produced beyond the academy is also exacerbated by biases against particular subjects, such as women's history. Finally, specific types of historical writing gained greater prestige within academic circles, with genres such as biography and local histories viewed as inherently less important.

Gender, subject, and genre intersect in the sexist biases that often condemn biographies of women written by women (Alpern et al. 1992; Caine 2010; Culley 2014; Mitchell 2000). Female biographers have faced challenges to the materials, methods, and merits of their work. The 'struggles to find sufficient and reliable documentation' meant biographers often deviated from the narrow forms of historical evidence, considering 'photographs and other nonliterary materials... oral evidence, the testimony of children, relatives, and friends of our subjects,' and to 'fill the gaps,' biographers also relied on 'unusual' methodologies (Alpern et al. 12). Biography was frequently accused of 'exaggerate[ing] the importance of individuals in history,' a charge easy to make about female subjects who did not participate in politics or public life (Alpern et al. 13). For this reason, historians of women have been forced to provide thoughtful analyses of the genre.[1]

The dismissal of female biographers reflects sexism within academia, and feminist researchers are not exempt from this bias. Gerda Lerner's early typology of the development of women's history consigned the history of women worthies, a phrase borrowed from Natalie Zemon Davis to the earliest, and by implication, less sophisticated phases of the field, and this belittling attitude continued well into the 1990s (Lerner 1975; Davis 1976; Hoff 1992). Bonnie Smith argues that a focus on 'women's achievements' by 'amateurs and a few professional historians carried women's history across a mine field of rebuke' long before the field found a place in academia (Smith 1993, 1049), yet the fear of association with amateurism continues to exist. As one scholar recently lamented, 'many historians of women and gender remain, to some extent, embarrassed by their field's origins' (Chernock 2013, 130).

This embarrassment may be compounded by the gendered ageism often attached to independent female researchers. Ageism in academia is a problem that has received increased attention in recent years ("Statement on Age Discrimination" 2017; Gullette 2018), but academics have long exhibited ageist attitudes, as in the 'elderly swells who dabble' condemned by one academic historian in 1889 (Kammen 1996, 108). Even when acknowledging independent researchers, scholars often denote their age, pointing to 'an elderly retired enthusiast' (Longair 2016, 117). While any individual might be described as 'a history buff...enthusiastic about some aspect of history without, the word implies, a serious, contextual knowledge' (Kammen and Wilson 2012), a gendered ageist variant exists in 'the stereotypical elderly female volunteer,' (Howe 1990, 44) in the 'gendered characterization of amateur (and local) history as the work of elderly, possibly eccentric, women' and in the trope of 'little old ladies in tennis shoes' (Boutilier and Prentice 2011, 5). Unwarranted assumptions about the poor quality of work produced beyond academia become an even greater problem for the older female independent scholar like Martin.

Critical Reception of *Chinatown's Angry Angel*

Four academic journals assigned *Chinatown's Angry Angel* to reviewers, a somewhat surprising occurrence given Martin's outsider status. The disparities between prevailing academic expectations and Martin's research practices became a point of contention in these reviews. Martin subtitled her biography the story of Donaldina Cameron. In this regard, Martin was like many local historians Kammen describes – individuals who 'came into the field [of history] from the newspaper world; ... interested in telling a good story, in attracting and keeping readers ... They gathered their information where they could and from whoever had a tale to tell. They repeated what they heard in such a way as to amuse and entertain' (1996, 106). Martin's preface details her motivation: 'In a time of turmoil when people search for identity, freedom and social reforms, it seems appropriate to tell the story of a woman who lived through another tumultuous period' (5). The implicit thesis that Cameron could serve as a role model was similar to the motivations of other academically trained historians at the time. Reflecting on the early days of the field, one historian remembered: 'the importance of uncovering the life stories of women forebears to serve as role models to define ourselves and our careers in a male-dominated, masculinized profession' (Banner 2009, 579).

Reviewers nonetheless found many faults with *Chinatown's Angry Angel*. Donald MacInnis, a Methodist minister who served as director of an academic think tank, praised the 'extensive research and interviews' conducted by Martin but decried the lack of 'scholarly analysis of the social, economic and demographic dynamics' (1979, 176–77). Philip P. Choy, an architect-turned-historian who taught at San Francisco State University, ignored Martin's original research contributions. The bibliographic essay in *Chinatown's Angry Angel* indicates Martin consulted books, magazines, church publications, and newspapers, as well as Cameron's correspondence from 1888 until her death, expense logs, professional writings, and official reports. Still, Choy claims Martin's 'story … is by no means new' and argues that Martin is simply 're-telling' and 'regurgitates' from a book published four decades earlier (1978, 321). Gunther Barth, a history professor at the University of California, Berkeley, expresses concerns about the lack of direct citations. Martin's preface anticipated this criticism. She emphasizes her adherence to the primary sources: 'for the conversations quoted in the text, I have recorded verbatim those repeated by Miss Cameron, her relatives, and friends. Other quotations come directly from her reports, her diary, notes for speeches, and her writings' (1977, 6–7). Nonetheless, Barth finds the 'lack of footnotes or specific references limits the usefulness of the study for scholarship' (1978, 508).

The most sustained criticism of Martin came from Laurene Wu McClain, a lawyer and scholar of international relations who taught history at the City College of San Francisco. In the *Pacific Historical Review*, McClain concurs with McInnis (1979) regarding the 'need for a scholarly analysis,' and like Barth, she questions the omission of direct references. However, McClain also claims that she left 'important questions unanswered' (1979, 304). In 1983, McClain expanded these criticisms into a full-length essay that contests three aspects of *Chinatown's Angry Angel*. She highlights the issue of 'attributed dialogue' (1983, 31) in relation to a particularly problematic passage in the biography. McClain introduces the excerpt with 'Mildred Martin quotes Cameron as having written,' which seems to accept Martin's explanation for the lack of footnotes (31), and her references reveal a reliance on Martin's book (35, fn2, fn 7, fn 11). However, in the following sentence, McClain adds the phrase 'assuming accuracy' in Martin's work which introduces doubts about its reliability (31). McClain also disputes Martin's interpretation of Cameron's nickname 'Lo Mo,' a colloquial form of mother given to her by mission home residents as a mark of their affection. While McClain agrees that early residents initiated Cameron's nickname, she claims Cameron made clear the 'expectation that [subsequent] residents would call her 'Lo Mo'' (30) even if the women were the same age or older than Cameron. Finally, McClain takes issue with Martin's depiction of Cameron as a beloved figure in Chinatown, suggesting 'there is little evidence that Cameron's efforts enjoyed wide support in Chinatown' (27).

With ambiguous reviews in academic journals and an article that directly challenged Martin, how did *Chinatown's Angry Angel* become the foundational text about Donaldina Cameron? Part of Martin's success can be attributed to her fortuitous timing. *Chinatown's Angry Angel* appeared as women's history became a well-established field. Graduate students picked up Martin's work in the decade after its publication. Peggy Pascoe's dissertation *Relations of Rescue*, completed at Stanford University in 1986 and published in 1990, took on the dominant social control interpretation of female reformers. This intervention led to the rehabilitation of women like Cameron and validation of Martin's research. Martin's biography of Cameron also appeared, although more briefly, in a second work of women's history. Judy Yung's dissertation in ethnic studies at UC Santa Cruz (1990), published as *Unbound Feet: A Social History of Chinese Women in San Francisco* (1995), also helped to legitimize Martin's biography.

The treatment of *Chinatown's Angry Angel* by Pascoe and Yung scholars offers insights into how we might credit our predecessors who do not conform to the most rigid scholarly practices. Based on their example, I derived four specific research practices to embrace amateurs fully: acknowledge, cite, discuss, and contextualize their work. These recommendations are framed by professional guidelines and augmented with additional examples from academic scholarship to reinforce that my suggestions do not require significant deviation from our current obligations and that precedents exist.

Four Practices to Subvert Academic Gatekeeping

All guidelines from historical associations spell out researchers' commitments to one another. What is less apparent is how independent researchers fit into these guidelines. The 2005 version of the American Historical Association Statement on Standards of Professional Conduct indicates, 'Membership in this profession is defined by self-conscious identification with a community of historians.' While this language disappeared in the 2017 revision, self-defined participants are still clearly addressed as part of 'the community of inquiry' ("Statement on Standards of Professional Conduct" 2019). The Canadian Historical Association defines 'Historians' as people who 'work in a variety of contexts' ("Statement on Research Ethics" n.d.). Some guidelines refer specifically to uncredentialed individuals. The Inclusive Historian's Handbook describes public history as a collaboration between 'professional practitioners' and 'partners having no formal academic training' (Bryans 2019). A guideline to museum ethics discusses 'museum work, whether volunteer or paid' ("AAM Code of Ethics for Museums" 2020). The Code of Practice for Professional Historians Association of New Zealand/Aotearoa succinctly references 'others' admonishing members, 'Give credit to others where appropriate,' while Parks Canada recognizes the 'knowledge, expertise and suggestions' of all 'Canadians' ("Code of Practice" n.d.; Parks Canada Agency 2018).

On this question of inclusivity, the field of local history provides an exemplary model. The Federation of Australian Historical Societies highlights the achievements of its volunteer members who 'collect documents and images, research and publish history, present public lectures, and exhibitions, protect and preserve built and place heritage, collect material objects and exhibit them in museums, and make an invaluable contribution to heritage tourism' ("About" n.d.). The British Association For Local History emphasizes that 'amateur and professional can meet and work profitably together' ("The British Association for Local History [BALH]" 2009). The American Association for State and Local History offers a sweeping invitation to all 'history-doers,' which includes individuals who 'work at a history organization, teach history, are studying public history or museum studies, volunteer at a historic house museum, research and write history in your spare time, or practice local history and public history in any other capacity' ("Membership" n.d.). I take the position that professional guidelines should apply to all 'history-doers,' not just to academically-situated colleagues.

Acknowledge

Researchers must acknowledge people whose assistance facilitated their work. For example, the Australian Historical Association requires that 'Members shall in published work or public statements make due acknowledgment of the work of others' ("Our Code of Conduct" n.d.). While it is more common to find archivists and librarians named, precedents exist to incorporate other individuals, including independent scholars. The author of a biography about Ida C. Craddock, a sexual reformer and popularizer of yoga, highlights the crucial roles of two non-professionals in his acknowledgments. The first individual 'amassed a remarkable archive,' without which his 'book could not have been written,' while the second person had the 'foresight' to preserve materials that 'would have been lost' (Schmidt 2010, 317). Similarly, in the case Martin, Pascoe discusses the challenges of finding sources that she faced as a doctoral candidate, noting that she located one 'treasure trove' of sources on a closet floor (1990, xxiii). Pascoe thanks Martin for the generous access to her 'personal research notes and photographs' (1990, viii). By incorporating Martin into her acknowledgments, Pascoe recognizes Martin's contribution to compiling materials about Cameron long before an archive existed. Martin's contribution is hardly unique. Local history associations have long emphasized the role of their members in preserving historical materials. In 1971, librarian and editor Whitfield J. Bell, Jr. commented, 'not a year passes that some library does not receive a collection made by some enthusiast for history.... such collections are among the principal contributions that anyone can make to the study and writing of history' (1996, 24).

Cite

Citations credit earlier works on which a researcher relied. The American Historical Association recommends 'generous citations' as a defense against possible plagiarism accusations, but such generosity should be considered more expansively ("Statement on Standards of Professional Conduct" 2019). Bell Jr. reminds us that independent historians have often preceded subsequent academically employed scholars. Their 'determination to present a truthful record' has 'furnish[ed] material for other, but not necessarily better, writers of history' (1996, 25). All researchers' contributions to the development of a subject should be credited in direct citations. Pascoe cites Martin only once in *Relations of Rescue*, but Yung carefully mines Martin's biography for the information it provides about Chinese women's lives in an era with scant historical documentation (1995, 39, fn85, 74–75, fn67). Yung notes that 'uncovering and piecing together the history of Chinese American women has not been an easy task. There are few written records to begin with, and what little material does exist on the subject is full of inaccuracies and distortions' (1995, 9). Yung relies so heavily on Martin's biography that she cites it almost as many times as she cites Pascoe's award-winning work. These citations create the trail of evidence that leads back to Martin, indicating her central role in creating Cameron's history.

Carolyn Karcher's biography of the nineteenth-century author and reformer Lydia Maria Child offers an excellent example of incorporating direct citations to a range of researchers. As Karcher notes, Child 'languish[ed] in obscurity' for nearly a century until freelance writer Helene Gilbert Baer published *The Heart Is Like Heaven: The Life of Lydia Maria Child* in 1964 (1994, xii). The following year, Milton Meltzer published *Tongue of Flame: The Life of Lydia Maria Child*. Although his biography aimed at a juvenile audience, Meltzer co-edit Child's correspondence, a move credited as 'the real breakthrough' moment in Child scholarship (Karcher 1994, xii). Karcher's footnotes meticulously place the references to Child's earliest biographers before indicating works by subsequent formally trained scholars. In providing details about Child's husband's involvement in a legal case, the first alerts the reader to the appropriate page in Baer's biography and Melzer's collection of her letters, only then citing a 1992 biography written by an author with training in history (Karcher 1994, 686).

Discuss

Direct acknowledgment and citations are the bare minimum that professional standards require. A generosity towards our intellectual debts should extend to a fuller discussion of works produced beyond the academy. Both Pascoe and Yung consider Martin's work as part of historiographical debates. In the process, both authors address McClain's criticisms of Martin and find them unwarranted. Pascoe confirms that the passage McClain questioned came from Cameron, thus quashing the notion that Martin was an unreliable researcher (1990, 250fn30). Both Pascoe and Yung also concur with Martin's interpretation of Camron's actions and reputation. Pascoe refutes McClain's assertion that Cameron coerced the Lo Mo nickname, stating, 'One historian has suggested that the use of the term ... was 'expected' ... but I have found no specific evidence to support her claim' (104). Yung also accepts the nickname and rejects McClain's claim that Cameron was disdainful towards the Chinese: 'Although some historians have criticized Cameron for her patronizing attitude and the regimented way in which she ran the Mission Home, those who knew and worked with her have only high regard for her work among the Chinese' (1995, 74). Even if such an extensive historiographical discussion does not occur in the text, expository footnotes should incorporate amateur work. Yung offers only one brief historiographical footnote in her work, but it incorporates Martin: 'For different assessments of Donaldina Cameron, see McClain, "Donaldina Cameron"; Martin, Chinatown's Angry Angel; Pascoe, Relations of Rescue; and Mason, "Social Christianity"' (327) In their discussion of Martin's biography, Pascoe and Yung both credit her work and validate its reliability as a source, clearing the path for subsequent scholars to rely on it.

Another excellent model for incorporating discussion of independent researchers as part of evolving scholarship may be found in Lynn Marie Hudson's biography of Mary Ellen Pleasant, an African American entrepreneur, which relies on a wide range of studies. In discussing a much-debated event in Pleasant's life, Hudson draws on Helen Holdredge, the first biographer of Pleasant, who, as she notes, 'became the single most influential person to shape Pleasant's legacy' while also amassing 'an extraordinary collection of materials' that make up her primary archive (2003, 4–5). Hudson (2009) next considers an 'unpublished and undocumented' manuscript attributed to a 'Pleasant enthusiast' before offering her account of what 'seems most likely' to have happened (25–26). Generosity here expands beyond acknowledgment and citation practices to credit all antecedents in scholarly debates, giving them a valid place in the literature.

Contextualize

Finally, subsequent scholars should consider the context of a work. The code of practice for The Professional Historians Association of New Zealand/Aotearoa requires members to 'acknowledge the diversity of historical scholarship and the right of others to take different approaches,' while the *Working Group on Evaluating Public History Scholarship* stipulates that historians should 'honor the range of scholarly methodologies employed in the profession.' Academics might bemoan the lack of scholarly context in a work they consider amateurish, but independent scholars writing for an audience outside academic might equally object that it is the academic who is missing the larger context. Among *Chinatown's Angry Angel* reviewers, only McClain mentions that Martin wrote a popular biography, not a scholarly tome. One self-described academic biographer notes that significant differences exist between a text produced for an academic audience and one meant for a general readership. Popular biographies 'often have shorter chapters … and try to find ways of avoiding footnotes and endnotes, which are thought to discourage the general reader' (Potter 2018, 392). Martin's original manuscript contains references, but like many popular biographies, the published book omitted them ("Guide to the Mildred Martin Papers" n.d.), although that did not preclude Young and Pascoe from relying on her work. Similarly, the author of *Thomas Hardy: A Companion to the Novels*, recommends 'several biographies written for an educated general audience' as 'entirely appropriate to supplement' the acknowledged definitive work and credentialed full professors from elite institutions, such as Jill Lepore, publish lightly sourced or unreferenced works when writing for a public audience (Morrison 2021, 29; Lepore 2014, 2015; "5 Questions for Jill Lepore" 2014). Finally, regarding Martin's fictionalized scenes, authors in the field of speculative biography have usedsimilar strategies to great acclaim (Curthoys 2006; Bahadur 2013; Fuentes 2016; Lindsey 2016; Hartman 2021). As Jane McVeigh reflects on the factual versus fictional biography split, form may be of less significance than content when it comes to telling life story (2018, 146). As these examples indicate, the claim that a fixed and unwavering set of research practicesunites academics is inaccurate. Variability exists; we simply accord some authors more latitude than others.

Conclusion

Researchers who have gained entrée to academia must attend to those individuals excluded by gatekeeping practices, both past and present. Mildred Crowl Martin's biography of Donaldina Cameron represents just one example in a rich vein of largely ignored historical writing that took place beyond the academy.[2] I encourage more scholars to recognize that so-called 'amateurs are not always ineffectual dabblers (nor are professionals necessarily more expert)' (Bell and Whitfield 1996, 22). Amateur status is just one of the barriers within the academy. In Martin's case, marginalization related to gender and age may have amplified the too-typical dismissal of work seen as amateurish. For other authors, race, social class, or educational attainment may exacerbate existing biases. We cannot allow old boundaries of occupation, compensation, audience, or publication to perpetuate the amateur/professional divide ("AHA Resolution Supporting Scholars off the Higher Education Tenure Track" 2019). Retire the term amateur and all it implies about legitimacy, control, and hierarchy. A generous scholarship would embrace all researchers fully for the contributions they make; acknowledge, cite, discuss and contextualize their work.

Notes

1. *Australian Feminist Studies* has played a leading role in considering the intricacies of the biographical tradition as scholarship. In 1989 the Australian Feminist Biography and Autobiography conference stimulated much research and writing on the topic (Curthoys 1989). Special issues on biography appeared in 1992 and 2004, and a third special issue in 2012 devoted to the career of historian Margaret Allen contained several essential pieces on the topic (Sheridan 2012; Hughes 2012). Outside of these thematic issues, many other significant articles also appeared (Somerville 1990; Jeffreys 1994; Kosambi 2001).
2. Another intriguing example is found in biographies of Biddy Mason, an enslaved woman who successfully won her freedom in California in 1860 and eventually became a prosperous property owner. Mason first appeared in lawyer-turned-historian Dorothy Gray's Women of the West (1976), still cited today. Grey builds on journalist Delilah L. Beasley's compilation of Mason's history (1919). History professor Marne L. Campbell has recently built on these predecessors to write about Mason (Campbell 2012, 2016).

Disclosure Statement

No potential conflict of interest was reported by the author(s).

References

"5 Questions for Jill Lepore." 2014. *Nieman Storyboard*, October 6. https://niemanstoryboard.org/stories/5-and-12-questions-for-jill-lepore/.
"AAM Code of Ethics for Museums." 2020. American Alliance of Museums. 2020. https://www.aam-us.org/programs/ethics-standards-and-professional-practices/code-of-ethics-for-museums/.
"About." n.d. *Federation of Australian Historical Societies*. Accessed August 29, 2021. https://www.history.org.au/about/.
"AHA Resolution Supporting Scholars off the Higher Education Tenure Track." 2019. American Historical Association. https://www.historians.org/jobs-and-professional-development/statements-standards-and-guidelines-of-the-discipline/aha-resolutionsupporting- scholars-off-the-higher-education-tenure-track.
Ahmed, Sara. 2017. *Living a Feminist Life*. Durham: Duke University Press Books.
Alberti, Johanna. 2014. *Gender and the Historian*. New York: Routledge.
Alpern, Sara, Joyce Antler, Elisabeth Israels Perry, and Ingrid Winther Scobie, eds. 1992. *The Challenge of Feminist Biography: Writing the Lives of Modern American Women*. First Printing edition. Urbana, IL: University of Illinois Press.
Arnold, John H. 2000. *History: A Very Short Introduction*. 1st ed. New York: Oxford University Press.

Bahadur, Gaiutra. 2013. *Coolie Woman: The Odyssey of Indenture*. Chicago: University of Chicago Press.

Banner, Lois W. 2009. "Biography as History." *The American Historical Review* 114 (3): 579–586.

Barth, Gunther. 1978. "Chinatown's Angry Angel: The Story of Donaldina Cameron." *The Journal of American History* 65 (2): 508–9.

Beasley, Delilah L. (Delilah Leontium). 1919. *The Negro Trail Blazers of California*. Los Angeles. http://archive.org/details/negrotrailblazer00beas.

Bell Jr., Whitfield J. 1996. "The Amateur Historian." In *The Pursuit of Local History: Readings on Theory and Practice*, edited by Carol Kammen, 21–32. Walnut Creek, CA: AltaMira Press.

Boutilier, Beverly, and Alison Prentice. 2011. *Creating Historical Memory: English-Canadian Women and the Work of History*. Vancouver, BC: UBC Press.

Bryans, Bill. 2019. "Collaborative Practice." The Inclusive Historian's Handbook. September 16, 2019. https://inclusivehistorian.com/.

Caine, Barbara. 2010. *Biography and History*. New York: Palgrave Macmillan.

Campbell, Marne L. 2012. "African American Women, Wealth Accumulation, And Social Welfare Activism In 19th-Century Los Angeles." *The Journal of African American History* 97 (4): 376–400.

Campbell, Marne L. 2016. *Making Black Los Angeles: Class, Gender, and Community, 1850–1917*. University of North Carolina Press. http://www.jstor.org/stable/10.5149/9781469629285_campbell.

Chernock, Arianne. 2013. "Gender and the Politics of Exceptionalism in the Writing of British Women's HIstory." In *Making Women's Histories: Beyond National Perspectives*, edited by Pamela S. Nadell, and Kate Haulman, 115–36. New York: NYU Press.

Choy, Philip P. 1978. "Review." *California History* 57 (2): 201–2.

"Code of Practice." n.d. Professional Historians Association of New Zealand/Aotearoa. Accessed April 2, 2021. https://phanza.org.nz/code-practice/.

Cronon, William. 2012. "Loving History." *Perspectives on History*, April 2012. https://www.historians.org/publications-and-directories/perspectives-on-history/april-2012/loving-history.

Culley, Amy. 2014. *British Women's Life Writing, 1760–1840: Friendship, Community, and Collaboration*. New York: Springer.

Curthoys, Ann. 1989. "Feminist Biography and Autobiography." *Australian Feminist Studies* 4 (9): 111–17.

Curthoys, Ann, and John Docker. 2006. *Is History Fiction?* Sydney: University of New South Wales Press.

Dagbovie, Pero Gaglo. 2007. *The Early Black History Movement*. Edited by Carter G. Woodson and Lorenzo Johnston Greene. Urbana: University of Illinois Press.

Dagbovie, Pero Gaglo. 2010. *African American History Reconsidered*. Chicago: University of Illinois Press.

Davis, Natalie Zemon. 1976. ""Women's History" in Transition: The European Case." *Feminist Studies* 3 (3/4): 83–103.

Des Jardins, Julie. 2003. *Women and the Historical Enterprise in America: Gender, Race, and the Politics of Memory, 1880–1945*. Chapel Hill, NC: University of North Carolina Press.

Dubois, Ellen Carol. 1991a. "Eleanor Flexner and the History of American Feminism." *Gender and History* 3 (1): 81–90.

DuBois, Ellen Carol. 1991b. "Making Women's History: Activist Historians of Women's Rights, 1880–1940." *Radical History Review* 1991 (49): 61–84.

Dymond, David. 2011. "Does Local History Have a Split Personality." In *New Directions in Local History Since Hoskins*, edited by Christopher Dyer, Andrew James Hopper, Evelyn Lord, and Nigel J. Tringham. Hertfordshire, UK: University of Hertfordshire Press.

Fuentes, Marisa J. 2016. *Dispossessed Lives: Enslaved Women, Violence, and the Archive*. Philadelphia: University of Pennsylvania Press.

Gray, Dorothy. 1976. *Women of the West*. Lincoln, NE: University of Nebraska Press.

"Guide to the Mildred Martin Papers." n.d. Online Archive of California. Accessed April 2, 2021. http://www.oac.cdlib.org/findaid/ark:/13030/kt8v19p9ck/.

Gullette, Margaret Morganroth. 2018. "The Monument and the Wrecking Crew: Ageism and The Academy." *AAUP*, May 9. https://www.aaup.org/article/monument-and-wrecking-crew.

Hamerow, Theodore S. 1990. *Reflections on History and Historians*. Madison: University of Wisconsin Press.

Hartman, Saidiya. 2021. *Wayward Lives, Beautiful Experiments: Intimate Histories of Riotous Black Girls, Troublesome Women and Queer Radicals*. London: Serpent's Tail Limited.

Hoff, Joan. 1992. "Introduction: An Overview of Women's History in the United States." Edited by Gayle V. Fischer." *Journal of Women's History Guide to Periodical Literature*, 9–38.

Howe, Barbara J. 1990. "Women in Historic Preservation: The Legacy of Ann Pamela Cunningham." *The Public Historian* 12 (1): 31–61.

Hudson, Lynn M. 2003. *The Making of "Mammy Pleasant": A Black Entrepreneur in Nineteenth-Century San Francisco*. Urbana and Champaign, IL: University of Illinois Press.

Hudson, Lynn M. 2009. "Lies, Secrets, and Silences: Writing African American Women's Biography." *Journal of Women's History* 21 (4): 138–40.

Hughes, Karen. 2012. "Micro-Histories and Things That Matter." *Australian Feminist Studies* 27 (73): 269–78.

Jeffreys, Elaine. 1994. "Woman, Nation and Narrative: Western Biographical Accounts of Jiang Qing." *Australian Feminist Studies* 9 (20): 35–51.

Kammen, Carol. 1996. *The Pursuit of Local History: Readings on Theory and Practice*. Walnut Creek, CA: Rowman Altamira.

Kammen, Carol. 2014. "Call: Water Buffalos, Wildabeests, and Gazelles." In *Zen and the Art of Local History*, edited by Carol Kammen, and Bob Beatty, 37–40. Lanham, MD: Rowman & Littlefield.

Kammen, Carol, and Amy H. Wilson. 2012. *Encyclopedia of Local History*. Walnut Creek, CA: AltaMira Press.

Karcher, Carolyn L. 1994. *The First Woman in the Republic: A Cultural Biography of Lydia Maria Child*. Durham, NC: Duke University Press.

King, Michelle T. 2011. "Working With/In the Archives." In *Research Methods for History*, edited by Simon Gunn, and Lucy Faire, 13–29. Edinburgh: Edinburgh University Press.

Kosambi, Meera. 2001. "A Prismatic Presence: The Multiple Iconisation of Dr Anandibai Joshee and the Politics of Life-Writing." *Australian Feminist Studies* 16 (35): 157–73.

Leavy, Patricia, and Anne Harris. 2018. *Contemporary Feminist Research from Theory to Practice*. New York: Guilford Publications.

Lepore, Jill. 2014. *Book of Ages: The Life and Opinions of Jane Franklin*. New York: Knopf Doubleday Publishing Group.

Lepore, Jill. 2015. *The Secret History of Wonder Woman*. New York: Vintage Books.

Lerner, Gerda. 1975. "Placing Women in History: Definitions and Challenges." *Feminist Studies* 3 (1/2): 5.

Lindsey, Kiera. 2016. *The Convict's Daughter: The Scandal That Shocked a Colony*. Crows Nest, NSW: Allen and Unwin.

Longair, Sarah. 2016. *Cracks in the Dome. Fractured Histories of Empire in the Zanzibar Museum, 1897–1964*. New York: Routledge.

MacInnis, Donald. 1979. Review of *Chinatown's Angry Angel, the Story of Donaldina Cameron* 57 (2): 175–77.

Martin, Mildred Crowl. 1977. *Chinatown's Angry Angel: The Story of Donaldina Cameron*. Palo Alto: Pacific Books.

"Membership." n.d. AASLH (blog). Accessed August 29, 2021. https://aaslh.org/membership/.

McClain, Laurene Wu. 1979. "Review." *Pacific Historical Review* 48 (2): 304.

McClain, Laurene Wu. 1983. "Donaldina Cameron: A Reappraisal." *Pacific Historian* 27: 25–35.

McVeigh, Jane. 2018. "Concerns about Facts and Form in Literary Biography." In *A Companion to Literary Biography*, edited by Richard Bradford and Jane McVeigh. Chichester, UK: John Wiley & Sons.

Mitchell, Rosemary. 2000. *Picturing the Past: English History in Text and Image, 1830–1870*. Oxford: Oxford University Press.

Morrison, Ronald D. 2021. *Thomas Hardy: A Companion to the Novels*. Jefferson, NC: McFarland.

Mott, Carrie, and Daniel Cockayne. 2017. "Citation Matters: Mobilizing the Politics of Citation toward a Practice of 'Conscientious Engagement'." *Gender, Place & Culture* 24 (7): 954–73.

Offen, Karen M., Ruth Roach Pierson, and Jane Rendall, eds. 1991. *Writing Women's History: International Perspectives.* New York: Macmillan.

"Our Code of Conduct." n.d. *Royal Australian Historical Society* (blog). Accessed August 12, 2017. https://www.rahs.org.au/welcome-royal-australian-historical-society/our-code-of-conduct/.

Parfait, Claire. 2020. "'Un-Sung Heroes of Afro-American Historiography': The Case of Joel Augustus Rogers." *IdeAs: Idées d'Amériques*, no. 16, October. doi:10.4000/ideas.9256.

Parfait, Claire, Hélène Le Dantec-Lowry, and Claire Bourhis-Mariotti. 2016. *Writing History from the Margins: African Americans and the Quest for Freedom.* New York: Routledge.

Parks Canada Agency, Government of Canada. 2018. "Parks Canada Guiding Principles and Operational Policies." 2018. https://www.pc.gc.ca/en/docs/pc/poli/princip.

Pascoe, Peggy. 1990. *Relations of Rescue : The Search for Female Moral Authority in the American West, 1874–1939.* New York: Oxford University Press.

Potter, Lois. 2018. "Writing Shakespeare's Life." In *A Companion to Literary Biography*, edited by Richard Bradford, 391–404. Chichester, UK: John Wiley and Sons.

Schmidt, Leigh Eric. 2010. *Heaven's Bride: The Unprintable Life of Ida C. Craddock, American Mystic, Scholar, Sexologist, Martyr, and Madwoman.* Basic Books.

Scott, Joan Wallach.. 1988. *Gender and the Politics of History.* New York: Columbia University Press.

Sheridan, Susan. 2012. "White Women Writing in the Contact Zone." *Australian Feminist Studies* 27 (73): 249–57. doi:10.1080/08164649.2012.700259.

Smith, Bonnie. 1993. "Woman's History." In *Encyclopedia of Social History*, edited by Peter N. Stearns, 1049–1053. New York: Routledge.

Smith, Bonnie G. 2000. *The Gender of History: Men, Women, and Historical Practice.* Cambridge, Mass.: Harvard University Press.

Smith, Nadia Claire. 2007. *A "Manly Study"?: Irish Women Historians 1868–1949.* New York: Palgrave Macmillan.

Snyder, Jeffrey Aaron. 2018. *Making Black History: The Color Line, Culture, and Race in the Age of Jim Crow.* Athens, GA: University of Georgia Press.

Somerville, Margaret. 1990. "Life (Hi)Story Writing: The Relationship between Talk and Text." *Australian Feminist Studies* 5 (12): 29–42. doi:10.1080/08164649.1990.9961695.

Spender, Dale, and Lynne Spender. 1983. *Gatekeeping: The Denial, Dismissal and Distortion of Women.* New York: Pergamon Press.

Spongberg, Mary. 2002. *Writing Women's History Since the Renaissance.* New York: Macmillan.

Spongberg, M., A. Curthoys, and B. Caine. 2005. *Companion to Women's Historical Writing.* London: Palgrave.

"Statement on Age Discrimination." 2017. *American Historical Association 2017.* https://www.historians.org/jobs-and-professionaldevelopment/statements-standards-and-guidelines-of-the-discipline/statement-on-age-discrimination.

"Statement on Research Ethics." n.d. Accessed April 2, 2021. https://cha-shc.ca/english/about-the-cha/statement-on-research-ethics.html.

"Statement on Standards of Professional Conduct." 2019. American Historical Association. 2019. https://www.historians.org/jobs-and-professional-development/statements-standards-and-guidelines-of-the-discipline/statement-on-standards-of-professional-conduct.

"The British Association for Local History (BALH)." 2009. The Historical Association. December 21. https://www.history.org.uk/primary/resource/2759/the-british-association-for-local-history-balh.

Townsend, Robert B. 2014. "Response to Kammen." In *Zen and the Art of Local History*, edited by Carol Kammen, and Bob Beatty, 37–40. Lanham, MD: Rowman & Littlefield.

Tuchman, Barbara W. 2011. *Practicing History: Selected Essays.* New York: Random House Publishing Group.

Tyrrell, Ian. 2005. *Historians in Public: The Practice of American History, 1890–1970.* Chicago and London: University of Chicago Press.

White, Deborah Gray, ed. 2009. *Telling Histories: Black Women Historians in the Ivory Tower.* Durham, NC: University of North Carolina Press.

Wilson, Carol Green. 1931. *Chinatown Quest: The Life Adventures of Donaldina Cameron*. Palo Alto: Stanford University Press.
Wilson, Amy H. 2017. "Amateur." In *Encyclopedia of Local History*, 25. Lanham, MD: Rowman and Littlefield.
Wright, Donald A. 2005. *The Professionalization of History in English Canada*. Toronto: University of Toronto Press.
Yung, Judy. 1995. *Unbound Feet: A Social History of Chinese Women in San Francisco*. Berkeley: University of California Press.

Index

acknowledge people 120
agency 10, 24, 38, 39, 60, 64, 67, 97, 106
Ahmed, Sara 114
amateurism 115–17
amateurs 114–23
anonymisation 73, 80, 82–5
Appadurai, Arjun 3
archival/archives 8, 9, 21, 22, 25, 26, 28, 48–51, 53, 54, 76, 77, 79, 80, 82, 84, 86; materials 2, 8, 9, 29, 82; research 4, 8, 18, 22, 29; theory 73, 75, 77, 79, 87; web 79–80
assimilation 95, 97, 111, 112
authority 25, 28, 64, 95, 106, 107, 110

Berriman, Liam 86
Birch, Maxine 11
Blaser, Mario 98, 99

Cadena, Marisol de la 98, 99
Campbell, Rebecca 40
care 6, 10, 12, 13, 40, 73–7, 80, 82, 83, 85, 87, 94–8
care-full risks 72, 73, 76, 85–7
caregivers 58, 60, 68
Caswell, Michelle 77, 82
Cifor, Marika 7, 77, 82
citations 39, 104–12, 114, 118, 120–1
colonial archive 19, 20, 22
colonialism 51, 75, 85, 94–9, 105
community archives 48–54, 77–8
compassionate research 12, 13
Cook, Terry 78
critical reception 117–19

decolonising methodologies 94–6
DeVault, Marjorie L. 5
digital archive 78, 79, 81, 83, 85, 86
divergence 98, 99
DIY academic archiving 72, 73, 77–9
domestic caregiver 57
Downes, Julia 36

Edwards, Rosalind 5, 80
Ellis, Carolyn 11, 12

ethical practice 43, 73–6, 80
ethical research 4, 35, 36, 40, 42–4

feminist research, methodologies 57, 58, 96
feminist research, practices 4, 115
feminists 73–7, 79–81, 85, 87, 106–8, 110; citational practices 106, 108; ethic of care 73, 75, 77, 83–5, 87, 93, 96; knowledge 109–11; practice of care 80–6; scholarship 94, 96
first nations women's life narratives 18–30
Fontes, Lisa A. 39

Gavey, Nicola 38
gender 20, 85, 97, 108, 116, 117, 122
generosity 120, 121
Gillam, Lynn 12
Gilligan, Carol 12
Gross, Glenda 5
Guillemin, Marilys 12

Haraway, Donna 52
Harkin, Natalie 20, 25
Heywood, Paolo 100
hospitality 48–52
Hudson, Lynn M. 121
human subjects 8, 50

Indigenous peoples 19, 41, 93–6, 98
innovation 72, 74, 85, 114
institutional ethics processes 35, 36, 42, 43
intellectual labour 106, 109–11
intersectionality 108–11
intimate interviews 9–12
invented traditions 72–4, 81
inventive ethics 72–87
invisible work 79, 80

Kelly, Liz 36, 43
Kirsch, Gesa E. 9
knowledge production 28, 59, 93, 94, 101, 104–6, 108, 111, 114

Laplanche, Jean 37
Latour, Bruno 96, 98

Lee, Jamie A. 78
logic of ownership 105, 111, 112

marginalised communities 39, 41
Martin, Karen 95
Mauthner, Melanie 5
McInnis 118
McLeod, Julie 74
Miller, Tina 11
Murphy, Michelle 76, 97

neglected things 75, 76
Noddings, Nan 12
non-innocent care 92–101

O'Connor, Kate 74
online grief communities 3, 6–9, 13
oral histories 27–30, 54, 78, 81, 83, 85
ownership 105, 109, 111, 112

Paget, Marianne A. 10
Palmisano, Stefania 74
Pannofino, Nicola 74
Pontalis, Jean-Bertrand 37
Puig de la Bellacasa, Maria 76, 94, 96, 97

radical hospitality 48–54, 78
recordkeeping 2–4, 10, 11, 13
relational ethics 4, 12, 13, 77
relationality 2–4, 49, 50, 79, 99, 100, 111, 112
research design 5, 10, 13
research knowledge 59, 68
research participants 3–5, 8, 9, 35, 73–8, 81
research relationships 9, 13, 74
review ethics boards (REBs) 2, 4, 5, 10, 11
Ribbens, Jane 80
Rifkin, Mark 101
Rigney, Lester 18, 95–7
risk management model 35
Russell, Lynette 26

Schmidt, Johanna 38
Scott, Joan Wallach. 35
settler colonialism 94, 97, 98

sexual violence 34, 35, 37–44; research 34–6, 39, 41, 43; researchers 35, 42; research ethics 39, 43
Simpson, Audra 94, 95
Smith, Cathy 95
social worlds 20, 93, 96–9, 101
Stengers, Isabelle 100
storytelling 20, 22, 24, 49, 50, 52
Strathern, Marilyn 100
subvert academic gatekeeping 114–23
Sundberg, Juanita 97
Sutherland, Tonia 78

take down approach 84–5
Tallbear, Kim 93
territoriality 106, 109, 111
Thomson, Rachel 86
Todd, Zoe 94, 97, 98
Tomlinson, Barbara 110
transcripts 78, 80–2, 84, 85
trauma 4, 10, 20, 29, 30, 37–40; model 35, 37–9, 43
Trinh, Minh-ha T. 105
Tronto, Joan 96
truths 20, 21, 25, 27, 29
Tseris, Emma 37, 38

use/less citation 110–12

Veracini, Lorenzo 95
victim-blaming world 39
victim-survivors 34, 36–9, 44
violence 26, 37–43, 84, 85

Walters, Maggie 95
Watson, Irene 94
web of care 83–4
Westmarland, Nicole 36
Whelan, Andrew 36
whiteness 107, 108
Wilson, Shawn 11
women 10, 20–3, 25, 27, 39, 59, 62, 63, 84, 116–18

zoomspace 60, 62, 64, 65